D1080461

THE ARCHAEOLOGY
OF THE ENGLISH CHURCH

*To Dr Harold Taylor, who inspired me to
pursue church archaeology, and to
Kirsty Rodwell, who has
contributed so much
to that pursuit*

THE
ARCHAEOLOGY OF
THE ENGLISH CHURCH

The Study of Historic Churches and Churchyards

WARWICK RODWELL

B. T. Batsford Ltd London

Frontispiece

1 Anglo-Saxon sundial and inscription over the door of St Gregory's Minster, Kirkdale, Yorks; c. AD 1055. *After Gough, 1789*

> 'Orm, son of Gamal, bought St. Gregory's Minster when it was all broken down and fallen, and he let it be made anew from the ground, to Christ and St. Gregory, in the days of Edward the King and Tosti the Earl, and Haward wrought me, and Brand the Priest.'

'This is the day's sun-marker at every tide'

0558/024

Typeset by Willmer Brothers Limited, Birkenhead, Merseyside and printed in Great Britain by
The Anchor Press, Tiptree
for the Publishers
B. T. Batsford Ltd
4 Fitzhardinge Street
London W1H 0AH

ISBN 0 7134 2590 3

D
726.5094'2
ROD

Contents

Acknowledgements

A book of this nature inevitably draws upon the labours and publications of many scholars, my debt to whom will be readily apparent from the text. The sources of the illustrations are individually acknowledged in the captions; those which are unattributed have been prepared by the author.

For the benefit of discussion and advice on numerous aspects of church archaeology, over the past decade, I am grateful to many scholars and friends, and in particular to Peter Burman, Paul Drury, Daryl Fowler, The Very Revd Patrick Mitchell (Dean of Wells), Richard Morris, Professor Philip Rahtz, Dr Juliet Rogers and Dr Harold Taylor. The signal contributions of Dr Taylor in the field of 'architectural archaeology' inspired me to venture into the subject, and the opportunity for practical investigation, on what seemed to me an adequate scale, was first provided by the Revd David Nash at Rivenhall in Essex. His friendship and encouragement since the day when I first knocked upon his Rectory door have been greatly valued. Indeed, in every church and cathedral in which I have been privileged to work I have received nothing but encouragement and generous assistance from those responsible for the worship, daily life and maintenance of the building.

My greatest debt must, however, be to my wife, Kirsty, who has assisted me continually and unstintingly, not only with the preparation of this book, but also with every aspect of church archaeology in which I have had an involvement, indoors and outdoors, above and below ground. I wish also to thank Sue Heathorn who typed the text. Finally, I am grateful to the Publishers and Series Editor for inviting me to contribute this modest essay on a slightly neglected aspect of British archaeology, but one which is immensely rewarding, as those who have been 'initiated' may testify.

The Illustrations

Preface

Countless books have been written on the history and architecture of churches, cathedrals and monasteries in the British Isles. Some writers have concentrated on individual buildings, while others have examined themes, architectural style, aspects of construction, use or decoration. Underlying most of these works has been the basic premise that our ecclesiastical heritage is a finite stock of buildings, furnishings and fittings for which the fundamental studies have already been undertaken, so that it remains only for us to re-discuss the material and re-order it according to our particular interests.

This falls far short of the truth. If we set aside the facade of inherited complacency and critically re-examine many of the theories put forward long ago (now often compounded into accepted 'fact'), we find that the foundations of our knowledge are less sure than they at first seemed. Furthermore, there are yawning gaps to be filled, and countless questions to be answered. Many of these questions have not been asked, or at least not seriously considered, in the past, simply because scholars have presumed that they were unanswerable. Obviously, the further back in history we go the more difficult it becomes to find the answers to questions, owing to the reduced survival rate of all kinds of evidence. But is this really the insurmountable problem that it seems? Fortunately, the development of modern techniques in church archaeology, particularly in the last decade, has revolutionized our approach to the subject. While not forgetting the legacies of previous generations, it is fair to say that the great campaigns of archaeological investigation at York Minster and Winchester Cathedral in the 1960s set the scene. These two projects showed that large-scale excavations in and around living cathedrals were not only viable but also yielded colossal returns in data of many kinds. In the 1970s the principles of modern archaeological investigation were extended to 'ordinary' churches and, most importantly, to their superstructures as well as to their buried remains.

This book sets down for the first time an introduction to the history, aims, methods and achievement of modern church archaeology. It cannot be a definitive statement, nor all-embracing, because the subject is still developing fairly rapidly and because most of the results of the major campaigns in church and cathedral archaeology of recent years have yet to receive full academic publication. Nevertheless a considerable corpus of new information has become available and an impressive range of new techniques pioneered and developed. I shall not give a blow-by-blow account of how to survey a church, conduct an excavation or draw up the results for publication. Each of these requires a manual to itself. Instead, I have outlined the general principles involved, drawing attention to major pitfalls and areas of common neglect, and, on the whole, avoiding the special complexities of the 'great churches' and monasteries.

Some chapters of this book are personal because they contain large slices of material derived from investigations which have been directed by my wife and me (e.g. Rivenhall, Hadstock, Barton-on-Humber and Wells Cathedral) and material derived from other projects with which we have had some direct association. This is inevitable in a subject in which rapid growth has outstripped publication. However, the problems encountered in studying, recording, excavating and publishing the four churches mentioned are together well representative of the whole spectrum of English ecclesiastical archaeology. Some of those sites had their beginnings in prehistory; the architecture of the buildings ranges from Anglo-Saxon to Victorian; their socio-religious status spans the gamut from proprietary chapel, through town church and minster, to cathedral; and their construction varies from rough rubble to moulded and sculptured ashlar on a monumental scale.

In short, I have attempted to provide a general account of church archaeology which will demonstrate for the interested amateur how much latent history there is in the average medieval church, which will suggest to the architectural historian new ways of extracting evidence from buildings, which will remind the documentary historian how the equation of written evidence with physical remains is a tortuous and dangerous occupation, and which will provide the student of archaeology with some insight into the wide ranging and at times difficult problems presented by archaeo-ecclesiology. No subject can call so loudly for a co-ordinated inter-disciplinary approach to its study. Because of its very complexity church archaeology is always challenging and stimulating, yielding unexpected results, often from the most unpromising material. There is not an ancient church in Britain whose history could not be enriched through archaeological study.

Warwick Rodwell

Clifton, Bristol
December 1980

1 The Archaeological Study of Churches

As a discipline church archaeology is both old and new. It is old in the sense that archaeologists, or antiquaries as they were then called, were observing and recording evidence relating to the physical histories of churches and monasteries as long ago as the twelfth century. The discipline is, however, new in that it has only been in the last two decades that the full-scale archaeological study of a selection of English ecclesiastical buildings has been attempted, drawing together in the process a wide range of specialist skills and services.

It will be as well, here at the outset, to look at the proper definition of 'church archaeology', since there are entrenched misconceptions in the minds of many, both inside and outside the archaeological profession. It is almost universally supposed that the archaeologist is a person who excavates for ancient remains, that anyone who studies buildings must be an architect, and that a person who studies documents must be an historian. That is an over-simplification, which has come about as an accident of social history. This is worth exploring.

Up to the First World War, ecclesiastical studies formed perhaps the strongest and most rapidly advancing branch of British archaeology. Its practitioners were mainly drawn from the ranks of architects and clergy: this was natural enough since they were the people most closely associated with churches and cathedrals. They called the study of tombs, stained glass and sculpture 'archaeology', and when they wanted to find out about buried remains or the demolished parts of buildings workmen were employed to dig trenches to answer the questions which were being posed. The person who superintended the work was the 'archaeologist' (although he would seldom style himself as such): he would report upon the findings and, if he were not himself an architect, he would probably engage an architect or surveyor of his acquaintance to prepare any illustrations which were needed.

However, after the turn of the twentieth century, the great wave of church restoration was over and nearly all the classic works on medieval architecture had been written. One of the more popular accounts, J. H. Parker's *Introduction to Gothic Architecture*, had by then run to fifteen editions. In the 1920s and '30s British archaeology developed a new character based upon emergent prehistoric and Roman studies; at the same time practising architects became less concerned with ecclesiology and the interests of the clergy in the historic past gradually dwindled.

The devastation of urban centres during the Second World War paved the way for the birth of 'medieval archaeology' in the 1950s, and as one small part of that new discipline excavations were mounted amongst the ruins of several bombed churches. Although some notable excavations took place on ecclesiastical sites in the 1950s and '60s, the modern concept of 'church archaeology' was as yet unborn. It was the threat of a new wave of self-inflicted devastation which brought about a reawakening in archaeo-ecclesiology. In 1968 the Church of England drafted and adopted *The Pastoral Measure*, a piece of legislation which was designed to unburden the diocesan system of those buildings which were deemed surplus to pastoral requirements. The options for disposal were simply: preservation by a trust as an ancient monument, conversion to another form of use, or demolition. The two latter options set the alarm bells ringing in the world of medieval archaeology, and the impending cataclysm was viewed as an opportunity for further excavations in and around churches.

In 1972 the Council for British Archaeology created its Churches Committee and shortly afterwards issued the first policy statement for Church Archaeology in this country (Jesson, 1973). Even at this stage, the concept of studying a church primarily through *excavation* was still paramount in the minds of archaeologists. But the early 1970s saw fresh

2 St Peter's, Barton-on-Humber, Lincs.: full-scale archaeological investigation inside the church. Here, the 'total' archaeology of a church is being studied: the roofs, the walls, the floors and the foundations. The excavation of the interior of the church took place 1978–81. In this photograph, taken in 1980, the floor levels and internal features from the tenth century to the twentieth have been removed, ready for the excavation of the pre-church deposits. For the plan see fig. 12. *Photo: author. Crown copyright*

moves which were rapidly to bring about the expansion of church archaeology into the multi-disciplinary subject which it is today. The crucial development was accidental and coincidental: a handful of 'conventional' archaeologists became interested in architectural history, and an equally small number of architectural historians turned to archaeological methodology as an aid to their studies. A union was struck up and archaeo-ecclesiology took off in a new direction. By 1975 the subject had regained the cohesion which it had been

well on the way to losing in 1900.

The upshot has been the realization that church archaeology must embrace the whole range of material available for study: the church building and its site, its furnishings, fittings and monuments, the graveyard and the boundaries and ancillary structures (fig. 2). Unfortunately, the misconception persists that the archaeologist is a person who digs for the remains of the material past. This view is as distorted as would be the supposition that a surgeon performs only amputations. Throughout this book, I have used the term 'archaeologist' to mean a person who undertakes or co-ordinates an investigation into the history of ecclesiastical buildings, sites and monuments. The process is that of 'archaeological investigation', which may or may not involve excavation.

Obviously, the church archaeologist is unlikely to embrace within his personal repertoire of skills all, or even most, of the

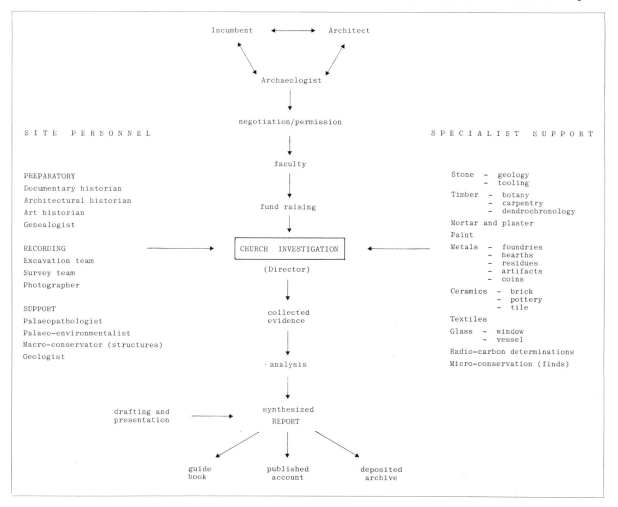

3 Diagram to illustrate the discipline of church archaeology, showing the principal procedures and personnel likely to be involved in the investigation of the average parish church. On the left is the basic complement of skills which will invariably be required on site, while on the right the main fields of technical speciality are listed; the need for the latter will vary according to circumstances

disciplines and sub-disciplines which together form church archaeology. He often therefore finds himself in the role of co-ordinator and director of investigations. He must at least have a general acquaintance with the whole range of material and problems which may require study, and be able to direct the attentions of specialists to those facets of the work with which he is not personally familiar (fig. 3).

Since churches have such long and rich histories (which may extend back to pre-Christian eras), and since there is so much historical, architectural, artistic and other material evidence to take into account, it is hardly surprising that ecclesiastical archaeology has been a late developer. In fact any church archaeologist who has previously worked in the fields of prehistory and proto-history will readily appreciate how the problems of studying the cultural evidence from those eras pale into significance when compared, say, with the complexities of the archaeology of a great cathedral. In due course we shall explore some of those complexities.

The elements of church archaeology

Once it is accepted that archaeology is the total study of the material past—and the etymology of the word admits no exclusions—then almost everything becomes significant; in particular there is no rule which decrees that the older or rarer an object is, the more absolute importance it accrues. Importance is relative. It is wrong to suppose that an Anglo-Saxon church must be more important than a Victorian church, or that the one should merit meticulous recording and the other should not—as, for example, in the event of proposed demolition.

This principle must always be borne in mind when an investigation is in progress, and the temptation, through pressure on resources or lack of personal interest, to record the earliest evidence exhaustively, and the latest most scantily or not at all must be resisted. There is one very good practical reason to support this rigorous and all-embracing approach: it is very rare for work of any period, however modern, not to owe a hint of its shape or form to something which went before. Put another way, it is exceedingly common for new work to copy, follow in outline, or in some way be influenced by existing or recently destroyed features in buildings, or elements in the landscape.

If one begins the study of a building, or of documents relating to it, from the point of view of the earliest evidence first, then the story which is unfolded usually contains errors and omissions which are only detected later, if at all, when the more modern aspects of the church's history are scrutinized. Although it may excite less initial enthusiasm, a study which begins with the latest evidence and is then taken back to the earliest, will produce a fuller and more reliable end-product. In the case of archaeological excavation there is, of course, no option but to begin with the most recent deposits and to work downwards to the most ancient; and it is entirely logical to adopt the same investigational approach to remains which are only partially buried or are not buried at all. This, it should be stressed, is only the technique of investigation; there is no reason why the final report should not be presented in chronological order.

In the ensuing chapters we shall look in detail at the discipline of church archaeology, to ascertain why it is important, what its application can tell us that we did not already know, and how its methodology should be applied to churches and chapels, cathedrals and monasteries.

2 The Development of Church Archaeology

The quest for knowledge of the religious past is so ancient that no date for the inception of church archaeology can be offered. One might argue, for example, that the monks of Ely were acting as archaeologists when they took a boat down the river Granta to Cambridge in AD 660, with a view to digging in the abandoned Roman town cemetery there, to find a good stone coffin which they could re-use as a receptable for the bones of the abbess Etheldreda. Bede, who recorded this event (*H.E.* IV. 19), described the coffin as 'a white marble sarcophagus of very beautiful workmanship, with a close-fitting lid of similar stone'. A description such as this could have been written by a nineteenth-century antiquary.

While this seventh-century excavation at Cambridge was not undertaken as a quest for antiquarian knowledge, the activities of the monks of Glastonbury in 1190 could be so described. They undertook an excavation in the

4 Anglo-Saxon leaden mortuary crosses
A Glastonbury: cross alleged to be from the tomb of King Arthur, but now lost. *After Camden, 1607*
B Wells: cross from Bishop Giso's tomb (height 16·5cm.). There is an inscription, taken from the Mass for the Dead, on the back face. *Drawn by Helen Humphreys. C.R.A.A.G.S. copyright*

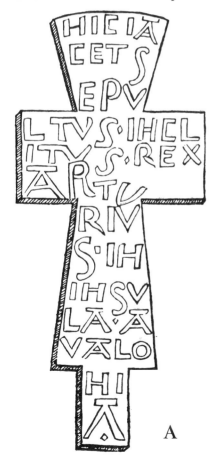

A

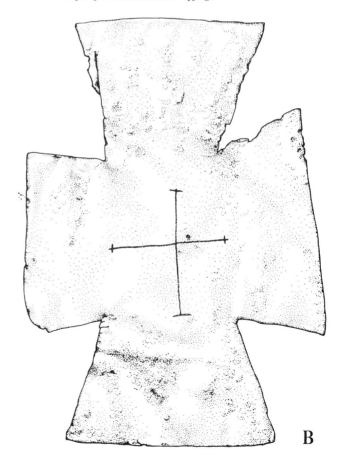

B

abbey cemetery to recover the bodies of the legendary King Arthur and Guinevere. The excavation was recorded in some detail by three contemporary writers: approximate dimensions were quoted and the leaden mortuary cross which was discovered was described (Radford and Swanton, 1975, 42–3). Incidentally, this cross (fig. 4A) was one of the first objects from an archaeological excavation to be drawn and published, albeit long after the discovery: it first appeared in Wm. Camden's sixth edition of his *Britannia* (1607). The fact that the skeletons excavated by the monks of Glastonbury were almost certainly not those of the legendary Arthur and his queen, and that the lead cross was probably a tenth-century falsification which was 'planted' to help support the famous legend, need not concern us here. The excavation of 1190 is not in doubt.

There were scores of excavations carried out in the Saxon and medieval periods for the purpose of recovering the remains of kings, bishops, saints and martyrs, details of a few of which happen to have been preserved by contemporary chroniclers. There is an archaeological dimension to some of these exhumations which is of considerable interest to us today (such as the translation of the Saxon bishops of Wells from the old cathedral to the new one, around AD 1200), but at the time there was more than mere antiquarian curiosity to motivate the work, such as was to become the norm later on (as, for example, when St Cuthbert was exhumed in 1827 and again in 1899). The primary function of these early 'archaeological' activities was to bolster up local ecclesiastical history, to demonstrate the antiquity, identity and respectability of a religious house, and to provide a stock of relics for veneration. In some countries there is still today an element of nationalism in archaeological motivation—a feature which is scarcely present in Britain.

Early archaeological records

It may be useful here to differentiate the two basic forms of ancient archaeological record. First, there are those records which we now regard as contributing to the archaeological study of churches, but which were originally the working documents of architects and masons and had nothing to do with antiquarianism. One thinks particularly of medieval building accounts; plans and other drawn material have

rarely survived from the pre-Reformation era. Examples of surviving drawings are the early ninth-century plan of the monastery at St Gall, Switzerland, the late twelfth-century plan of the plumbing at Canterbury Cathedral, and, much later, the many Victorian architects' specifications for reseating and restoring churches.

Secondly, there are those records which were produced in the light of the antiquarian interest aroused by the Renaissance. Records took the form of maps, plans, sections, elevation drawings, sketches, notes and inventories, and their primary purpose was to immortalize evidence of the past, not to provide a utilitarian document for the present. There was a major exception in the case of the records made of classical antiquities. Many of these were drawn during the Renaissance, specifically as models for the construction of new buildings. Thus, for example, in 1665 Sir Christopher Wren went to France (since he could not afford the journey to Rome) to study dome construction for the new St Paul's.

Renaissance-period and later antiquaries advanced the study of all aspects of antiquity far beyond the limits of recording adopted by the medieval chroniclers. The men who travelled around the country making drawings and collecting information, between the mid-sixteenth and mid-eighteenth centuries were laying the foundations of antiquarian studies, upon which the Georgians and Victorians were to build. Classical, secular and ecclesiastical antiquities were all subjected to intense scrutiny. It is ironical that Henry VIII, the man who brought about the Dissolution of the Monasteries and caused a greater devastation of the architectural heritage than time, neglect and two world wars were subsequently to inflict, was also responsible for the appointment of the first 'King's Antiquary'. John Leland, who had formerly been the King's chaplain, was appointed to the new post in 1533, with the commission 'to search for records, manuscripts and relics of antiquity, in all the cathedrals, colleges, abbeys and priories of England'. Leland was really the first 'rescue archaeologist' employed by the British government, since he was travelling about the country making records, literally while the monasteries were being looted and demolished around him. If only he had had a camera!

When he returned from these itineraries in 1542 Leland devoted the last few years of his life

Fig. 5. p. 200.

5 The first published illustration in British archaeology was this Saxo-Norman chancel arch at Lewes, Sussex (Camden, 1586). In 1587 the ruinous church was restored and the arch moved outside, where it can be seen over the doorway in the small picture (Gough, 1789). The whole church was demolished in 1839

to the assimilation and publication of his material. The principal work which appeared in his lifetime was *The laboryeuse Journey and Serche for Englandes Antiquities; A New Yeares Gyfte to Kynge Henry the VIII in the 37 yeare of his Regne* (1549). Most famous and important for church archaeology, however, is *The Itinerary* which was eventually published in 9 volumes (1710–12; reprinted 1964). Casually presented observations and quaint descriptions of ruins often provide vital clues for the archaeologist. Thus Leland's description of the vanished Norman cathedral church at Bath has recently helped archaeologists to reconstruct that once-important building: 'John (of Tours) pulled down the old church of St Peter at Bath, and erected a new, much fairer (one), and was buried in the middle of the presbytery thereof, whose image I saw lying there 9 years since; at which time all the church that he made lay to

waste, and was unroofed, and weeds grew about this John of Tours' sepulchre. . . . Oliver King let almost all the old church . . . go to ruin. The walls yet stand.'

After Leland came William Camden. In 1586, at the age of 35, he produced his monumental *Britannia*. This was the first illustrated book on British archaeology, albeit there was only one picture (Kendrick, 1950, 151). Significantly, that illustration was of the Saxo-Norman chancel arch in the church of St John-sub-Castro at Lewes, Sussex (fig. 5). In 1587 the ruinous church was restored and the chancel arch was taken down and rebuilt, in a different form, in the south wall of the nave; this is recorded in a later edition of *Britannia*, with the arch drawn out in its new form and a sketch of the church provided to show its new site (Gough's ed. 1789, I, 200–1 and pl.XII). The whole church was demolished and rebuilt in 1839.

This example demonstrates the importance of the records made by the early antiquaries and how archaeological developments can be traced from one edition of a book to another. In fact, Gough's edition of Camden's *Britannia* is

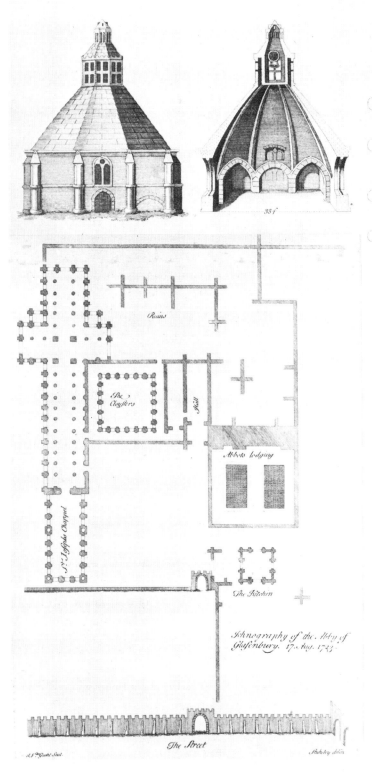
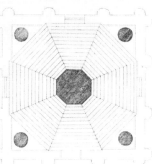

6 Glastonbury Abbey, part of Stukeley's survey of 1723. He prepared a ground plan of the abbey ruins, together with several sketches and detailed drawings, including a full orthographic set (plan, section and elevation) of the abbot's kitchen. *After Stukeley, 1725*

packed with interesting archaeological records. Thus he included plans and elevation drawings of some relatively minor churches, like Tickencote, Rutland (Gough, 1789, II, pl.V, after Stukeley). He also thought it worthwhile to publish a plan, drawn to scale, showing the position and alignment of every grave slab in the floor of Lincoln Cathedral, as it was 'before the late new paving' (Gough, 1789, II, pl.VIII). Furthermore, as a result of observations made below floor level, Gough published a reconstructed ground plan of the Norman cathedral and discussed its relationship to the demolished Roman city wall (1789, II, pl.IV).

Outstanding in the seventeenth century was William Dugdale, whose *Monasticon Anglicanum* (1655 and later) was illustrated with detailed engravings, including the first pictorial record of the west front of Wells Cathedral, with every extant statue shown in its niche. Thirty years later the Duke of Monmouth's soldiers were probably responsible for the destruction of the lowest tier of statuary.

The greatest antiquary of the early eighteenth century was William Stukeley, whose *Itinerarium Curiosum* was published in 1725, with a second, enlarged edition in 1776. Stukeley himself was responsible for many of the published drawings, which included a range of ecclesiastical structures and monuments. He illustrated Glastonbury Abbey, for example, with two of his famous 'prospects'—a full ground plan, a longitudinal section through the Lady Chapel—and a trio of measured drawings of the Abbot's kitchen, showing an elevation, cross-section and plan (fig. 6).

After Stukeley came antiquaries like Samuel Lysons, whose archaeological activities were of great breadth: he was an excavator, a student of classical antiquities, an architectural historian and a topographical artist. His contribution to church archaeology in Gloucestershire ranks amongst the finest of county studies (Lysons, 1791). He recorded many features of churches which were later rebuilt or destroyed during 'restoration' campaigns: e.g. the chancel arch of Elkstone church (fig. 7).

By the late eighteenth century detailed architectural drawings of superb quality were being produced by men such as John Carter, and accompanied by texts which attempted to define and discuss architectural history (e.g. Carter, 1780–94 and 1798). The onset of the Gothic revival brought about detailed studies of surviving medieval architecture, not simply out

7 Elkstone, Glos., chancel and sanctuary arches: eighteenth-century drawing of Norman detailing in the church before 'restoration'. Illustrations frequently provide a good impression of the state of decay into which these buildings had fallen, even if the effect is slightly exaggerated. *After Lysons, 1804*

of antiquarian interest, but also because architects who were engaged in restorations and new works needed manuals of style and ornament, and moulding-profiles in order to provide correct detailing. In due course fanaticism overtook common sense and sound judgement, giving rise to mid-nineteenth-century dogmas on what constituted 'correct' Gothic architecture (Clarke, 1969).

Nineteenth-century achievements

In the opening years of the last century architectural, archaeological and topographical recording blossomed and men like John Britton and Thomas Rickman published seminal works. Their volumes were the foundations for the classification and dating of architectural detail. Britton turned out in a quarter-century an amazing five volumes of *Architectural Antiquities* (1807–26) and five volumes of *Cathedral Antiquities* (1814–35): these are indispensable for details which have since vanished. Rickman's volume, *An Attempt to Discriminate the Styles of Architecture in England from the Conquest to the Reformation*, first appeared in 1817 and quickly ran through many editions (most useful are the second,

8 The tower of St Peter's, Barton-on-Humber, Lincs.
Left Drawing made for Rickman to illustrate his
contention that the tower was largely Anglo-Saxon with
a Saxo-Norman top stage. Although it fulfils that
purpose, it is remarkable for its fundamental inaccuracies
and for the fact that the western baptistery has been
omitted and the great arch which provided a
communication between it and the tower is represented
as a modest doorway. Both the round-headed and
triangular-headed panels on the south face are shown
with one bay fewer than there actually is. *After Rickman*,
1819

Right Dating from the turn of the nineteenth-century,
this drawing shows the tower in the condition which
must have obtained at the time of making the previous
illustration. Here, the artist has not taken the liberty of
showing the triangular belfry openings without their
blockings; indeed his honesty has extended to the
inclusion of the vicar's laundry in the picture! It is
always unwise to accept a single antiquarian illustration
at face-value unless the reliability of the artist is well
known

9 Antiquarian illustrations of church ruins
Upper The north-west tower of St Augustine's Abbey Church, Canterbury, an elaborate and very important survival from its period. This drawing was made by Stukeley in 1722, exactly 100 years before the tower collapsed. Nothing of significance now remains. *After Stukeley, 1725*

Lower The west front of St Botolph's Priory Church, Colchester, in the early nineteenth century. This survives largely as seen here, except that the site has been 'cleared' for public display with the consequent destruction of much archaeological evidence. *After Dugdale, 1846*

10 Reconstructed plan of the early twelfth-century church at Bath Abbey. Nothing of this building now stands above ground, except a fragment of arch of the south triforium which is encapsulated in the upper parts of the present Tudor church. The foundations of the Norman nave and aisles lie beneath the modern floors and the parts marked in solid black on the plan were recorded by J. T. Irvine during restoration works in 1867–72. The Norman central tower, transepts and eastern arm are all lost below modern roads, but an excavation in 1979 by Tim O'Leary for the Bath Archaeological Trust, in the centre of the Orange Grove roundabout, revealed part of the north-eastern apsidiole. When put together, there is just sufficient evidence to ascertain the basic form of this great and important church, which was built by Bishop John de Villula to serve not only the abbey but also to be the new cathedral for Somerset, after the demotion of Wells. The closest English parallel for the plan is St Augustine's Abbey, Canterbury, but the ultimate derivation of the type is the church of St Martin of Tours (of which city Bishop John was, incidentally, a native)

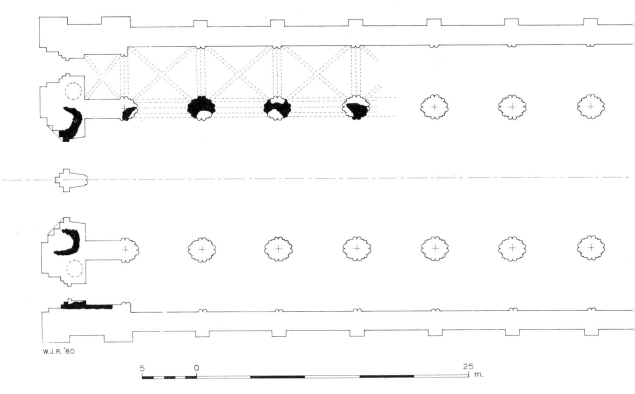

W.J.R. '80

5   0   25 m.

1819, fourth, 1835, and fifth, 1848).

Rickman's approach was archaeological: he divided English architecture into periods, on style (viz. Norman, Early English, Decorated and Perpendicular); he produced classifications and typological sequences for architectural features and decorative details; and he observed that buildings could exhibit stratification in their fabrics. That is to say, a relative chronology for distinctive features could be established by studying the order of construction in those buildings which exhibit several different architectural styles. Rickman's most celebrated observation was that at St Peter's, Barton-on-Humber, Lincs., where a Saxo-Norman belfry crowns a tower which is clearly of a different, and earlier, style (fig. 8). He therefore securely identified Anglo-Saxon work, and was able to transfer his deductions about the Anglo-Saxon style of building to other church towers which he considered to be of similar design (Barnack, Brigstock, Earls Barton, etc.). This enunciation of the principles of archaeological stratification in buildings was not effectively extended to buried remains for more than half a century.

The excavation of buried remains associated with religious buildings had begun in Rickman's time, and the first serious attempt to open up the floor of a church for archaeological study is probably to be accredited to John Browne, a Yorkshire antiquary. After a fire in 1829, he laid bare the remains of the Norman crypt under the choir of York minster (Browne, 1847); following a further fire in 1840, he excavated in the nave (Morris II, 1979, 44). Excavations, however, were still a comparative rarity until the end of the nineteenth century, at

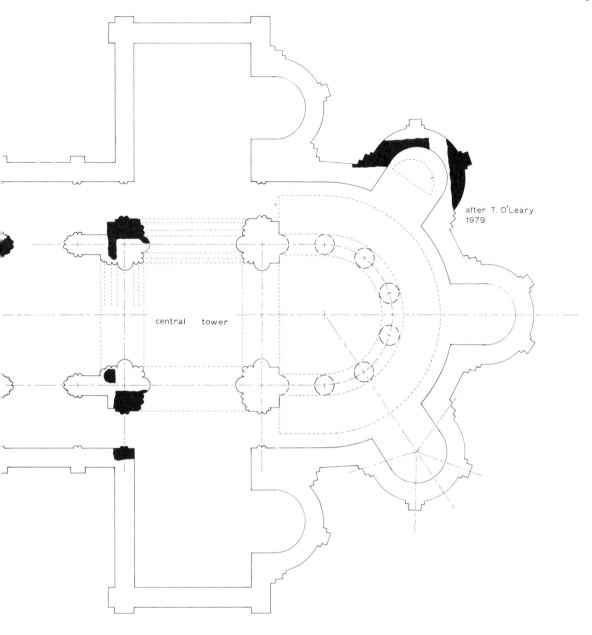

central   tower

after T. O'Leary
1979

least in and around standing buildings. On derelict sites there developed a positive fervour to excavate in trenches, or sometimes clear large areas, in order to recover the *plans* of religious houses. Thus in 1834 excavations began on the cathedral site at Old Sarum, Wilts., in 1850–51 at Tutbury Priory, Staffs., and in 1889–90 at Hulne Priory, Northumb., while at Vale Crucis Abbey, Pembrokeshire, excavations seem to have been more or less continuous from 1882 to 1894. By 1900 the trickle of investigations was turning into a flood: the long series of

excavations was begun at St Augustine's Abbey, Canterbury and continues to the present day; in 1907 Haughmond Abbey, Salop., was investigated; the following year Glastonbury Abbey began to be disinterred, a process which continued intermittently thereafter down to 1979; and in 1912 St Botolph's Priory, Colchester, was summarily cleared (fig. 9). These are but a few examples.

Excavations and observations, by the score, took place in churches and cathedrals in almost every year in the second half of the nineteenth century. Virtually all were occasioned by restoration programmes, such as Stow, Lincs., 1850; Monkwearmouth, Durham, 1855; Bath Abbey, 1863; Jarrow, Durham, 1866; Hexham Abbey, 1881; and St Martin's, Canterbury, 1895. Many restoration programmes were carried out over the course of some years, and archaeological discoveries were frequently being reported for up to a decade after work began, or in some cases longer.

With the great enthusiasm for church building and restoration largely spent by the end of Victoria's reign, the rate of archaeological discovery tailed off rapidly. This coincided with the upsurge of attention being paid to ruined sites, such as those just noted. A few belated restorations of Victorian type were still being carried out, especially in rural areas, down to the First World War. Thus in 1913 the interior of St Peter's, Barton-on-Humber, was being refloored, the walls were stripped and pointed, and small-scale excavations were carried out, yielding results which were to puzzle archaeologists for the next 65 years.

Between 1840 and 1913 hardly a working day passed without the discovery of archaeological evidence in medieval churches up and down the country. The vast majority of this information was simply not recorded. Nevertheless the number of observations committed to paper in the form of notes, sketches and measured drawings was impressive, and has still not been fully digested or published. When one looks through the sheaves of notes and drawings produced by James Irvine, the immense labour of recording archaeological evidence cannot fail to impress. Irvine was clerk of works to Sir Gilbert Scott and was employed on a number of major restoration schemes, such as Bath Abbey (1863–72). The evidence which he recorded so meticulously, more than a century ago, is sufficient to allow the reconstruction of the greater part of the ground plan, and some of the superstructure, of the Norman abbey church (fig. 10; Cunliffe, 1979; O'Leary, forthcoming). Irvine's even more remarkable study of the Anglo-Saxon chapel of St Laurence, Bradford-on-Avon, Wilts., during the period 1871–81, when he was responsible for its rehabilitation, remained virtually inaccessible until it was edited and published by Dr H. M. Taylor in 1972.

In the nineteenth century, archaeological recording was tackled on a small scale by many antiquaries, and on a large scale by few.

Outstanding among the latter were the Rev. Prof. Robert Willis, Charles Clement Hodges, Sir Harold Brakspear and James Irvine. In the early years of the present century they were succeeded by Sir William St John Hope, Roland Paul, Dr John Bilson, Bligh Bond and Sir Charles Peers. Then in the inter-war period Peers, Sir Alfred Clapham and Prof. A. Hamilton-Thompson overshadowed all others. Alongside these men, whose widely based activities included much archaeological recording in and out of church buildings, was another group of scholars, best known for their treatises on architectural style and detail. Their work followed on from Thomas Rickman's (p. 21). There was Augustus Pugin, *Specimens of Gothic Architecture* (1823), J. H. Parker, *Glossary of Gothic Architecture* (1836), F. A. Paley, *Manual of Gothic Mouldings* (1845), R. and J. A. Brandon, *Analysis of Gothick Architecture* (second ed. 1874), and Francis Bond, *Gothic Architecture in England* (1905). This was to be the last great work of architectural synthesis for many years. Bond was a remarkable scholar who, in a space of less than ten years, wrote a series of volumes covering many aspects of archaeo-ecclesiology, the majority of which still remain standard works. They included: *Fonts and Font Covers* (1908b), *Screens and Galleries* (1908) *Woodcarvings* (1910), *Dedications* (1914) and *The Chancel of English Churches* (1916). These examples serve to remind us of the diversity of study-themes which have to be encompassed in church archaeology.

Towards modern archaeology

When archaeologists began to take to the field again after the First World War, there was a marked shift of interest, as already observed. Churches were no longer being restored, so that opportunities for excavation and structural recording seemed to be few; and such a plethora of text-books and learned papers had been written by the previous generation that there seemed very little remaining to be done in church archaeology of the traditional kind. Hence the shift of attention to the excavation of ruined castles and abbeys. This approach, started and fostered by H.M. Office of Works, began c. 1900.

Unfortunately, excavation was almost invariably seen as fulfilling two objectives: first, the recovery of 'the plan' of the buildings, and,

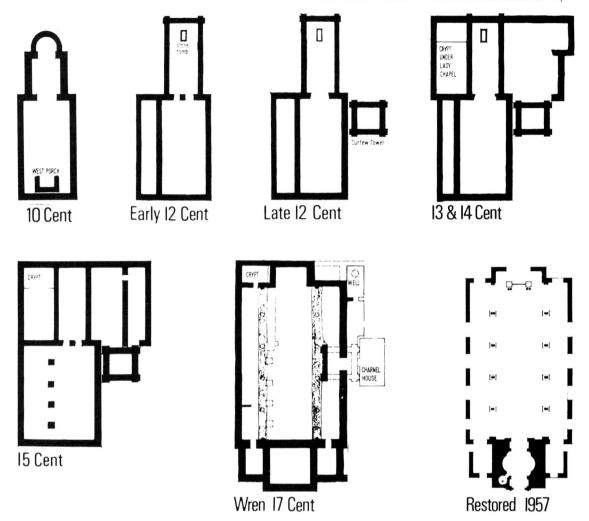

10 Cent   Early 12 Cent   Late 12 Cent   13 & 14 Cent

15 Cent   Wren 17 Cent   Restored 1957

11 St Bride's, Fleet Street, London. The development of the church plan as revealed by excavation after wartime bombing. The feature labelled 'west porch' is probably part of a free-standing cemetery structure ante-dating the tenth century; cemetery features of Roman date were also present (not shown). *After Morgan, 1969*

secondly, the general clearance of sites for display to the public, where this was possible. Many of the excavations were thus undertaken by gangs of workmen who were directed, from a distance, by an eminent architectural historian, such as Hope, Peers or Clapham. One ruin after another was cleared in this way, usually with scant attention being paid to archaeological stratification, either in the ground or in the fabric of the buildings. For some reason which is difficult to explain, the concept of preparing detailed elevation and section drawings of medieval ecclesiastical buildings had faded away, in favour of studying the evolution of plan-forms. There were some notable exceptions, such as the important but insufficiently detailed elevations which were drawn of the Anglo-Saxon church of St Peter, Bradwell-on-Sea, Essex. A set of tinted drawings was prepared in 1919 by the then Office of Works in advance of the rehabilitation of the building (RCHM, 1923, 17 pl.).

Perhaps the most important single work of synthesis to emerge during the inter-war years was Sir Alfred Clapham, *English Romanesque Architecture* (1930 and 1934). Although this contained a heavy emphasis on plan-forms, mouldings, sculpture and certain other architectural features were also discussed in fuller detail than had been attempted hitherto. In his first volume, on the pre-Conquest period, Clapham was following in the footsteps of Prof. G. Baldwin Brown, the most versatile and far-

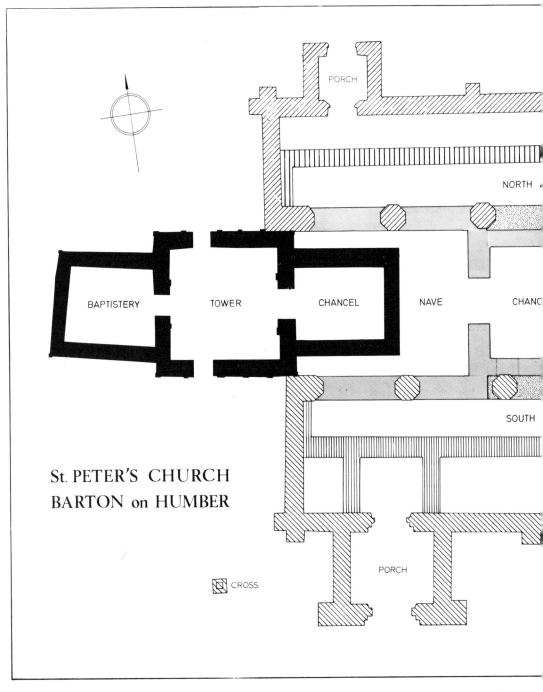

PORCH

NORTH

BAPTISTERY   TOWER   CHANCEL   NAVE   CHANC

SOUTH

St. PETER'S CHURCH
BARTON on HUMBER

CROSS

PORCH

sighted of all Anglo-Saxon scholars. In the early years of the century Baldwin Brown had published a series of volumes, under the title *The Arts in Early England*, on the archaeology of the Anglo-Saxon period, a substantial component of which was church archaeology. Most facets of the subject were touched upon, and in many respects his detailed reasoning and shrewd observations remain unsurpassed today.

The Second World War led to a new kind of church archaeology: the excavation of the parish church. Several dozen medieval churches and one cathedral (Coventry) were either obliterated or seriously damaged by bombing in the early 1940s. The end-product of

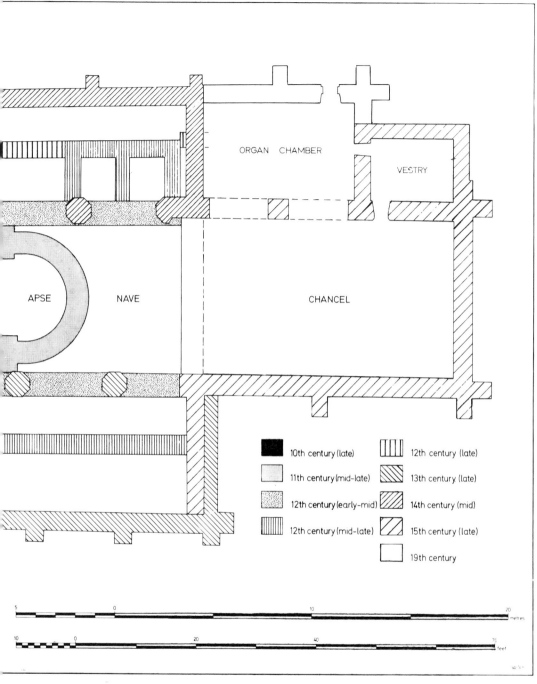

ORGAN   CHAMBER

VESTRY

APSE   NAVE   CHANCEL

■ 10th century (late)	12th century (late)
11th century (mid-late)	13th century (late)
12th century (early-mid)	14th century (mid)
12th century (mid-late)	15th century (late)
	19th century

metres

feet

this devastation varied considerably: some churches have remained as ruins, virtually untouched down to the present day, others have been tidied up and made into landscape features, while quite a number were restored or rebuilt; a few have been erased from the landscape and their sites lost beneath modern urban development.

12 A 'nest' of churches revealed through internal excavation at Barton-on-Humber (see also figs. 13 and 49). The outline of the present church is represented by the outermost walls on this plan. Although the late medieval parts of the church still stand, together with the Anglo-Saxon west tower (fig. 8), nothing could be seen of the early medieval building until excavation took place: the eleventh-century apsidal church and its twelfth-century aisled successor were entirely unknown. *Drawn by Kirsty Rodwell. Crown copyright*

The coming again of war, and the sight of the first few casualties, brought home to architectural historians that there was no adequate record for the vast majority of British parish churches. Thus in 1940 the Central Council for the Care of Churches (later the Council for Places of Worship) called for an emergency programme of church recording, and obtained a government dispensation which allowed a special release of photographic materials to facilitate such recording. In the event, not a great deal was done. This is a pity, because most of that which has been lost is irretrievable. The situation in Britain stood in marked contrast to that in Germany, where extensive architectural records had been made before the war. Thus the Germans knew exactly what they had lost and had the option of using their records to 'recreate' buildings if they so wished. We had no such option for post-war architectural resuscitation.

The most serious losses through enemy action were naturally in the cities, particularly in London (e.g. St Bride's, St Mary Aldermanbury, St Alban Wood Street, St Lawrence Jewry, St Mary le Bow, St Olave's, Christchurch Newgate, St Swithun London Stone, and parts of several monastic houses such as the Carthusian Charterhouse and the Austin Friars) and in Bristol (e.g. St Maryleport, St Peter's, St Augustine the Less and the Temple Church). Losses in the countryside were, relatively speaking, few and far between. Even with its close proximity to London, the total number of churches bombed in Essex was only four out of more than 400 (Shopland, Great Coggeshall, Danbury and Little Horkesley), although there were several 'near misses'.

In every case known to me, the rubble of wartime church bombings was summarily cleared away without so much as a thought for archaeological recording. In all but a handful of instances this academic neglect extended to the subsequent redevelopment of the site. Those few instances are now the classics of early parish-church excavation. The best known is St Bride's, Fleet Street, London, where Prof. W. F. Grimes excavated the complete interior of Wren's church before the rebuilding of the mid-1950s (fig. 11). In 1961 he excavated St Swithun London Stone, in Cannon Street, where an office block now stands. Of St Alban Wood Street, excavated 1961–2, only the tower remains amidst the concrete jungle; and the last

in the series excavated by Grimes (1968) was St Mary Aldermanbury, where the foundations form part of an ornamental garden. In Bristol, only one ruined church was subjected to proper excavation, St Maryleport. Prof. Philip Rahtz examined this site in 1955 when redevelopment was thought to be imminent; that was a quarter of a century ago, and the area is still semi-derelict today.

These post-war investigations were important because they not only introduced the concept of parish-church excavations, but they also demonstrated just how complex these seemingly modest little buildings were. In each of the instances mentioned it was found that the bombed church was only the latest in a long sequence of churches and other structures which had occupied that site since the Roman or Saxon periods. In some cases the foundations of previous churches rested one upon another, as it were 'stacked'. Otherwise, the foundations of the later and larger buildings enveloped those of the earlier phases, forming a 'nest'. Later we shall examine the processes which gave rise to these phenomena; for the sake of convenience they may be distinguished as a 'nest of churches' (figs. 12 and 13) and a 'stack of churches'.

Church archaeology today

In the 1950s and '60s there was then a slight movement towards modern church archaeology, in the sense of excavation, but still nothing approaching a unified study of church buildings, both above and below ground, and of their immediate environs. The breakthrough was made at Winchester. Here, from 1961 to 1971 Prof. Martin Biddle directed a major campaign of excavation in the medieval city, a project which was backed up by intense historical and topographical studies. Unfortunately, there could be no substantial architectural input to this project because the buildings investigated had all long since been levelled to the ground.

From the archaeo-ecclesiastical point of view there were three prongs to the attack at Winchester: first, the study of the two successive Anglo-Saxon minsters which now lie beneath the Cathedral Green; secondly, the excavation of part of the Bishop's Palace; and thirdly, the meticulous examination of a small, but hopefully typical, piece of medieval townscape. This last aspect involved the

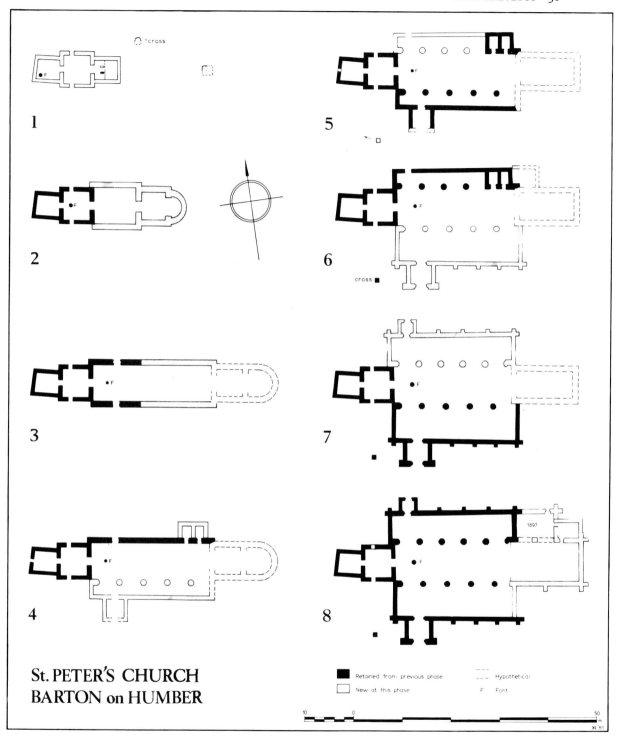

St. PETER'S CHURCH
BARTON on HUMBER

■ Retained from previous phase   --- Hypothetical
□ New at this phase   F Font

13 Development plans of St Peter's Church, Barton-on-Humber, extrapolated from the master-plan of the building (fig. 12). The fine and important Anglo-Saxon tower (fig. 8) dominated the development of this church, causing each successive enlargement to take place to the east. It is more common for the chancel arch to remain the fixed point, from which expansion was effected both to east and west. *Drawn by Kirsty Rodwell. Crown copyright* excavation of a block of land in Lower Brook Street, where there had been medieval houses, streets and churches (St Pancras, Brook Street and St Mary, Tanner Street). For the first time it was now possible to examine the below-ground dimension of a pair of small urban churches and their surroundings, in its entirety. Everything could be, and was, dissected stone by stone.

A different set of circumstances obtained at Wharram Percy, Yorks., where John Hurst and Prof. Maurice Beresford have been leading a campaign of excavation and survey on the site of the deserted medieval village since 1950. The parish church of St Martin stood in ruins and was thus an ideal candidate for detailed architectural study and excavation, both inside and outside. This took place in the years 1962–74 and was an important step forward in church archaeology. The excavation was carried out in unhurried circumstances, but because of its necessarily piecemeal nature problems of correlation and interpretation were encountered. Nonetheless the difficulties and rewards attending the total investigation of a standing church were encountered and tackled at Wharram Percy for the first time in British archaeology (Hurst, 1976).

Concurrently, this kind of investigation was being taken a stage further at Rivenhall in Essex, where the author and Kirsty Rodwell directed a project between 1971 and 1973. Here, a new kind of problem was being tackled: how to investigate and record a parish church which, far from being derelict, was in daily use and was about to undergo a substantial restoration. A complete structural study of the church was organized, together with its monuments, furnishings and fittings; and an excavation was undertaken around much of the exterior of the building (Rodwell and Rodwell, 1973). Also at Rivenhall, excavation was undertaken in a corner of the churchyard, well away from the church itself, to investigate the archaeological losses incurred through modern grave digging (the graveyard is still in use). The logistics and tactics of investigating a 'living' church and its surroundings were found to be very different from those pertaining to disused sites (Rodwell and Rodwell, 1976).

The investigation at Rivenhall was essentially an outdoor one, and the logical corollary was to investigate a living church from the interior. In 1974 this was tackled at Hadstock, Essex, by the same team which had worked at Rivenhall.

Hadstock is a church in use which needed an almost total reflooring. Through the immense goodwill of all concerned, it was possible to close the building completely for three months while full-scale archaeological investigation took place beneath the floors (Rodwell, 1974 and 1976). This was subsequently extended to the walls, roof and superstructure of the tower in 1976 and 1979. The methods adopted at Rivenhall and Hadstock were combined and refined for tackling a much larger project at Barton-on-Humber, begun in 1978. Here, the full-scale structural study and excavation of a complex, redundant urban church are in progress, with simultaneous investigations taking place internally and externally (fig. 2; Rodwell and Rodwell, 1981).

The 1970s also saw three important research projects launched, involving the investigation of Anglo-Saxon parish churches of the first rank. From 1971 to 1976 excavation and structural study took place at Deerhurst, Glos. (Butler, Rahtz and Taylor, 1975; Rahtz, 1976a; Taylor, 1977a); in 1974 a similar programme was begun at Repton, Derbyshire, which still continues (Taylor, 1977b; 1979); and in 1972 a long-term study at Brixworth, Northants., through architectural recording and analysis, was instituted (Parsons, 1977; Cramp, 1977a). These projects have already yielded impressive results, with the promise of much more to come.

So much for parish churches; let us turn now to monasteries. In the 1950s and '60s very little work was undertaken on a substantial scale, which was partly a reaction to the many quasi-archaeological clearances of religious houses in the inter-war years and earlier. But advances have begun to be made in recent years in monastic archaeology of the Anglo-Saxon period, where our knowledge has hitherto been very scant indeed. Much of the new material has come from Prof. Rosemary Cramp's excavations on the twin Northumbrian monasteries of Jarrow (1963–71) and Monkwearmouth (1959–71). Substantial areas of the Anglo-Saxon monastic churches and the associated claustral buildings have been examined, providing the most completely understood pair of plans of English pre-Conquest monasteries (Cramp, 1969; 1976a; 1976b). At the opposite end of the country, the only extensive plan of a Celtic-British monastic complex was recovered by Dr C. A. R. Radford at Tintagel, Cornwall (Radford, 1935; 1955).

The archaeology of cathedrals has received a

pitifully modest amount of attention in the present century. We have mentioned the excavation of the site of the Old Minster at Winchester, and the only other instance where work on a notable scale has taken place is York Minster (1967–73). Here, in the latter part of that period, Derek Phillips directed an impressive campaign of excavation and structural recording, both inside and outside the cathedral, at the same time as complex engineering works were in progress to save the building from collapse. This project transformed previous hypotheses about the early development of the Minster (Phillips, 1975). To the south of the cathedral at Wells excavations in 1978–80 revealed the site and part of the plan of the Anglo-Saxon minster-cathedral, providing a valuable comparison for the work at Winchester (Rodwell, 1980a; 1980c).

Since 1950 there has been a resurgence of interest in ecclesiastical architecture and art, and considerable advances in the study of these subjects are once again being made, mainly in specialist avenues of research, such as stained and painted glass, floor tiles and timber work. A good deal of this reasearch was, until the mid-1970s, being undertaken without reference to the buildings as a whole, and thus such obviously interrelated subjects as floor tiles, wall paintings and window glass were too often seen as separate entities rather than as components in the decoration of medieval buildings. Nor was the study of architectural stonework proceeding hand in hand with that of structural timberwork.

The architecture of the Anglo-Saxon period has been a hotly disputed subject for more than 150 years (summarized by Hunter, 1976) and in the last three decades there has been a flood of papers by Lord Fletcher, E. D. C. Jackson, Dr E. C. Gilbert, Dr E. A. Fisher and Dr H. M. Taylor. The most significant contributions have been made by Dr Taylor, who was responsible for the compilation of an immensely detailed inventory of pre-Conquest and Saxo-Norman churches (Taylor and Taylor, 1965), followed by a volume of analysis and synthesis (Taylor, 1978). He has also contributed many detailed studies of particular buildings and problems, and an important paper on 'structural criticism' which sets out the basic principles for the analysis of standing buildings (Taylor, 1972a). It was not until 1978, however, that the first study of Anglo-Saxon church

carpentry was published, following a gradual realization by scholars that there is a significant quantity of timberwork from this early period still extant (Hewett, 1978). There is a vast amount of surviving medieval timberwork in churches, particularly in roofs and screens, and Cecil Hewett's study of this branch of archaeology has been described as 'epoch making': see, for example, his *Church Carpentry* (1974a) and *English Cathedral Carpentry* (1974b).

The Victorians pioneered the study of medieval stone mouldings, but the subject went into an almost total eclipse between the publication of Bond's *Gothic Architecture* in 1905 and a renewed interest which developed in the early 1970s. Mouldings are now being studied in a systematic manner which was unheard of only a few years ago. Foremost in this field have been the works of the late Stuart Rigold on Romanesque mouldings (Rigold, 1977), and Dr Eileen Roberts and Dr Richard Morris on later medieval mouldings (Roberts, 1977; Morris I, 1978; 1979). The study of mouldings, probably more than any other aspect of building detail, has brought us close to the individual characters of medieval masons and it has been possible to identify the work of one man, or one workshop, in buildings which are many miles apart, or in buildings which are restricted to a discrete geographical locality (e.g. Roberts, 1979). Also on the subject of medieval architects, craftsmen and building practice, a stream of original works has flowed from the pen of Dr John Harvey in recent years. These provide essential background reading for the architectural archaeologist (e.g. Harvey, 1954; 1972; 1975; 1978). Nobody has done more than Harvey to ferret out the names, origins and careers of medieval architects and craftsmen (see especially Harvey, 1974).

Thus, architectural historians and art historians have become increasingly aware of the need to understand and record buildings as multi-dimensional entities, and to apply to them the practical, theoretical and analytical techniques of archaeology. They have also been very active in promoting architectural conservation, as at the west fronts of Wells and Exeter Cathedrals, and in drawing public attention to the ecclesiastical heritage and the dangers which it now faces (Binney and Burman, 1977a; 1977b). Archaeologists, for their part, extended their sight horizons in the 1970s to the study of church buildings in their environment and they have, coincidentally, drawn attention to the ways in which the ecclesiastical heritage is being eroded (Jesson, 1973; Morris II, 1977). Some of the 'threats' are obvious, while many are insidious (Rodwell and Rodwell, 1977). But there is still no room for complacency: much progress needs, for example, to be made in above-ground archaeology of the 'great' churches. To date, the problems of studying, recording and interpreting what might be called the 'architectural archaeology' of cathedrals and like buildings have not really been tackled in Britain. This is one of the great challenges for archaeologists in the late twentieth century: a start was made in 1980 when a comprehensive recording programme was instituted on the west front of Wells Cathedral.

Yet a third viewpoint, which is currently being voiced, comes from the genealogists and others concerned with churchyard monuments. These features too have suffered depredations and their proper recording has become a matter of urgency. In response to the need, methods of recording, based on archaeological principles, have been developed (Jones, 1976; White, 1977).

The destructive urges of modern society, coupled with the undeniable need to repair and adapt church buildings, have therefore caused a wide range of specialist interests to coalesce in such a way that church archaeology has undergone a reincarnation and is now developing along lines which only a decade ago were virtually inconceivable. But the organization of church archaeology in Britain is still elementary compared to that in some Continental countries, particularly Germany, Holland and Scandinavia. In the first two countries there is a tradition of large-scale excavation and thorough study, while in Scandinavia there are tighter controls on archaeologically destructive activities in churches. In terms of both protecting the ecclesiastical heritage and of producing high quality survey-inventories there can be no doubt that Denmark stands in the European forefront (Wilson, 1973; Olsen, 1976).

3 Why Investigate Churches?

'Churches are particularly unedifying as archaeological sites: the structural sequence is difficult to read and usually impossible to date.' This was published in 1978 as the considered opinion of one archaeologist, who continued, 'Artifacts are rare, and the only biological deposits susceptible to analysis are generally those of human bones, normally so numerous that their incidence can be disentangled from each other, and from structures, only with elaborate and often unrewarding efforts' (Carver, 1978). This is fallacious. The underlying contention is that churches, as a whole class of archaeological evidence, are not worthy of concern, or, as Richard Morris has observed, 'whereas we are now comparatively technically well equiped to take advantage of opportunities for investigation, we lack the sense of academic purpose which was available in the intellectual climate of the nineteenth century' (Morris II, 1981, para. 1.1). Why should this be so?

The answer lies in the divergent courses taken by academic studies in the twentieth century, brought about by increasing specialism. We have all too often taken a narrow view of archaeology, at the expense of the real comprehension of history; in so doing some scholars have almost persuaded themselves that there is no longer a place for general and wide-ranging ecclesiastical studies, or for a reassessment of our basic stock of acquired knowledge. 'Most insidious of all is the belief that almost everything worth knowing about churches is already known . . . and an idea exists that little remains to be done apart from dotting the i's and crossing the t's' (Morris II, 1981).

While it is probably true that 'we know more about the Christian Church and Christianity than any other religion that was ever practised', it is a gross exaggeration to claim that 'we know what everything in a church was for, and what happened there on every day of the liturgical year' (Carver, 1978, ii). In fact, pre-nineteenth-century liturgical arrangements in English churches represent one of the greatest voids in our knowledge.

This points to the crux of the matter: the study of ecclesiology has been highly selective. Certain aspects—most notably Gothic architecture, sculpture and art—have been well, but by no means exhaustively, studied. Other aspects, such as church origins and sites, liturgy, graveyards and basic structural histories, have been so little investigated that answers are lacking to both the general and specific questions which are now being asked of the material.

Professor Baldwin Brown's assessment of the problems pertaining to church origins—to take just one aspect—has remained virtually unassailable for three-quarters of a century. His chapter, 'The Village Church: the circumstance of its foundation', examined the historical, topographical, archaeological and place-name evidence and was a masterly exposition of current knowledge (Baldwin Brown, 1903). Slowly, with the acquisition of new knowledge, mainly derived from archaeology, and the reassessment of old evidence and hypotheses, fresh approaches to the material are being tested. (e.g. Brooke and Keir, 1975, ch. 6; Biddle, 1976; Morris II, 1981; Thomas, 1980).

The quest for knowledge

An interest in the past is a component of human nature and it is the principal foundation upon which the British tourist industry thrives. Tourists take an interest in everything around them and have an insatiable appetite for guided tours, booklets, postcards, slides and souvenirs of all kinds. The more that is offered, the more they will take. While many visitors to churches, cathedrals and monasteries seem content to wander around with little or no understanding of what they are looking at, an equal if not greater number have a positive or latent interest in learning something of the history of the building and its past usage. By far the commonest question which is asked by the visitor concerns the origins of the place: How far does this church go back? Where is the earliest part of the building? What is the oldest thing you have found? The sight of an archaeological excavation is sufficient to spark off showers of questions about the early history of the building or locality.

Yet how seldom can questions such as these be answered, however significant the place. Fundamentally, it makes little difference whether one is looking at a chapel or a cathedral: the documentary historian can recall the earliest written reference to the place and the architectural historian can point out the oldest window or doorway. But these are merely identifiable points on a timescale of unknown length. There is an increasing realization that documentary evidence is highly selective and cannot always be taken at face value (p. 175; Butler, 1976; Owen, 1976); furthermore, it is often found that when a critical appraisal is undertaken the written material cannot be unequivocally associated with the architectural (Taylor, 1976). To complicate the matter even further, it is frequently obvious that stylistically datable architectural features such as windows and doorways are not original to the walls in which they are now set, and are merely squares in a patchwork quilt. We shall explore these themes in due course (Chapter 5).

The advent of archaeological excavation in and around churches has added many new dimensions, including the revelation that multiple building phases, in timber and in stone, are commonly present even in simple rural churches, but are now completely masked and their very existence has thus remained unsuspected. Such was the case at Asheldham (Drury and Rodwell, 1978) and Rivenhall in Essex (Rodwell and Rodwell, 1973; 1977; forthcoming).

Something in writing

The interested visitor, upon entering an historic church, usually looks about him for a guide-book or information board, but more often than not he will be disappointed. A survey undertaken in the Chelmsford Diocese in 1974 showed that in 60 per cent of the medieval churches no information was displayed relating to the building. In 11 per cent there was an information board, usually listing a few architectural and historical details in a brief and uninviting manner. The remaining 29 per cent of churches had a guide-book or leaflet of some kind on sale, and of these 10 per cent could be classed as worthy productions (whether large, illustrated guides or merely a few pages of typescript), while the remainder were inaccurate, incoherent and badly produced. Many of the finer churches in the diocese had no guide, and the number for which there was a ground plan available totalled 5 per cent.

Those who attempt the writing of a church guide are only too well aware of the difficulties of finding competent architectural descriptions, details of structural development and, most particularly, information relating to the early history of the building and its environs, especially for the pre-Norman era. Hence it comes as no surprise to find that the opening paragraphs, even in basically sound guide-books, tend to comprise a garbled account of local Roman and Anglo-Saxon history and archaeology. There are frequently mentions of prehistoric implements, the Romans 'passing by', and the Saxons with their 'pagan shrines' in the mythical forests. So often we read that the first church was built by the Normans, and is 'doubtless' on the site of a 'heathen temple'. One could quote from scores of church-guides from all over the country to illustrate the drivel that has been written in the name of history, and which is constantly being reiterated and embroidered upon. It is indeed rare for the local topography of a church to be described, analysed or mapped, yet it is here, in and around the ancient focus, that real local history lies, awaiting recognition and recording.

For the majority of medieval churches there exists no proper architectural description and only one or two general illustrations. Virtually all churches receive a mention, albeit often brief, in Prof. Nikolaus Pevsner's monumental series, *The Buildings of England*; while those churches which lie in regions surveyed by the Royal Commission on Historical Monuments will have been described in moderate detail in the published inventories (pp. 54 and 82).

Reports for series such as those cited have necessarily to be prepared in a hurry, to be sparsely illustrated, and to concentrate on the principal visible features of churches. Detailed structural analyses, full working drawings and a comprehensive set of photographs cannot be prepared under such circumstances. Yet it is only when a survey of that kind is attempted that the real history of a building begins to emerge, and even then it is but the tip of the iceberg, for there is always far more which is concealed from view.

In Britain there is no Commission, or other body established by the Church or State, charged with recording ecclesiastical monuments. Hence the English records are haphazard and of varying quality. This is in sharp contrast to the Swedish and Danish approach, where detailed inventories are being prepared on a systematic and scholarly basis. Dr David Wilson has drawn attention to the British deficiencies, but there is no remedy in sight: 'the inventories published so ably by the Danes and their fellow Scandinavians could well serve as a model for a similar project in this country where day by day churches are becoming derelict, being demolished or neglected, and where in fifty years time there may be no surviving record' (Wilson, 1973).

In Britain there are only semblances of policies for safeguarding historic monuments, and there is a strongly implied philosophy: while a structure is standing, ignore it. There is no effective provision for the architectural recording of buildings, except when a crisis arises, and even then the resources are so inadequate that the response can be little more than a token effort. Thus when a church is declared redundant under the *Pastoral Measure 1968* the Royal Commission on Historical Monuments is notified so that it may record the building. In practice, the record will normally consist of between 6 and 25 monochrome photographs of first-rate quality. Thereafter, the church may be demolished or converted to another use without a set of detailed drawings being produced, not even a plan.

Through an accident of history, an unfortunate division exists, whereby the recording of buildings is a charge on the Royal Commission on Historical Monuments, the study of historical documentation is deemed to be the preserve of Record Societies and the Victoria History of the Counties of England, and archaeological 'rescue' excavations are controlled by the Directorate of Ancient Monuments and Historic Buildings (Department of the Environment). Despite the title, there is no overall provision for the archaeological investigation of buildings. Fortunately, however, there have been several instances in recent years when detailed archaeological study and recording has taken place on the above-ground structure, despite official disapproval at first, at the same time as a rescue excavation has been conducted in or around a church (e.g. Rivenhall and Hadstock, Essex; Little Somborne, Hants.). Thus, under present arrangements, the recording of 'threatened' churches is haphazard and, at best, partial. Churches which are technically not threatened are simply ignored. Familiarity breeds contempt: we assume that because a structure is 'safe' today it will be the same tomorrow and for ever after. This problem was succinctly but forcibly enunciated in 1872 in a Parliamentary Report: 'Practically, it is impossible to ascertain what particular monuments are specially exposed to danger from malicious injury, neglect, or misdirected zeal for "church restoration". A church which seems, today, liable to no molestation, may, tomorrow, at the suggestion of an ambitious architect, an ignorant committee, or a speculator in glazed tiles, be turned inside out.'

Despite all the losses incurred in the later nineteenth century, to which that report was addressed, no lessons were learned: permanent safety of unrecorded buildings was the tacit assumption in 1939, but by 1945 hundreds of churches in Britain (and hundreds more in Europe) had been flattened, gutted by fire or shaken into an unsafe state by bomb-blast. They, for the most part, were not recorded: now they cannot be. The 1970s have been characterized by non-wartime terrorist bombings in Britain; it so happens that these were not directed at churches, but they could well have been.

Vandalism and accidents bring about the sudden destruction of several medieval churches in England every year by fire and other means. Again, the loss usually precedes the record. The following is a sample from the pages of my own case-books over a ten-year period: 1968 Iken, Suffolk gutted by fire; 1969 Woodford, Essex, gutted; 1971 Alresford, Essex, gutted and partly demolished subsequently; 1972 Hagworthingham, Lincs., tower collapsed; 1974 Writtle, Essex, chancel burnt out; 1976 Frating, Essex, tower demolished as allegedly unsafe, by order of the district surveyor (fig. 14); 1978 Downham, Essex, gutted by fire; and 1979 Ickleton, Cambs., eastern parts burnt out. This last example was one of five churches fired by a single arsonist. Yately, Hants., was another such victim.

14 Frating, Essex: modern destruction
Left A fine fourteenth-century tower attached to a small Saxo-Norman church. This photograph was taken a few days before demolition contractors moved in, following the issue of a 'dangerous structure notice' by Tendring District Council in 1976.
Right All that remains of the tower today are two jagged lumps of rubble walling. Not only has this impressive landmark been lost, but so too has its archaeology without a proper record being made. *Photos: author*

Redundancy and its aftermath

When an Anglican church is deemed surplus to pastoral requirements, or beyond economic repair, it may be declared 'redundant' under the *Pastoral Measure 1968*. It is then subject to a clearly defined legal procedure, which takes a minimum of three years. This procedure ultimately determines the church's fate. It may take one of three forms: first, preservation as an ancient monument (by the Redundant Churches Fund, Department of the Environment, a special trust, or some other body with powers of guardianship); secondly, conversion to an alternative use (a community building, museum, dwelling, warehouse, etc.); or, thirdly, demolition. Only in exceptional circumstances is a partial demolition permitted (i.e. the creation of a 'controlled ruin'); total destruction is the norm with this option. The site may then either be left as a graveyard or sold for commercial redevelopment; the latter frequently happens in towns (Binney and Burman, 1977b, 155–75).

Whichever option for disposal is eventually decided upon there is likely to be an archaeological implication. We can consider the third option first, since this is the most drastic.

Obviously, if a church is to be demolished or seriously altered a full archaeological record should be made before work begins; and if below-ground disturbances are anticipated, the only way to record the evidence which will be destroyed is by advance excavation. When the irrevocable step is taken and demolition authorized, it should be controlled, especially if the building is an ancient or multi-period structure. Neither dynamite nor the ball-and-chain is a suitable instrument of demolition. An old building is like a piece of knitting: unpick it carefully and you will recover something useful from the destruction of the original object. Careful dismantling of a church will always lead to the recovery of historical data, as well as re-usable architectural hardware.

The processes involved in converting a church to a new use are generally destructive of archaeological evidence, both above and below ground. Floors may be dug up to lay new foundations and insert a damp-proof course; extensions are often erected; ground levels may be lowered around the building; drains, sewers and cess-pools constructed; old plaster and rendering may be removed; decayed woodwork and stonework replaced; and monuments, furnishings and fittings removed or resited. Some conversions involve destruction on a massive scale, as at All Saints, Oxford, where the entire interior of the church was dug out to a depth of more than 10 feet to construct a library basement. Some of the excavation was by archaeologists, the rest by bulldozer. Perhaps the most ironical of all, was the conversion of St Mary Castlegate, York, into a Heritage Centre: the concept of heritage preservation was taken lightly, and again machinery was brought into the church in order to rip out the interior. This action revealed important evidence relating to the Anglo-Scandinavian period, but proper recording was not possible in the circumstances and much was probably lost.

From the architect's plans and specification, it is seldom apparent just how much archaeological damage will be done during a church conversion. I have never known a conversion take place according to plan: there are always last-minute revisions, discoveries of sinking floors, subsiding foundations, or bulging wall-cores. Time and again builders dig holes where they are least expected, and hitherto unknown architectural features are invariably discovered when work is in progress, while other details which were thought to be safe get destroyed through ignorance or accident. Finally, whatever archaeological controls may be imposed during the conversion process, there is nothing effective that can be done to safeguard the building and the site from depredation in future years, after they have passed from ecclesiastical to secular control. It is unnecessary to discuss church conversions here in further detail since that has been done elsewhere, from archaeological and other points of view (Rodwell and Rodwell, 1977; Tudor-Craig, 1977; Binney and Burman, 1977b, 188–204).

The third and most desirable option for the disposal of a redundant church is for it to be vested in a body with guardianship powers, with the intention that the building will be maintained and cared for as an ancient monument and will be accessible to the public. This is basically static preservation. In theory there should be no need for anything to be lost, damaged or destroyed, and the usual intention is to preserve the complete ensemble of furnishings, fittings and graveyard monuments. However, theory and practice can, and usually do, differ. Many churches which are designated for preservation are, at the moment of handover, in a dreadful state of neglect or are even dangerous. One of the factors which often precipitates a declaration of redundancy is the decayed state of the building and the parish's inability to raise the necessary funds to return it to good order. Thus, when the Department of the Environment took over St Peter's, Barton-on-Humber in 1978 the floors were sodden and rotten; and when the Redundant Churches Fund assumed responsibility for Redbourne Church, Lincs., in 1980 the east wall of the north aisle had collapsed, the roof of the south aisle was falling in and the south-east chapel was completely roofless.

Preservation is not therefore a static situation, and restoration works are usually undertaken by the guardianship body. These may be nothing more than a few running repairs to gutters and glazing, but they may involve the demolition of much of the building and the consolidation of the rest. This happened at Lassington, Glos., where the Anglo-Saxon nave of the church was demolished as part of a 'preservation' scheme. At Little Somborne, Hants., the Redundant Churches Fund initiated extensive restoration works, which involved drainage excavations around the exterior, reflooring the interior, removing the rendering from the south wall, stripping internal plaster, and completely relaying the roof. A programme of archaeological investigation was fully integrated into this project (Biddle, 1975b).

St Peter's, Wickham Bishops, Essex, was a derelict church on the brink of demolition in 1960 and is now vested in the Friends of the Friendless Churches. Reroofing has taken place, much of the window tracery has been renewed, and the whole exterior of the building is being reconditioned in such a way as to remove or obscure most of the archaeological evidence which the wall surfaces formerly exhibited. This work has not been recorded.

Archaeology and the living church

It is legitimate to ask whether, with some 8,500 churches in England which are still largely or wholly medieval in fabric, we should be too concerned about the relatively small number of buildings which have become redundant? First, however, the redundancy casualties are not so few in number that they can be ignored: in the first ten years of operation of the *Pastoral Measure 1968* one thousand buildings have been declared redundant, of which about half could be described as substantially medieval. Many of the remainder are not without archaeological interest. Secondly, a church is made redundant on pastoral grounds, not on the basis of its historic merit. Thus there are redundant churches of all ages, from Anglo-Saxon to twentieth-century buildings. Thirdly, and perhaps most importantly, living churches are not significantly 'safer', archaeologically speaking, than redundant ones.

This far-reaching statement needs support. A living church is not a static building either: it is subject to restoration and alteration to a greater extent than is perhaps generally realized. We may look back on Victorian restorations and condemn them as unnecessary, excessive or insensitive, but churches were generally in a poor structural state at the end of the Georgian era, and restoration was inevitable, although the extent to which it was taken is a matter for censure (fig. 15). It is now a century or more since the great wave of church restorations was undertaken, and many buildings have had very little done to them in the intervening period. It is not therefore surprising that we are approaching the crest of a new restoration wave. The scheme for State Aid

to Churches in Use came into operation in 1978 and is providing a vast sum of money for church repairs which was previously not available.

This is all to the good. The money will help to put many churches into good order which were actually or potentially falling into decay and ruin. Unfortunately, there are signs that the increased cash-flow is also aiding excessive restoration in some churches. The basic relevant fact is that church restoration is a continuous process and that at any given time there are several hundred churches undergoing building works, the great majority of which have archaeological implications. Furthermore, church extensions, new vestries, toilets and other facilities are being built in many places. New works at cathedrals are generally on a larger scale: visitors' centres, treasuries, cathedral schools, workshops and so on.

While new work and alterations to existing structures can clearly pose archaeological problems, it is seldom appreciated by the non-specialist how far-reaching are the results of even conservative restoration. The meaning of the term 'restoration' is widely misunderstood. There are two distinct forms of restoration. The first, and literal, meaning is 'to return to a former condition'. This can seldom be done precisely. An alabaster tomb, for example, can be restored by cleaning, fixing together broken parts, filling cracks, etc. This is really the process of 'conservation', or taking care of what actually exists. The second, and more commonly implied, meaning of 'restoration', is the renewal of damaged or missing parts in the same form as they originally existed, or as they are believed to have existed. Thus restoration, as generally practised, is the destruction of something original and its replacement with a replica (fig. 16) (for an architect's view, see Schofield, 1977).

Having said this, it must at once be admitted that restoration is an essential process in the maintenance of old buildings, it being inevitable that archaeological evidence will be destroyed both by nature and by man. There are many ways in which evidence may be lost and these, together with examples, have been fully discussed (Rodwell and Rodwell, 1977, ch. 9). To summarize: archaeological evidence below ground is destroyed every time the soil is disturbed, whether that be for the digging of graves or drains, or laying foundations, new floors or pipes; above ground, evidence is destroyed or masked when stone and timber

15 St Mary's, Deerhurst, Glos., the church and Priory Farm from the south, 1794 and 1979. Victorian 'restorations' have removed the high-pitched chancel roof (which might well have been of late Saxon date), completely changed the character of the south porticus, and altered windows and doorways. Despite the unpromising looking exterior, this church has, upon archaeological investigation, yielded the most significant evidence yet available for the development of a complex, multi-cellular building of the Saxon period. See also figs. 88–9. *Photos: author, the upper after Lysons, 1804*

16 A fourteenth-century window is seen here partially dismantled for the renewal of decayed tracery and mullions, presenting an opportunity to record the geometry of the window and the profiles of the original mouldings. Piecemeal replacement of masonry has led in many instances to the complete removal of medieval work without record. *Photo: author*

repairs take place, when plaster or rendering is stripped and renewed, when walls are rebuilt, refaced or repointed. Damage can be insidious and unsuspected: thus, stripping old plaster or cutting conduits in it for cables can easily destroy hidden medieval wall paintings; and whenever timberwork is treated with a liquid preservative it may be ruined from the point of view of radio-carbon dating.

In the churchyard there is just as much

archaeological evidence as in the building itself, and this evidence is destroyed when funerary monuments are broken up or removed from their original sitings, when boundaries are demolished or rebuilt, and when earthworks are levelled.

Enough has been said to demonstrate that natural decay and all forms of interference with a church, its contents or surroundings will bring about a loss of historical information. This information is unique to each site and it is irreplacable. Often it can only be detected, recorded and interpreted through archaeological techniques: the techniques themselves can be simple or sophisticated, and they are being improved all the time. A great deal of the archaeological evidence encapsulated in churches is obvious and, through trained eyes, may be interpreted with a minimum of effort. But even more evidence is not obvious: it is concealed in the ground, under floors, behind plaster, hidden by a ceiling or by cobwebs in a belfry.

No ancient church in Britain has been studied to exhaustion—indeed most have not been studied at all—and every one could be made to yield more of its unwritten history through archaeological investigation. We shall explore the evidence and the methods of recovering it in subsequent chapters.

Are churches especially important?

Before leaving this section we should face the question which is frequently asked as to the relative importance of churches, compared with other types of archaeological site. There is no simple answer to this: it depends upon the kind of archaeological data which are being sought, and the way in which investigations are to be undertaken. In theory, at least, a church should not be especially different from any other kind of archaeological site which incorporates upstanding structures, such as a castle or a manor house. In practice, however, the logistical problems of investigating churches can be considerable, and bewildering to those who lack familiarity with the whole field of ecclesiology. Sadly, there are many archaeologists and others who believe that there is nothing more to be gained from a church investigation than a series of plans illustrating development phases, and a lot of embarrassing bones. This is the equivalent of the pre-war attitude to the excavation of Roman villas: the sole or primary objective was to ascertain the plan of the main dwelling.

There is also the unfortunate attitude, exemplified in the opening quote to this chapter, that a Christian graveyard is just a sea of unstratified bones, and that burials will have destroyed everything which might otherwise have been found in or around a church. The disinclination to treat Christian burials with the academic respect they deserve is a legacy of our long history of excavation on pagan cemeteries, particularly Roman and early Anglo-Saxon, where pottery, jewellery and other 'grave goods' have dominated funerary studies.

These preliminary remarks are necessary because church archaeology is such a complex subject and one which has only recently become re-established, in its full and proper sense, in the annals of British archaeology. There will thus inevitably be misunderstandings and prejudices which will take a generation or so to expunge.

We shall be looking in detail at the kinds of evidence which a church can yield in later chapters: so of the general points, the first and most important is that churches easily constitute the most completely surviving class of archaeological monument. Hence, it is possible to test all observations, hypotheses, statistical studies, and so on, against a known and finite background. At any one time in medieval England there were at least 12,000 parish churches, plus cathedrals, chapels and monasteries. The numbers of buildings in each of these categories varied from century to century, as new structures were put up and old ones abandoned. But within a fairly fine tolerance the total of ecclesiastical buildings at any given period can be calculated. While there has been about a ninety per cent destruction toll on monastic buildings (the sites of most are known), the survival rate of parish churches and cathedrals is very high: at least 8,500 are still substantially medieval, while many more incorporate early elements in post-medieval fabrics. In not more than 0·5 per cent is both the church building and all knowledge of its site lost.

Churches are of course numerically overtaken by a few classes of site, such as Bronze Age barrows and medieval manors, but the survival of evidence is at a much lower level. Barrows, for example, once probably outnumbered churches by five to one, but the vast majority have been destroyed or mutilated, so that there is precious little left to excavate. Manor houses, on the other hand, survive to this day in far greater numbers, but many no longer incorporate any trace of a medieval building, and in not a few cases sites have been shifted too. The contrast with churches is marked: only in exceptional circumstances have they 'migrated', at least until fairly recent times.

The church is normally the oldest surviving building in a settlement, so that *ipso facto* it usually provides for the topographical archaeologist the earliest fixed point in the local post-Roman settlement history. Very often too the road pattern and major boundaries immediately around the church are demonstrably of early date. Indeed sometimes one can detect that the church was an introduction into a pre-existing and very ancient landscape. On other occasions it is clearly to be seen how a settlement has developed around a church, or how a market place may have been established beside the gate of a monastery or cathedral. Where a medieval manor house and church stand cheek by jowl, the church often began as a proprietary chapel, the implication here being that the manor house was established first. Almost everywhere the position of the medieval church is pivotal in settlement history.

Next, the position of the church in social history should be recalled. It was not just a building used on Sundays and feast days. In most villages it was the only public building, and was in continuous use. An amazing range of activities took place in the body of the church, in upper-level chambers, in the porch and in the churchyard. In many churchyards there were other buildings too, and town churches were intimately involved with markets and with guilds of craftsmen and merchants. The church was focal to medieval life, serving not only spiritual and sepulchral requirements, but also fulfilling a wide range of social, commercial and educational needs. In the Middle Ages the Church and the Crown were the principal patrons of the arts and providers of work for skilled craftsmen in virtually every trade. It is not therefore surprising that ecclesiastical buildings comprised the greatest store-houses of medieval art and architecture in the land. Much of that achievement still remains, and more can become available through the labours of the archaeologist.

The great volume of documented history pertaining to the Church is unrivalled in any other branch of archaeological study: there are cartularies, registers, wills, archdeacons' acts, terriers, vestry minutes, faculty papers, tithe awards, tombstones and painted inscriptions. All these sources of data are inseparable from the physical evidence and must be considered side by side. Taken together they admit precision where it would otherwise be unattainable. Phases' of building work, particularly in monasteries and cathedrals, can often be ordered into long sequences with many dated fixed-points. These critical points and sequences provide the foundations for much of the dating of medieval and later architecture, art and artefacts.

Finally, there is the range of evidence. At a basic level, there are the observable regional and local styles of art and architecture, the foreign influences, evidence of itinerant architects and craftsmen, and of course the time-scale from the sixth century to the present day. At a more refined level, there are all the component parts, the historical styles, the trademarks of individual craftsmen and of gangs of labourers, which together make up the fabric of an ancient church. All this we tend to take too much for granted and speak loosely of, for instance, Kempley, Glos. as a 'complete' Norman parish church, or of Salisbury as a 'single-period' Gothic cathedral. We may glance at the west front of Lincoln cathedral and accept it as a two-period construction (Norman and early English), and compare it with the west front of Wells as a single-period work (Early English), Yet these are massive over-simplifications, for there are at least four architecturally distinguishable building phases in each of those west fronts. And each phase will have involved an architect who drew up the plans, craftsmen who did the physical work of construction and artists who applied the decoration. They were all human beings who will have made mistakes and developed new ideas as they worked, so that in points of detail, at least, the end-product will have differed from the original intention. Furthermore, it must not be forgotten that no medieval building, or indeed very few parts of buildings, can be seen today in anything like the state in which they were left by their creators: the passage of time, the activities of 'reformers' and despoilers, and the hand of the 'restorer' have erased perhaps 95 per cent of all medieval ecclesiastical art which once existed in this country. The survival rate amongst the applied arts is much higher, although related closely to age.

Enough has been said to dispel any latent idea that because churches exist in their thousands, and because so many embody medieval architecture and ornament in their fabrics, they are fully or even largely comprehended in their historical, topographical, artistic and architectural dimensions. It is only through archaeological investigation that fragmentary architecture can be recreated, destroyed decoration be revisualized, medieval architects' lost plans redrawn and the individual contributions of artists, craftsmen and labourers may be detected, appreciated and recorded. It is to the techniques of study that we must now turn.

4 Church Surveys

There are several distinct meanings of the term 'survey' as used in architecture and archaeology. First, there is the detailed study and recording of a site or monument, in which an attempt is made to note down, draw or photograph as much information as possible: that is an 'intensive' or 'detailed' survey. Secondly, there is the wide-ranging but superficial examination of a group of sites, or a large geographical area, in order to record information in general terms, not in detail: that is a 'non-intensive' or 'general' survey. These represent the opposite ends of a continuous scale. There is also a third kind of survey, undertaken by architects, the 'survey of condition'. It normally comprises the detailed examination of a single church, from the point of view of its structural stability, general state of repair, condition of decorations, etc. It is a strictly utilitarian survey, rather than an academic one.

All three kinds of survey are relevant to archaeo-ecclesiology and will be discussed in turn, but first the general background must be examined. These surveys, as we now understand and operate them, are of recent conception. But the principle of examining and recording the condition of a building, making a schedule of its contents or preparing an inventory of associated property is as ancient as any form of record keeping. Any survey, no matter what its original purpose or date, which contains structural or topographical information that can specifically be tied to a church or its associated property, is of interest to the archaeologist. There are, of course, many documents which contain incidental structural and topographical evidence but which should not be classed as surveys: most Anglo-Saxon and medieval sources of ecclesiastical information fall into that category, but there are some notable exceptions.

Surveys from the past

It is unfortunate for church archaeology that the greatest property inventory in English history—the Domesday survey of 1086—did not really concern itself with ecclesiastical sites and buildings: monasteries, churches, chapels and priests were regularly mentioned under entries for some counties, but not for others. The reasons why this should be so are not wholly clear and need not detain us here. Thus, for example, the differences in approach of the Domesday surveyors are demonstrated in the adjacent counties of Suffolk and Essex, where respectively c.360 and 17 churches were recorded. Yet it is clear when information of all kinds is assembled that there were probably between 400 and 450 churches in Suffolk by 1086, while for Essex there is a strong presumption in favour of a minimum of 350. Domesday records 176 churches in Kent, but it so happens that there are three near-contemporary surveys which list the churches of the Dioceses of Rochester and Canterbury, bringing the eleventh-century total to just over 400 (Ward, 1932; 1933).

Such early surveys tell us some of the places where there were churches, but give little further information of relevance. Approaching the material from a different angle, the Domesday survey provides a good deal of information on the lands held by religious houses and bishops. Thus in Northamptonshire estates were held by the church of St Remigius of Rheims, nine religious houses (including the abbey of Grestain) and four bishops (of Lincoln, Coutances, Durham and Bayeux). The usual inventories of the estates are given, covering types of land, acreages, men of various ranks, livestock and a few other details; but even on these ecclesiastically owned estates the local churches are scarcely ever mentioned.

Although the Domesday survey was not intensive by modern standards, it nonetheless provides a wealth of topographical data for ecclesiastical studies. Unfortunately the art of map making was unborn in 1086, and throughout the survey was the underlying assumption that an estate was a more-or-less static entity for which descriptions of location were unnecessary. This naturally causes great difficulties in mapping estates.

The medieval cartularies (official records) possessed by monastic houses sometimes contain precise topographical information, but on the whole they do not constitute surveys in the sense which is meant here. The inventories which were produced from 1535–50 in conjunction with the Dissolution of religious houses are quite different. These could be very detailed and include mention of many buildings by name, a note of the quantities and values of the re-usable materials in those buildings (lead, glass, timber, paving, etc.) and a full inventory of the goods and chattels in the establishment (down to bed linen and broken furniture). There are also schedules of work preserved which tell us about the numbers of craftsmen involved in dismantling monastic houses, how much they were paid, how long they took about the task, and so on. The demolition contractor's record of work on the priory church at Lewes, Sussex, is a good example. Paraphrased, we read:

A vault on the right side of the high altar that was held up by four great pillars, having about it five chapels: all this was down on Thursday and Friday last. Now we are plucking down a higher vault. . . . We brought from London 17 men, three carpenters, two smiths, two plumbers and one man who keeps the furnace. Each man attends to his own office. Ten of them hewed the walls about, among which were three carpenters; they made the props for undersetting while others broke and cut away the walls. On Tuesday they began to cast the lead. . . . (Wright, 1843, 180–1).

Accounts such as this have considerable value for the light they shed on buildings which have been mutilated or have entirely disappeared, and for helping to interpret evidence uncovered by the archaeologist during excavation. Thus, for example, the Cluniac priory at Prittlewell, Essex, was suppressed in 1536 and partly demolished. Nothing was known of the church until its site was rediscovered and partially excavated in the 1950s and '60s (Helliwell, 1958). But the full survey and valuation prepared in 1536 told us that there was a Lady Chapel and a Rood Chapel, both in 'the body of

the church', altars to St John and St Thomas, and a vestry. All these areas, together with the quire, were furnished: each was inventorized separately and the value of every item stated. There were alabaster tables, organs, hand-bells and candlesticks; altar cloths, hangings, carpets and cushions; chalices, censors, crosses and pyxes; vestments, copes old and new, mass books and antiphoners (Burrows, 1953). This inventory and the excavated evidence are entirely complementary: each helps to illuminate the other.

Inventories of materials are not only helpful for the understanding of demolished buildings, but they may also contribute to the archaeological study of standing structures. Although easily overlooked, there is a kind of Newtonian law which governs demolition: what comes down must go somewhere. Where did all the materials from the suppressed monasteries go? More than half of those materials are, to this day, probably incorporated in standing buildings. Thus it is relevant for the archaeologist to study who bought what, and where he took it, at the Dissolution. Lists of purchasers were often recorded, sometimes with specific destinations for the materials. The reuse of lead and carting of rubble were often mentioned in contemporary records, the latter being particularly significant to the investigator who is trying to discover the origin of moulded stones which may turn up in a post-medieval barn or garden wall. Some shipments of materials were to places so far distant from the demolished building that one would never guess what had happened without the documented clue. For instance, stone from the demolition of St Augustine's Abbey, Canterbury, was shipped to Calais in 1541. Similarly there are numerous local traditions, of varying reliability, of roofs, architectural stonework and fittings being taken from suppressed monasteries and re-erected in parish churches and manor houses. Thus to take again the example of Prittlewell Priory, it is said that one of its roofs was taken to Wickford Church (12 miles) and another to Rochford Hall (3 miles). We shall return later to the redistribution of materials and the archaeological problems of detection and interpretation (pp. 68–70).

Surveys of church buildings and property have more commonly survived from after the Reformation. The archdeacons in each diocese undertook regular surveys of condition and their reports, known as 'Visitations', have survived in large numbers. These reports covered both churches and their contents: they concentrated more on recording what was wrong or what was missing, in contrast to the Commissioners at the Dissolution who recorded only what was present. Visitations do, however, often record church plate, bells and other essentials. Typical items listed as wants and dilapidations in the Archdeacon of Colchester's Visitations of 1683 include the following (Pressey, 1940).

Structural defects. The east window wants glazing; the church wants paving; the chancel is out of repair; the church roof wants tiling; the steeple wants new shingling; the leads over the south aisle want mending; and the buttress on the south side of the church to be repaired.

Furnishings and fittings. The church to be new whited; there are no ornaments belonging to the communion table; the pulpit cushion to be new covered; the font wants mending; the pulpit cover wants mending; there is a chalice without a foot; and there are five bells but they are out of order.

Church property. The fence about the churchyard wants repair; the alders and other trees rooting near the church to be cut down and stubbed up; the parsonage house very ruinous; and the vicarage barn is out of repair.

Many of the items listed in visitations have a direct bearing on the archaeological study of church property, providing close dating for works of restoration and improvement. Occasionally demolitions were recorded, as at Little Holland, where in 1683: 'The Church is adowne and has bin downe for about 24 yeares. There are three bells which lie in Sir Thomas Darcyes yard.' As we approach recent times, and especially the nineteenth century, inventories and surveys of church property become more numerous and contain more detail. There were, for example, the great surveys (with maps) prepared for tithe commutation in the late 1830s, glebe terriers and the detailed architectural surveys which were often drawn up as a preliminary to major restoration campaigns.

Architects' inspection surveys

The need to restore, enlarge or rebuild ancient churches, from the closing years of the eighteenth century to the end of the nineteenth, gave rise to the preparation of architectural surveys and reports. These mark the beginning of the modern 'survey of condition'. The survival of documents from the first half of the period is not great, but for the second half large numbers of survey notebooks, plans, specifications and faculty papers are extant. Plans for reordering and reseating are amongst the commonest survivals. Many architects drew plans only to illustrate their proposals, but some prepared measured surveys of churches as they stood prior to restoration. These are especially valuable to the ecclesiastical archaeologist since they provide records of church interiors in their late medieval or Georgianized forms.

Even more valuable are architects' survey books in which measurements, ideas and observations were noted in varying amounts of detail, according to the disposition of the architect concerned. Thus when G. E. Street restored Tackley Church, Oxon., in 1864 he submitted a plan showing proposals to the parish in the usual way: that plan—still in the possession of the parish—is a unique document. Sometimes two or three copies of plans were made, but often there was only one, and that may now be lost. It is always a great joy to discover survey documents which were not known to survive: thus in 1980 Benjamin Ferrey and J. T. Irvine's schedule of works proposed for the west front of Wells Cathedral, made in 1870, unexpectedly came to light. This is most fortuitous because archaeologists and architects are trying to ascertain the condition of the front prior to the restorations of the 1870s and later. In this case it so happens that several photographs taken *c.* 1860 are available for comparison. J. T. Irvine, whom we have already mentioned (p. 26), was not strictly speaking an architect, but a clerk of works. He nevertheless undertook surveys and prepared notes of the greatest historical interest on buildings such as Bath Abbey and Peterborough Cathedral. One could multiply these examples with countless more.

Looking beyond architectural papers relating to individual churches, and in particular those which were provided for professional reasons, there are also vast numbers of survey notebooks which have accumulated and still are accumulating in architects' offices. These often take the form of day-books, and thus any one might contain material relating to dozens of buildings. To the archaeologist and historian these are primary record material and should never be destroyed. Sadly, most were, and still are being, destroyed or lost beyond recall. Such losses are highlighted by the incredible wealth of information contained in that material which has survived. Outstanding in this field is the Chancellor Collection of architectural drawings, survey notes, sketches and correspondence. The architectural practice of Beadle, Son and Chancellor was established at Finsbury Circus, London, in 1853 and finally closed at Chelmsford in 1965. The two leading figures of the practice were Frederic Chancellor and his son Wykeham, who were both keen antiquaries and published profusely; they were involved in restorations, extensions and new buildings for scores of churches in the London-Essex area.

In the architectural milieu in which the Chancellors worked drawings and notes were sacrosanct: the originals were never discarded, and hence a complete portfolio of the architectural practice has come down to us. Nowadays there is a regrettable tendency to treat outdated surveys, drawings and the like as irrelevant lumber. It cannot be said too strongly that the loss of twentieth-century architectural records will be viewed as no less a tragedy in years to come than we now view the loss of so many Victorian records. All unwanted architectural material should be deposited in an appropriate archive: the Diocesan (County) Record Office, the National Monuments Record (London) or a Cathedral Library, as appropriate (see also pp. 168–70).

Architects' surveys of churches were, comparatively speaking, few in number during the first half of this century, excepting those commissioned for the reinstatement of war damage. However, church surveys assumed a new dimension with the introduction of the *Inspection of Churches Measure 1955*. This provided for every parish church to be inspected by an architect and a survey report produced, at not less than five-yearly intervals. These reports (Quinquennial Surveys) constitute a significant class of historic documents in the making. They will be as important to future generations as are seventeenth- and eighteenth-century archdeacons' visitations to us (although visitations are still performed they have long since ceased to be concerned with architectural matters).

Quinquennial surveys vary in content and presentation but in essence their function is to list everything which is at fault in the church (not only the fabric but also major furnishings and fittings, and the boundaries) and to recommend an order of priority for remedial works. In practice, of course, not everything recommended is done in the quinquennium, or even at all. But surveys, together with faculty papers, provide a superb running commentary on the condition, maintenance and other developments in Anglican churches, regardless of age. When working on the archaeology and history of a church, the investigator will often find himself needing to refer to surveys of the 1950s and '60s.

General archaeological surveys

This heading covers a multitude of forms of investigation and study, and there is one important difference between surveys in this category and the two previous. We have moved from purely utilitarian operations and obligatory surveys to investigations carried out on a voluntary or academic basis. The same will apply to the fourth category, detailed surveys.

While there is a long tradition in British archaeology of producing weighty, academically inspired corpora of certain classes of sites and finds, often of a very esoteric character from the point of view of the non-specialist, there has been little attempt, until recently, to tackle wide ranging non-intensive surveys. In purely architectural and art-historical terms, some surveys of this nature were produced well back into the last century, but the archaeologist generally fought shy of such an approach until the early 1970s. Then in 1973 the idea was widely adopted and there was a perhaps ill-considered rush to embark on regional, county and district surveys at a general level, choosing various topics such as historic towns, villages, barrows, industrial monuments, cropmarks and so on. Most of these surveys were undertaken by archaeological units and county archaeological societies. But in the midst of this surveying euphoria there was a noticeable reluctance, especially at certain official levels, to embark on surveys of ecclesiastical subjects. On the one hand the uninformed view was put forward that since we know so much about churches they do not need further attention for the time being; on the other hand was the fear expressed by those better informed that the subject was of such enormous breadth that it was impossible to tackle it usefully with the available resources. As ever, a happy medium could have been found if sought.

In the event, several sample surveys were

tackled in various parts of the country, with differing terms of reference. So far only two of these—the first to be undertaken—have been published, but reports on two or three more are likely to follow. Only limited discussion of the aims and achievements of general archaeo-ecclesiastical surveys can therefore be offered here. By coincidence, both the available reports relate to Essex churches, although the problems and principles enunciated in these are of country-wide relevance.

As has been observed, church archaeology was stimulated by threatened redundancies in the wake of the *Pastoral Measure 1968*. The first fear of archaeologists was that medieval churches would be lost through demolition, their second was for the destruction of hidden or buried evidence through building works associated with the conversion of churches to new uses. At local-authority level the initiative was first taken by the Planning Department of Essex County Council which, in 1974, undertook a survey of the 30 redundant and disused churches in the county. In the published report (Essex County Council, 1976) the churches are considered as components in the landscape, as historic buildings requiring new uses, sensitive restoration and mainten-

ance, and as complex archaeological sites in need of study and recording. This, incidentally, is the only survey in the group under discussion which was prepared directly under the auspices of an official body: the remainder were tackled on a part-time or only semi-formal basis.

While the potentially dramatic effects of redundancy rightly claimed attention, it was also appreciated by some archaeologists that even greater, although less obvious, threats to church archaeology were the ordinary processes of restoration, maintenance and adaption of churches in regular use. Out of this realization grew the other Essex survey. It was undertaken in 1973–74 under the auspices of the Essex Archaeological Society with the remit to examine and report upon all parish churches and former church sites, antedating 1750, in the Archdeaconry of Colchester: that is a strip of varied countryside stretching from the east coast at Harwich to just south-east of Cambridge. The survey area included the

17 Map of the diocese of Chelmsford showing the extent to which historic churches have been lost through total or partial demolition. In the great majority of cases there is little or no record of what has been destroyed; some of the demolitions took place several centuries ago. *After Rodwell and Rodwell, 1977*

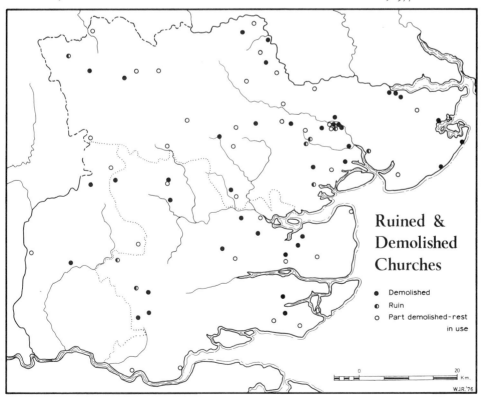

Ruined & Demolished Churches

● Demolished
◐ Ruin
○ Part demolished—rest in use

Borough of Colchester and 220 medieval churches and sites. The study covered approximately half the Chelmsford Diocese and the published report (Rodwell and Rodwell, 1977) set the survey in its diocesan context. It is worthwhile to examine this survey and its findings since, to a greater or lesser extent, it has acted as a model for most other church surveys.

It might be thought remarkable that we should not know just how many medieval churches there were in the Archdeaconry, or in the Diocese, but that was the case, and indeed still is the case in most dioceses. Lists of parishes published in diocesan handbooks give no real clue to the numbers of churches in the area, let alone those which are medieval. Thus in the Chelmsford Diocese there were 515 parishes in 1975, a reduction from more than 550 twenty years earlier, although an increase from 415 in 1750. But even that figure still did not give the number of extant medieval parish churches, since more than 40 buildings were found to have been demolished or have fallen into ruin (fig. 17). In some instances these 'lost' churches survive as picturesque overgrown ruins, while others have been completely flattened and now lie beneath fields or have been built over. Thus the initial task of the survey was simply to discover what the ecclesiastical heritage comprised and to record the present state of each building or site.

In order to simplify the recording a *pro forma* was devised (fig. 18) which has been used, with some modifications, for surveys in several parts of the country (Rodwell and Morris, 1976). The purpose of the *pro forma* was to assemble in an orderly fashion succinct statements, highlighting the salient points of each case. It in no way attempted to be comprehensive; the sections and sub-sections are largely self-explanatory. Basically sections 1–3 record location, principal published references and a brief description of the architecture and its dating. Sections 4 and 5 record the structural state of the building, pointing to defects which have archaeological implications. Section 6 is a statement on the condition and use of the churchyard, and Section 7 draws attention to known and potential archaeological discoveries in the immediate vicinity of the church. In sections 8 and 9 recent disturbances with archaeological consequences are noted, together with known and possible future threats. Finally, the last section is for a succinct, statement on the archaeological and historical interest of the

church and its siting, pointing to particularly interesting aspects of the building, avenues of potential research, threats and opportunities for investigation. A sample entry for section 10 might read as follows:

Archaeological and Historical Assessment. A large, well preserved late Norman church with traces of Anglo-Saxon fabric, probably built on the site of a Roman villa and evidently lying in a pre-medieval planned landscape. Little Victorian restoration or modern disturbance, except for the unfortunate reflooring of the chancel in 1978 in concrete paving slabs—archaeological deposits probably destroyed—no observations made. External ground levels high, walls and floors very damp, requiring extensive drainage works (Quin, Survey 1980, p. 7). Traces of medieval wall paintings revealed by peeling plaster. Superb alabaster tomb of 1608 to the Smyth family with much original colouring, badly cracked and affected by dampness—urgently in need of conservation. Fine graveyard with many excellent C18 monuments—must be preserved intact. Extensive opportunities should arise for archaeological study in the near future.

The net result of the survey of the Archdeaconry of Colchester was to provide a basic list of churches with details of their age, siting, general condition and relative archaeological and architectural importance. The data thus assembled can be used in a variety of ways to extract various classes of information, such as: all churches rebuilt in the nineteenth century, churches isolated with manor houses; churches with high ground levels and preserved archaeological deposits; churches where extensive drains, vaults or heating ducts have been dug and thus damaged the below-ground archaeology. The Colchester survey report also contained a full discussion of the agencies which cause damage (i.e. 'threats') to the archaeology of churches, above and below ground, inside and outside.

Surveys on the same lines have been carried out in the dioceses of Wakefield and Bradford, part of The Archdeaconry of York and small parts of several other dioceses. Other surveys, while still of a general nature, have been oriented towards the investigation of different classes of evidence. Thus churches in North Yorkshire (Bradford Diocese) were also surveyed from an architectural and art-historical point of view, with extensive photographic recording; this project formed part of a postgraduate study at the University of Bradford. In the Diocese of Southwell a survey organized with the assistance of the Manpower Services Commission investigated the ruined and redundant churches of Nottinghamshire: measured plans, elevation drawings and

ESSEX ARCHAEOLOGICAL SOCIETY   CHURCHES SURVEY

CHELMSFORD DIOCESE (ARCHDEACONRY OF COLCHESTER)

1. DEDICATION   PARISH
   CAT. No.   N.G.R.   Est. Population
   VICAR/RECTOR
   DATE VISITED   REPORT BY
   LOCATION: − in town/in village/edge of village/isolated with hall/isolated

2. REFERENCES
   RCHM   Published plan: adequate/sketch/none

   Guidebook:

3. ARCHITECTURAL DESCRIPTION
   Principal materials
   and apparent dating:
   Nave:

   Chancel:

   Tower/spire:

   North Aisle:

   South Aisle:

   Porches:
   Chapels:
   Other:

4. STRUCTURAL CONDITION − External
   Ground level & drainage:

   Walls & parapets:

   Tower:

   Windows & doorways:

   Roofs:

5. STRUCTURAL CONDITION − Internal
   Dampness in walls/floors − not serious/serious/very serious
   Floors:

   Walls:

   Roofs:

   Furnishings:

   Wall paintings: Floor tiles:

Heating system:

6. CHURCHYARD & ENVIRONS
   Size: Condition:
   Exceptional monuments:
   Apparent extent of burial:
   Present burial: regular/occasional/never.
   Earthworks − within:
       − enclosing:
       − adjacent:

7. ARCHAEOLOGICAL RECORD
   Reused materials:

   Finds from churchyard:

   Finds within 0.5 km. :

8. RECENT DISTURBANCES
   To structure:

   To floors:

   To graveyard:

9. POSSIBLE THREATS
   To structure:

   To floors:

   To graveyard:

   To adjacent, possibly related, sites:

   Proposed extensions:

   Possible redundancy:

10. ARCHAEOLOGICAL & HISTORICAL ASSESSMENT

18 Recording form devised for a general survey of the archaeological significance and potential of 220 churches in the Chelmsford diocese. The form is printed on both sides of a sheet of A4-sized paper; its use is discussed in Rodwell and Rodwell, 1977.

extensive photography were the basis of the record. A survey of this kind was sufficiently detailed for the hitherto unnoticed structural complexities of a seemingly simple rectangular building like Elston Chapel to be appreciated, but not fully understood. That brings us to the verge of detailed archaeological surveying which will be considered in Chapter 6.

A different order of problem in the study of redundant churches exists in East Anglia, where Neil Batcock has prepared an impressive and fairly detailed survey based on the Norwich Diocese (Batcock, forthcoming). There, redundancy has been an acute problem for centuries and an incredible number of fine, and not so fine, medieval churches have simply been abandoned. When work began on the survey in 1976 it was vaguely appreciated that something in the order of 200, or about one quarter, of the ancient churches of Norfolk were disused or ruinous (fig. 19). By 1979 the true position was

established: 33 disused but intact churches; 21 largely intact; 41 major ruins; and 110 sites where nothing now stands above ground level. That gives the staggering total of 256 churches; nor is that a gross number because a further 71 sites have been identified where churches are believed to have existed but where nothing survives to be seen.

The need for general surveys is admirably demonstrated by the Norfolk project. Identifying abandoned churches was only part of the survey: an extensive photographic record was made and comparisons drawn between the present state of these structures and their state in the early nineteenth century (when many were recorded by engravings). Even in those dioceses where one might feel that there is no real problem of ruined churches, it is deceptive how many sites have slipped out of public view. At the start of our Essex survey only four or five ruins sprang readily to mind; but upon completion 47 sites of ruined and demolished churches had been identified. Most fell in the latter category. The situation in Essex is more likely to be typical of England as a whole than the extreme figure from Norfolk. These

19 Hindolveston, Norfolk. In the early nineteenth century the church stood as a substantial aisled building of late Perpendicular style, but now all that remains above ground is the ivy-clad west wall of the tower. *Photos: Neil Batcock. Copyright Norfolk Archaeological Unit*

calculations do not, of course, take any account of ruined and demolished chapels of non-parochial status or of former monastic houses. Neither class of site has been surveyed as yet on a county basis.

Surveys of a general nature have, to a very great extent, been motivated by 'rescue' considerations, the dominant feature of British archaeology in the 1970s. As we have observed, it is not just the buildings themseves which are at risk through restoration, redundancy and other disruptive processes, but also their furnishings and monuments. In connection with the former, surveys of church contents are being undertaken all over the country by voluntary groups from the National Association of Decorative and Fine Arts Societies (NADFAS). On the second aspect, the Victorian Society has launched a survey of nineteenth-century cemeteries in Britain. This is a large and difficult task, since the non-specialist public has not yet come to terms with the value of Victorian monuments. In 1976 I was told, with an air of satisfaction and achievement, by an incumbent how he had smashed up every Victorian tombstone in his large and moderately important churchyard. He had annihilated a chapter in the history of his community. Organized vandalism of this nature has become all too common, and indeed Knaresborough Parochial Church Council received a Civic Society commendation for devastating its churchyard. In the Birmingham area 30 out of 71 graveyards have been destroyed and in 1977 a survey was conducted of what remained. It was found that about 16,500 tombstones still survive and are in need of recording, since the total is being depleted at a disturbing rate (Sage and Taylor, 1978). A survey of religious sites in Bristol, where redundancy and destruction are acute problems, has paid particular attention to Nonconformist chapels and graveyards (Dawson, 1977).

Surveys of monuments of intrinsic importance have been made, specifically with conservation in mind, in the Diocese of Lincoln and in the Archdeaconry of Wells (begun 1980). Finally, under the heading of general surveys, the Council for British Archaeology's 'Urban Churches Survey' should be mentioned (Keene, 1977). This is a colossal undertaking which cannot be faulted in principle, but in practice is never likely to reach fruition: the aim is to assemble a dossier of information and complete a *pro forma* for each pre-Reformation church which has existed, or still does exist, in every town in Great Britain. Simply to have a check-list of all those churches would be a valuable tool for scholars; but the requirements of the *pro forma* are such that very extensive research, particularly on the documentary side, has to be undertaken before each entry can be completed. This is, then, an intensive survey applied on a general scale. It could be completed, over a time-span of several decades, if groups of competent historians and archaeologists in major towns and counties worked together in a systematic manner to search, digest and abstract all relevant material.

Detailed archaeological surveys

It is a matter of opinion as to when a general survey becomes sufficiently comprehensive to qualify as a detailed survey. There are so many different angles of approach, interests and objectives that there cannot be a standard form of detailed survey. Obviously such a survey must involve close first-hand study of a church (or its environs) and the examination of relevant primary sources of manuscript and printed material. In the preparation of the written assessment it is desirable to follow the general format adopted by the Urban Churches Survey, details of which may be obtained from the Council for British Archaeology. Many of the sections on the *pro forma* are of equal relevance to urban and rural church surveys: those categories which are not relevant in any particular case can simply be passed over. The information which is entered upon the *pro forma* is, it must be stressed, not a haphazard collection of observations and notes, but 'a reasoned summary of all aspects of the church's development' (Keene, 1977, 8). In order to achieve that full and careful analyses need first to be undertaken of all the classes of evidence involved. The record of the survey should therefore be maintained at two levels: first, the detailed file of information containing photographs, drawings, field notes and full references to historical sources, and, secondly, the synthesized data entered on the recording form.

The Urban Churches Record Form is divided into twelve sections, as follows:

A. Identification (location, siting, basic chronology)
B. Origin and outline history
C. The structure (description and dating)
D. Site and setting

E. Clergy
F. Parochial status
G. The parish
H. Guilds and fraternities
J. Chantries, obits and lights
K. Other liturgical evidence
L. Value
M. Potential for future investigation

A detailed survey need not, by definition, involve extensive historical research, as envisaged by the progenitors of the Urban Churches Survey: it can be confined to the physical remains. The processes involved in undertaking surveys of the material evidence will be discussed in the respective sections on recording church buildings (Chapter 6) and graveyards (Chapter 8). Here it will suffice to give some examples of recent surveys which have been conducted with detail in mind. At Deerhurst the work of surveying the complex fabric at the east end of the church has been accompanied by investigational techniques which have revealed much hidden evidence both above and below ground (Butler, Rahtz and Taylor, 1975). At Brixworth a long-term survey project is in hand which, up to 1980, has involved only a modest amount of structural interference. The Brixworth Archaeological Research Committee has very wisely adopted the view that there is so much of the church fabric which can be surveyed without the application of destructive investigational techniques, and so much documentation waiting to be searched, that it would be premature to rush into excavation or other irreversible forms of investigation (Cramp, 1977a; Stones, 1980). Detailed surveys of St Peter's, Bradwell-on-Sea (by Jane Levitan, unpublished) and of the west end of St Peter's, Tichfield (Hare, 1976) have added enormously to our knowledge of the Anglo-Saxon fabric of both buildings.

Survey drawings of medieval churches were of course prepared in their hundreds in the nineteenth century, but few drawn surveys have been tackled in recent years. One such modern survey is of the redundant church at Ubbeston, Suffolk; this is an example of a 'measured sketch' survey, a method of providing a basic set of drawings which can be produced rapidly (Carr, 1976).

When time and money were of no great object, Victorian architectural surveys were often of extremely high quality, each drawing being a work of art in itself. One of the finest, most detailed, and superbly published architectural surveys undertaken in Britain was that of Hexham Abbey church by C. C. Hodges (1888). He recorded the building, its monuments and furnishings with a thoroughness which is an example to modern archaeologists (fig. 20). While the presentation of Victorian surveys was almost an end in itself (which all too frequently concealed unfortunate inaccuracies), the analytical and interpretive aspects, so essential in archaeological surveys, received scant attention. There was, until very recently, only a vague appreciation that even a supposedly single-period building is often incredibly complex, and that nothing short of stone-by-stone study can reveal its constructional history. With this in mind, John James has undertaken a study of Chartres Cathedral which easily surpasses all other building surveys to date. Many years of full-time study, during which something in the order of a million measurements have been taken, have led to the publication of the first volume of *The Contractors of Chartres* (James, 1979). On a humbler scale, the stone-by-stone study of the west front of Wells Cathedral was begun in 1979.

Finally, on the subject of surveys, the long-standing commitment of the Royal Commission on Historical Monuments (RCHM) to the recording and publication of buildings has given rise to the surveying, in varying degrees of detail, of several thousand parish churches and other religious monuments. Since 1908 the RCHM has systematically been surveying buildings of all kinds and publishing inventories for counties and cities. For at least two-thirds of the churches in those counties which have been covered the only authoritative architectural descriptions of the churches yet published are those in the survey volumes themselves. The depth of coverage and its reliability are variable: the more recent the survey the higher the quality of the published account. In the earliest RCHM volume, devoted to Hertfordshire (1911), each medieval church was described, with the principal dimensions given, and significant contents listed. Only a few churches of particular architectural interest were illustrated with photographs and plans. When the Commissioners came to survey Essex (1916, *et seq.*) it became policy to include a measured sketch plan at a scale of 48ft to 1in. (1:576) to illustrate every medieval church for which a detailed plan was not given. In more recent volumes, such as that for north-east

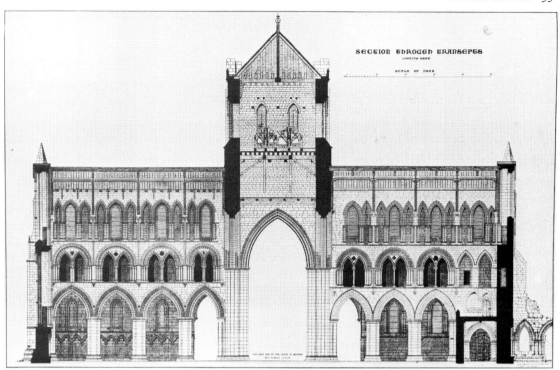

SECTION THROUGH TRANSEPTS
LOOKING EAST
SCALE OF FEET

20 Hexham Abbey, Northumberland. North-south sectional elevation through the transepts; an example of one of the many superb measured drawings produced by the Victorian architect, C. C. Hodges. *After Hodges, 1888*

Cambridgeshire (1972), carefully drawn plans, with differentiation according to period, are published for all early churches, and in many cases measured elevations of arcades, profiles of mouldings, and details of sculptured stones are also included. Furthermore, photographic coverage has greatly increased in recent years.

The climax in British archaeo-ecclesiastical surveys has recently been reached with the completion of RCHM inventory volumes devoted solely to York Minster and Salisbury Cathedral Close, respectively. These will be published in the mid-1980s. In technical accuracy and quality of presentation the RCHM surveys now equal, if not surpass, those of nineteenth-century architects. Unfortunately, the resources available to most archaeological and architectural institutions today are too slender to permit the kind of detailed recording and high standard of publication for which we are, and should be, aiming. In view of this one can only regret the decision made in 1980 by the RCHM to discontinue the systematic production of county inventories (Fowler, 1981).

In the early years, the surveyors of the RCHM employed recording forms for churches; these were useful when surveys were non-intensive. The completed *pro forma* for each church was retained in the Commission's files, and it often bears information which was noted at the time of inspection but was not subsequently published. In more recent years the *pro forma* has been discontinued in favour of writing a structured narrative account. A check list and instruction sheet provides the necessary guidance for describing the church and all its accoutrements in a systematic order and under a series of well defined headings. The published account follows the same order. It is strongly recommended that the essence of the system devised and tested over so long a period by the RCHM be adopted by all investigators who are undertaking architectural surveys. There should be twelve sections to the report, viz.

1 *Parish and dedication*
2 *Situation* and map ref.
3 *Structural materials* of:
(a) Walls
(b) Dressings
(c) Roofs
4 *Historical development*, with dates and scale plan
5 *Comparative value* as a monument, with mention of any special features
6 *Architectural description*, with measurements and dates (for order of description see below)
7 *Fittings* (for order of description see overleaf)

When compiling the architectural description (section 6), the following order should be maintained: generally work round the building from east, to north, to south and finally to west. Descriptions of east-west walls should begin at the east and work westwards; and north-south walls at the north and work southwards. The description of component parts of the church should follow as nearly as possible the order: chancel, north vestry, north chapel, south vestry, south chapel, central tower, north transept, south transept, nave, north aisle, south aisle, west tower, north porch, south porch, west porch. Uncommon structural features, such as transeptal chapels, tomb chambers, attached priests' houses, etc., should be described immediately after the parts to which they are most closely connected. Crypts and charnel vaults follow the parts under which they occur and vaulting, clerestories and upper chambers follow the parts to which they belong. Finally, roofs are grouped together but are described in the normal order.

The account of each component part of the building should also follow an internal logic. Thus the description of each wall will begin at ground level, with the plinths, followed by string-courses, buttresses and parapets. Windows, doorways and other openings are then described, working from east to west or north to south. For arches and doorways the following are noted: (a) date; (b) number of orders; (c) shape of arch or head; (d) label; (e) responds or jambs. Windows are more complicated and need to include the following: (a) date; (b) number of orders; (c) type of tracery; (d) shape of head; (e) external label; (f) external and internal jambs; (g) rear arch; (h) internal label.

The description of a church's fittings (section 7) may be even more complex than the architecture, and since so many articles have alternative names it is not possible to evolve an all-embracing system. Basically, the RCHM lists and describes fittings in alphabetical order according to common names and categories, as follows:

1 Altars
2 Bells and bell-frames
3 Benefactors' tables
4 Biers
5 Books
6 Brackets
7 Brasses and indents
8 Candelabra and chandeliers
9 Chairs
10 Chests
11 Churchyard crosses
12 Clocks
13 Coffins and coffin lids
14 Collecting boxes and shovels
15 Communion tables
16 Communion rails
17 Consecration crosses
18 Cupboards
19 Doors
20 Easter sepulchres
21 Fonts
22 Font covers
23 Galleries and their staircases
24 Glass
25 Hatchments
26 Helms, etc. (funeral)
27 Hour-glasses and stands
28 Images
29 Inscriptions and scratchings
30 Lecterns
31 Lockers
32 Monuments (all kinds)
33 Niches
34 Organs and organ cases
35 Paintings
36 Panelling
37 Piscinae
38 Plate
39 Poor-box
40 Pulpit
41 Rain-water heads
42 Recesses
43 Reredos
44 Royal arms
45 Screens
46 Seating
47 Sedilia
48 Staircases (wooden)
49 Stalls
50 Stoups
51 Sundials
52 Tables of Credence and Decalogue
53 Tiles and paving
54 Weathervane
55 Miscellanea (including architectural fragments not in situ)

Where other well-defined categories of fittings are present, such as dog-tongs, hat-pegs, sword-rests or stoves, they are best placed alphabetically within the list, rather than relegated to 'miscellanea'.

Archaeological, architectural and historical surveys of all kinds—from the wide ranging and non-intensive, to the extremely detailed—are valuable and worth undertaking, as long as the ground has not already been covered in more or less the same way. The important point to remember is to 'see the end of the job before you begin' and to make sure that the end is a worthy objective and that the means are available to achieve it. Consistency of approach throughout is essential, and the final report, whether published or lodged in an archive, should be prefaced with a concise statement of the aims, depth of coverage and all sources consulted. A survey is of little value if it is not systematic, fully referenced and useful to later scholars as a foundation upon which to build.

5 Looking for Evidence

If Sherlock Holmes were ever to be canonized he should be adopted as the patron saint of church archaeology. His investigational techniques must be possessed by every archaeologist: an enquiring mind, a capacity for clear and logical thought, a cautiously sceptical approach to the obvious, a meticulous interest in seemingly trivial detail, and a determination to solve problems. The ways of collecting evidence and the uses and abuses to which it has been put have varied greatly during the past century. Thus, for example, until about fifty years ago it was common for antiquaries to equate a church on a hilltop or on a mound with the site of a 'heathen temple' and to describe prominent earthworks surrounding a churchyard as a 'British camp' or a 'Roman fort'. The discovery of a Roman coin, a few sherds of pottery or a burial of pagan type, anywhere in the near vicinity of such a church, was enough to clinch the desired identification and provide the justification for a rambling excursus on local or national history. The significant point about these writings, of which there are thousands of examples in journals, magazines and guide books, is that their authors took a small piece of evidence—real enough in its own right—wished an interpretation on to it and then wrote a story around it. The concept of examining a piece of evidence in its local topographical and chronological setting was not often pursued with rigour: thus centuries (and sometimes millennia) became conflated and history was envisaged as a series of start-and-stop events. As colourfully as it was often portrayed, and as eloquently as it was usually written, this was nonetheless only pseudo-history. It was, and in some less well-informed quarters still is, believed that the early (i.e. unwritten) history of a community could be interpreted in that simple form.

In the inter-war years, when a more technical and rigorous approach to archaeological interpretation became widely adopted, earlier writings understandably fell out of favour. In the 1950s, and more especially the 1960s, archaeologists became scientifically minded and more numerate, but less literate. Scorn was liberally poured upon much that had been done and written in the 'pre-scientific' age: words such as 'camp, mound, alignment, ceremonial and ritual', which had been all-pervasive in pre-1930 writings, were either relegated to strictly limited uses or banished altogether from serious literature. The gathering of scientifically respectable data and the denigration of almost everything that did not constitute solid evidence or 'fact' (notwithstanding that both are undefinable and far from absolute) led to the growth of pseudo-scientific archaeology and academic sterilization. The study of ancient religion, ceremony and ritual—and thus of life itself—suffered a lengthy eclipse, from which we are now gradually emerging.

The reawakening of interest in the archaeology of religion—pagan as well as Christian—has opened a new epoch in conceptual archaeology. Religion, superstition, ritual and ceremonial *were* the moving forces of public, private and commercial life throughout the world until very recent times, and of course they still are in what we choose to call 'backward' communities. In an age when we seek to explain everything in rational terms and to apply scientific techniques to all forms of enquiry, we are apt to minimize or wholly forget the basic human element which was, and is, always present.

These introductory remarks remind us that the evidence for which we are looking will often appear to the twentieth-century investigator to be unintelligible, incredible and irrational. In short, it will not be susceptible to conventional scientific investigation or mathematical proof of the kind which spawns the signature *quod erat demonstrandum*.

Evidence is material which we chose to admit, and facts are evidence which we chose to accept. It is therefore vitally important in such a complex field as ecclesiastical archaeology to try to place oneself, as the investigator and interpreter, alongside the medieval architect or artisan and to appreciate the problems which he faced, the constraints under which he worked and the beliefs which he held. Then, and only then, do we have a chance of understanding the evidence before us.

A systematic approach

This chapter is concerned with the superficial study of ecclesiastical buildings and sites: that is to say the observation, examination and provisional interpretation of evidence which is readily accessible. The more detailed, intense and accurate approaches which involve structural investigation and excavation will be considered in Chapters 6 and 7.

One is often asked by interested persons, including archaeologists, who may or may not have some general knowledge of architectural history, how to elucidate the development of a building. Likewise questions such as 'which is the oldest part of the church?', 'how can you date that wall?' or 'how do you know that is a Victorian replacement window?' abound when conducting architectural tours of churches. Naturally answers to all these questions are given on the basis of experienced observation and analogy. Experience cannot be imparted through the pages of a book: it has to be gained through practical work with at least some supervision from a competent instructor. Buildings are like people: some are easy to work with and understand, while others seem to defy all attempts to establish a working relationship. This chapter is therefore directed at the novice who wishes to learn about churches by looking intelligently at them. He must be the Sherlock Holmes of architecture and work according to rules which were laid down more than 150 years ago. 'In the examination of styles it is essentially necessary that the enquirer should have a clear head, free from system, and that he be a careful collector and comparer of facts; and in this, above all noting carefully the construction of the masonry' (Simpson, 1828, ii).

The first essential is some good background reading, in order to become familiar with the range of church types which has been constructed in Britain over the past 1400 years: look at plans, building materials, architectural styles and regional characteristics. There are countless general books on parish churches: for a straightforward and well illustrated account of churches, their functional attributes and architectural development there is probably nothing better than G. H. Cook, *The English Medieval Parish Church* (1954, *et seq.*). In his *English Parish Churches as Works of Art* (1974), Alec Clifton-Taylor gives a good general introduction to church buildings, their fittings and decoration, together with a regional list of significant examples. These introductory works should be followed by a serious study of the major textbooks on architectural history, of which the most comprehensive and best illustrated is Francis Bond, *English Church Architecture* (1913).

Most non-specialist books contain a glossary of technical terms, of which there are unfortunately an enormous number: a basic list, with illustrations, will be found appended to any volume in the series, *The Buildings of England*. The coverage of terms applicable to furnishings and fittings is extensive in the excellent illustrated NADFAS guide, *Church Furnishings* (Dirsztay, 1978).

The next step is to visit as many churches as possible and to look at the architecture and form of each building in detail, using a plan and a reliable description as a guide. Cathedrals, abbey churches and other large or complex buildings are best avoided altogether at this stage. It is useless to visit churches merely to stare at the buildings or take photographs. A worthwhile visit—if the intention is to learn—must have purpose, structure and guidance. The purpose should be to examine buildings of a particular plan or date, logically beginning with Anglo-Saxon and Norman churches of fairly simple form, followed by good examples of each successive architectural phase. The structure of a visit concerns the methodical order of inspection of each church, and its site: it is easy to obtain a confused impression of a building and to miss details unless a disciplined approach is maintained. Finally, sound guidance is perhaps the most important of all: the student needs to take with him a good, detailed architectural guide to the individual church and to read it, line by line, as he examines the relevant parts of the building. Short of having personal, on-the-spot tuition from an architectural historian, this is the best way to learn about architectural styles, details and dating. An unhurried approach is essential: there must be time to read the description of a feature, look at it, touch it, write notes, make a sketch, take a photograph, or what you will.

The source of instruction is all-important. It is a sad fact that very few churches sell guide books which are both detailed in their architectural descriptions and reasonably accurate. Even those guides which do at first sight appear to contain authentic descriptions are not always as sound as they could be. They frequently copy or paraphrase entries from RCHM inventories or perhaps from learned journals, and in so doing dates are all too often wrongly quoted. Regrettably, there are no readily available detailed architectural descriptions for the majority of English parish churches, and the only published descriptions which can be recommended, more or less without reservation, are those contained in the inventories of the Royal Commission on Historical Monuments. The individual entries are seldom lengthy, but they do describe buildings systematically, with every feature of substance being mentioned. Good plans are essential to the study of churches and these are generally to be found in RCHM inventories, but seldom elsewhere (see also p. 54). The student should therefore aim to begin with churches for which suitable publications exist. A full list of the areas covered by the RCHM is given on p. 182. While other county-based studies exist—and some are excellent, such as the series, *The Buildings of England*, and *Suffolk Churches* (Cautley, 1937)—they do not contain systematic architectural descriptions and cannot be used as primers.

The more keen or experienced student will of course seek out individual monographs and articles published in the journals of national and county archaeological societies and take these along on his visit. The better known a church is, or the more outstanding or unusual its architecture, the more likely it is to have been the subject of various scholarly writings. It is essential to compare the written account with the physical evidence on site: if the relevant book cannot be borrowed it is usually possible to obtain a photocopy. Needless to say, published architectural descriptions are by no means always correct, and the discerning archaeologist can often spot crucial evidence for date or sequence in the fabric which has been overlooked by previous commentators. In fact the majority of published descriptions of churches are woefully naive.

This point needs expansion. Time and again one reads descriptions such as: 'the nave is the oldest part of the church and is of the twelfth-century; the chancel was built in the late fourteenth century'. A description like this, however much it may be embellished with other detail, basically conveys the impression that the church was built *ab initio* in the twelfth century, was single-celled, and that the chancel was added as a unit in the fourteenth century. The description might otherwise have been written thus: 'there is a twelfth-century south doorway in the nave, and the remains of several small round-headed windows, now blocked; the chancel is dominated by a large, late fourteenth-century east window, with two smaller but matching windows in the north and south walls'. The difference of approach as shown by these two descriptions is fundamental and must be thoroughly understood at the outset. In the first description the visible architectural detailing (not quoted in full) is used to date the whole building, while in the second the datable features are described but the building *per se* is left undated. In this example the true architectural sequence might have been as follows: the nave with its round-headed windows is late Anglo-Saxon, a new Norman doorway having been inserted two centuries later; the chancel, originally a square Anglo-Saxon structure, was doubled in length and completely refenestrated in the late fourteenth century.

The principle enunciated here is certainly applicable to seven or eight out of every ten medieval churches: put simply, it warns against using 'datable' architectural features (especially windows, doorways and arches) to provide a date for the shell of a building. We shall look at numerous examples of inserted and reset architectural features in due course. The havoc they cause to dating will be apparent. The novice in architectural archaeology will not find it easy to grapple with complex structural sequences—especially since most published church descriptions ignore the problem—but he must be aware that it exists.

Let us return now to a hypothetical church visit. Upon arrival at the church resist the temptation to rush straight inside: the external form of the building must first be appreciated. Starting at the main doorway (most commonly on the south side of the nave), walk slowly around the building, keeping ten yards or so from the walls. The circuit should run from the south side of the nave, eastwards around the chancel, along the north side, around the tower or west end, and back to the starting point.

Observe the fabric of the walls, the quoins, the roofs and gables, the superstructure of the tower, and any unusual excrescences and blocked or mutilated features. Upon entering the church examine first the nave and aisles, then the chancel, followed by any transepts or other appendages, and finally the tower. It is surprising how many visitors to churches fail to notice either what they are walking on or what is above their heads. Floors, roofs and ceilings are all part of the structure of a church, just as much as the walls and windows.

After a detailed internal inspection of the church, where written descriptions and plans can be studied in relative comfort, a second perambulation of the exterior is useful, followed by an examination of the churchyard, its monuments, boundaries and any other structures.

To recapitulate: the student beginning in ecclesiastical archaeology should make structured visits to churches which are representative of the principal architectural styles, using only an RCHM inventory or other well authenticated description of the building as his guide. After a good selection has been examined, only then is it sensible to turn to the larger, more complex and multi-period buildings. These take much longer to comprehend and almost invariably the intelligent observer can pick out details belonging to the earlier phases of the church's history which have not been commented upon in published accounts. When looking at a multi-period building it is important to remember that it is likely to have changed shape and size many times and that the simplest way to set the sequence firmly in mind is to draw a series of sketch plans, one for each architectural phase (fig. 13). For reasons of economy, as well as long standing tradition, published architectural accounts are seldom accompanied by more than one plan and that is normally composite, showing the phasing of the fabric as it now stands (e.g. fig. 12). The two forms of representation should be distinguished as 'development plans' and a 'phased plan', respectively. The publication of series of development plans have become widespread practice in recent years, largely as a result of detailed archaeological investigations, although Bond long ago used development plans to illustrate his 'Planning and growth of the English parish church' (Bond, 1913, 177–277).

It is now time to move on from the essentially instructive activity of looking *at* previously recorded evidence to the research approach of looking *for* new evidence. It is not difficult to spot features and details of construction which might be significant to the history of the church, but it is another matter to be able to date and interpret them. Many features cannot be fully explained by mere inspection, however experienced the observer. In such cases they can only be recorded and one or more possible interpretations offered, based on the knowledge that a proper archaeological investigation would probably amplify the evidence, confirming or rejecting a provisional interpretation. As in all branches of historical study, it is essential to distinguish between facts and interpretation. The former do not change, even if opinions as to their validity do.

When looking for hints of an architectural sequence in the fabric of a church one is normally confined to ground level, except perhaps for access inside the tower; the use of scaffolding and ladders takes us into the province of detailed investigation, which will be pursued in the next chapter. Here we shall confine our observations to those forms of evidence which are readily accessible without special equipment. However long a checklist of features for inspection or however many case studies were given here, they could never hope to cover all eventualities, so that it must suffice to mention some of the most fundamental lines of enquiry into common features. The examples are all authentic, but some have been simplified to illustrate more succinctly the points in question.

The plan

No proper study of a church can begin until a medium-scale (e.g. 1:200) accurate plan has been obtained. The amount of information which can be gathered from a plan alone is considerable. If a detailed plan is not available, a sketch plan is still worth consulting but its limitations, if known, must be borne in mind. The commonest faults in sketch plans, produced for example by many nineteenth-century antiquaries, are the assumptions that walls meet at right-angles and that wall thicknesses are generally constant. In reality, both vary a great deal. Distorted angles may represent carelessness in the original setting out of the plan, or they may be tell-tale evidence for later alterations which for a variety of reasons

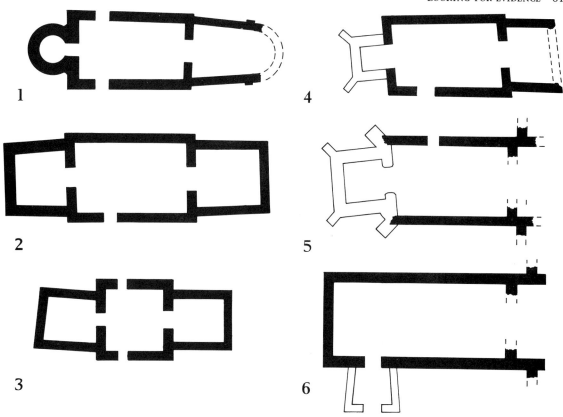

21 Misaligned parts of Anglo-Saxon churches

1 Framingham Earl, Norfolk. Tapered chancel with apsidal termination: an uncommon but deliberate plan-form (see also Winchester Castle Chapel and St Nicholas, Angmering, Sussex).

2 Little Bardfield, Essex. West tower trapezoidal in plan owing to an error of setting out.

3 St Peter, Barton-on-Humber, Lincs. Western baptistery deflected through the influence of earlier features on the site, only revealed through excavation.

4 Chickney, Essex. Nave and chancel set out as parallelograms, presumably owing to an error in the method used for establishing right-angles.

5 Hadstock, Essex. The original nave was shortened and the new west end established without bothering to check the angles.

6 Breamore, Hants. A trapezoidal Norman porch was added through careless setting out; the error equates with the thickness of one side wall, a very commonly found fault.

could not be marked out with precision (fig. 21). Variations in wall thickness nearly always betray different constructional phases.

The majority of the smaller English churches will have begun their existence as single or two-celled buildings; others will have had a quire, perhaps with an axial tower above, and side chapels (*porticus*) or transepts from the outset; an even lesser number will have been provided with transepts and aisles *ab initio*; and finally there is the small residue of buildings with unusual or extremely complex plans. It is generally found that the more complex the building, the more constructional phases there are to reckon with. While many a monastic church was laid out as a large aisled or transeptal building, few parish churches were similarly planned from the beginning. On fig. 22 a basic classification is given of ten common forms of church plan. These, if certain variations are permitted (such as the form of the east end and the position of the tower, if any), encompass all but a very few of the plan types found in England after the Norman conquest, and most before.

Development of the plan—by addition

In the Anglo-Saxon and medieval periods there was nearly always a reluctance to demolish a church and begin completely afresh. Thus buildings tended to grow piecemeal, in response to changing liturgical needs, fashion, or the inflow of finances. Continued change over many centuries often results not only in the

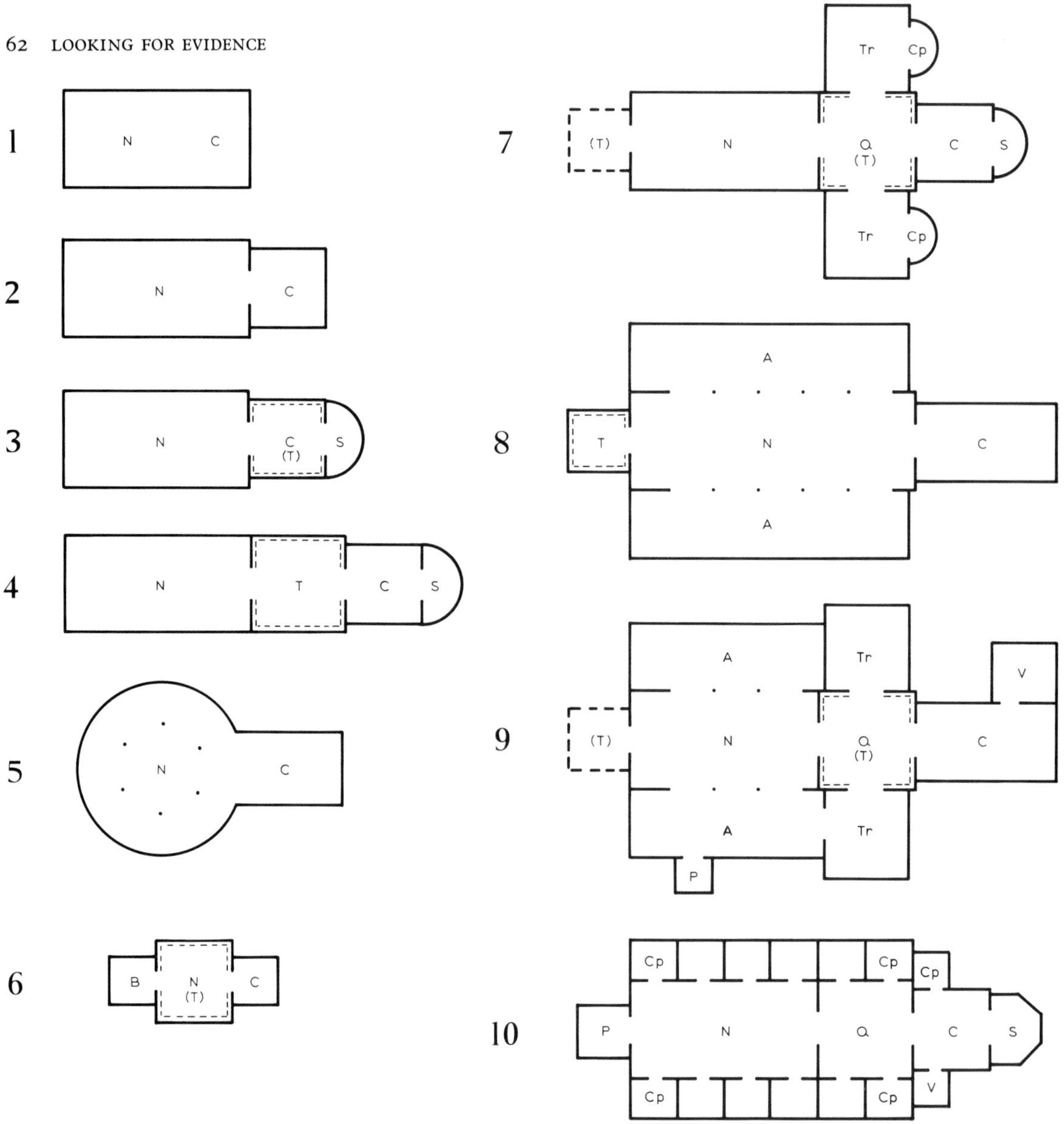

22 Basic types of church plan and component parts
A aisle B baptistery C chancel Cp chapel N nave
P porch Q quire S sanctuary T tower, Tr. transept
V vestry
1 single cell 2 two-celled 3 three-celled 4 four-celled
with axial tower 5 circular nave 6 turriform, with
western baptistery 7 transeptal usually with central tower
10 multi-cellular, with numerous side-chapels or *porticus*

original church being wholly replaced, but
some of the earlier additions too. It is important
to bear this in mind because there may be
several phases in a church's development
unrepresented by any fabric above ground
(p. 107).

The linear enlargement of a small church
could be effected in two ways: by extending the
chancel eastwards or the nave westwards. Early
chancels were often roughly square in plan, and
if later elongated the position of the original east
wall can usually be detected from vertical cracks
(sometimes buttressed over) and traces of
former quoins (i.e. salient angles of a building;
fig. 21.1). The extended chancel at Farley,
Surrey, is a straightforward example, showing
the vertical joint and traces of former quoins
(fig. 23). Almost invariably there will also be
visible differences between the old and new
masonry on any type of addition. An apse may
have been employed as an original eastern
termination or as a modification. Small offsets
may have been left to punctuate the junction
between the old and new work: these may be

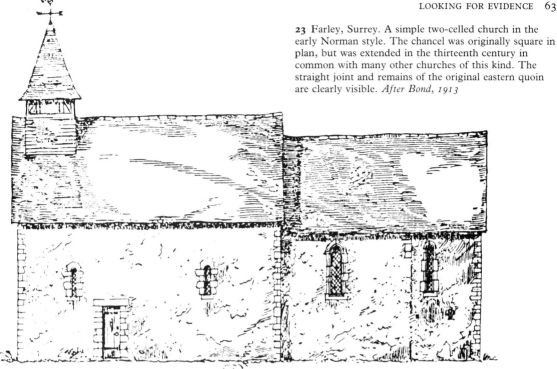

23 Farley, Surrey. A simple two-celled church in the early Norman style. The chancel was originally square in plan, but was extended in the thirteenth century in common with many other churches of this kind. The straight joint and remains of the original eastern quoin are clearly visible. *After Bond, 1913*

unequal, cracked or buttressed. A plinth may have been formed around the base of the apse when there was none on the remainder of the building, or *vice versa* (fig. 24.2).

The same principles apply to western extensions to the nave. The new work may be entirely out of keeping with the old and marked by buttresses, plinths and string-courses. The new walls may not align precisely with the old, and even a slight accidental misalignment on the north and south walls can be detected by eye (fig. 24.1). Towers were commonly added to the western ends of naves; the west wall was sometimes thickened to take the additional weight, but was usually rebuilt in whole or in part. The rebuilding need not be symmetrical, especially if there was a weak corner which needed strengthening (fig. 24.2). The accommodation in a small church could also be increased by lateral widening: i.e. the provision of transepts and, or, aisles. Transepts tended to be built in symmetrical pairs, more often than singly; aisles, on the other hand, were nearly always added one at a time. Many churches only ever gained one aisle. A square central space, the crossing (quire), lay between the transepts, separating the nave from the chancel, in the majority of cases. The crossing was generally surmounted with a tower.

Visible evidence for the addition of transepts, especially if there are now also aisles and eastern chapels on the building, is not easy to find. The places to look are in the external angles between the transepts and nave; if the church is aisleless the junctions between the western sides of the transepts and the nave may be revealing, as may the spacing of windows. On the eastern sides of the transepts it may be possible to find the original corners of the nave and the sequence will be obvious enough if the nave-transept junction is an awkward one, with a salient angle and straight joint (fig. 24.3). If the transepts and crossing were all built as one work, there will be no joints of this kind to find, and the fabric of the old and new parts will probably be keyed together.

By contrast, evidence for the addition of aisles is usually the simplest of all to find: straight joints and offset angles abound. Aisles were frequently built with regular buttressing and with plinths which are integral with the buttresses but which stop abruptly where the new work meets the old (fig. 24.3). Early medieval aisles were quite narrow, while later ones could easily be as wide as the nave. It was therefore common practice for Norman aisles to be more or less doubled in width in later centuries, and the tell-tale evidence for this having happened is sometimes discernible in the west end of an aisle: there may be a straight

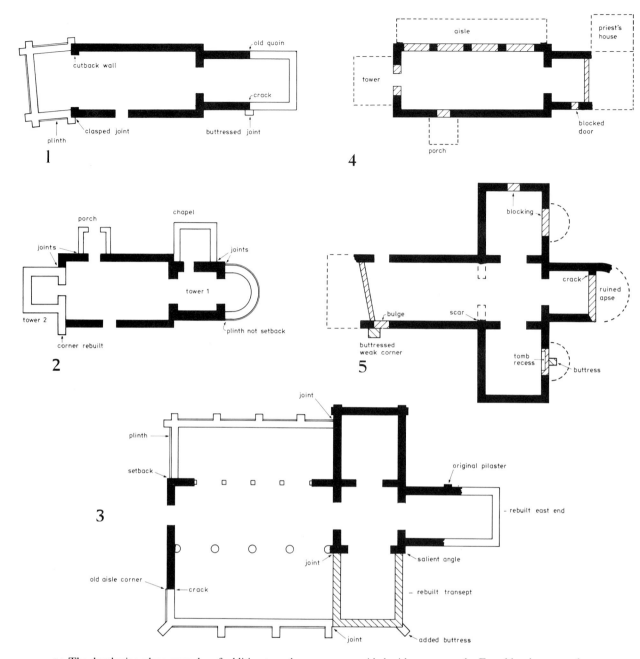

24 The developing plan: examples of addition to and deletion from a church

1 Extension of a simple church both to east and west; notice the misalignment of the new work at the west end and its distinctive character, having buttresses and plinths.

2 Rebuilding and extension combined. An axial tower has been replaced by a new one at the west end; a new sanctuary has been built (the old one having been demolished by the fall of the tower), and a late medieval chapel added.

3 A Norman aisled transeptal church modified on several occasions. First, a wide north aisle replaced the narrow original, leaving only the arcade as evidence for the early work. Secondly, the south transept was rebuilt, and thirdly the south aisle was widened and

provided with a new arcade. Fourthly, the east end was rebuilt, following the lines of the old foundations so that the plan at this point remained unchanged.

4 A drastically reduced church. In various stages the aisle, tower, porch and former chantry priest's house have been demolished, and the chancel reduced in length. The north arcade has been blocked and the tower arch reduced in width to form a west door.

5 The contraction of a large Norman tri-apsidal church, partly in response to liturgical changes. The west end has collapsed and been crudely shortened; the crossing has been thrown in with the nave by removing the western arch; and the unwanted apses have been shorn off. The opening to the southern apse has been utilized for a tomb recess, weakening the blocking and necessitating the addition of a stabilizing buttress.

joint or a discontinuous plinth (fig. 24.3). The junctions between aisles and pre-existing western towers are often clearly marked in the vertical plane, as at Deerhurst, Glos., Corbridge, Northumberland, or Bardsey, Yorks. The last is especially interesting because the west elevation shows not only how the aisles have been wrapped around the tower, but that they in turn are of two periods, having been doubled in width. Similar observations and reasoning may be applied to all other, generally late, medieval excrescences such as porches, chapels, vestries and priests' houses. Relatively modern additions—boiler houses and organ chambers—obey the same rules.

Development of the plan—by deletion

Not all developments were progressive: some could take the form of retraction or amalgamation. If the east end of a chancel became unsound and there was insufficient money available to undertake a proper rebuilding the expedient might be adopted of walling off a smaller area and letting the rest go to ruin. A chancel which is now shorter than it is wide has fairly certainly been reduced. Straight

25 Ovingdean, Sussex. Blocked arches indicating a former south aisle to the nave and a chapel against the chancel. Note that a medieval window has been set in the filling of the nave arcade, while the arch in the chancel wall is also clipped by the lower part of a small lancet. The blocking of these arches has therefore taken place in the Middle Ages. *After Bond, 1913*

joints, eastward projecting buttresses and scars may provide visual confirmation (fig. 24.4). The cost of rebuilding a collapsed or dangerous western tower was very great and since a tower was not an essential element in a church it could be deleted altogether. The mouldings of the tower arch might be left *in situ* or removed entirely and the aperture blocked with masonry. Sometimes a doorway was created in the opening (fig. 24.4). Dwindling populations in certain rural areas in the post-medieval period frequently led to the abandonment of one or more aisles, the arcades of which were then blocked, often with windows or a doorway being inserted at the same time. A blocked arcade is one of the easiest alterations to spot (e.g. Ovingdean, Sussex, fig. 25).

Large transeptal churches, especially those which once had a primarily monastic function, with a secondary parochial use, have in many instances been savagely reduced in size, so that only a tiny fraction of a medieval church formerly of massive proportions now stands. At Waltham Holy Cross, Essex, the nave and aisles were retained, at Chepstow, Mon., the nave alone, at Abbey Dore, Heref., the presbytery and transepts, at Crowland, Lincs., the north nave aisle, at Little Malvern, Worcs., the chancel, and at Little Dunmow, Essex, only the Lady Chapel. In all such cases it is not difficult to see that the present church is only a fragment of a much greater building complex. The ruins of adjoining parts may still stand, as at Wymondham and Binham, Norfolk. The growth of a parochial church into a much larger monastic building is seen at Lastingham, Yorks., not strictly speaking in a ruinous state, but as an arrested development. The attempt to found a new abbey in 1078 was abandoned ten years later, leaving a partially completed eastern arm.

Not all large churches in the early medieval period were monastic, and some which were undoubtedly parochial from the outset have proved too monumental for later needs, with consequent drastic reduction. Central towers had a habit of collapsing and were often not rebuilt, so that the crossing and nave might be thrown together as one unit; scars and misalignments usually betray the former presence of a central tower (fig. 24.5). Such was the case at Hadstock, where the length of the nave was increased eastwards, and a reduction from the west followed later. The new west end could have been built slightly askew or the thickness of its wall might differ from that of the adjoining nave walls (fig. 24.5).

A church with many different roof slopes and awkward structural junctions is vulnerable to the ingress of rainwater and costly to maintain, and it is not therefore surprising to find that chapels and other potentially troublesome excrescences were often trimmed away, leaving vertical scars on wall faces. Openings which formerly led into these amputated limbs had to be blocked and opportunities were often taken in such circumstances both to economize on building materials and to provide recesses for tombs and cupboards (fig. 21.5). These features lead on to a consideration of the vertical dimension in church analysis.

Stratified elevations in churches

Stratification is the sequential relationship which can be demonstrated between one wall and another. Although the term is commonly used in connection with geological and archaeological deposits in the ground, stratification is equally a feature of upstanding structures. Indeed, when discussing churches it is meaningless to differentiate as though there were two kinds of stratification: ground level is merely the point at which strata disappear from normal view, be they walls, floor levels or soil layers. It is often stated in manuals of archaeology that the lower strata must be older (i.e. deposited earlier) than the upper strata in any given sequence. While this is broadly speaking true of floors and soil layers, it is not always fully appreciated that this is far from an inalienable rule in structures. It does not matter whether the building projects above ground: there are many circumstances under which the older work is found to have been underlaid by newer work. The most obvious demonstration of this is in blocked arches and doorways: in strict stratigraphical terms the newer masonry is surrounded, and overlaid, by the older masonry. Other examples include the underpinning of walls and the insertion of string-courses. While simple blocked features can easily be recognized for what they are, greater difficulty is experienced when there is a succession of alterations more or less on the same spot. Likewise, a straight joint, although indicative of two periods of work, does not of itself give any clue which is the earlier. Thus a straight joint may reliàbly indicate the addition of an aisle, or the extension of a chancel, but when the joint occurs, say, part-way along an aisle or nave wall the sequence may not be self-proclaiming and must be elucidated on the basis of related evidence, such as the architecturally assigned dates of windows.

When an extension was well built straight joints were avoided wherever possible, the new work being keyed in with the old. This could be achieved with deceptive neatness in buildings of ashlar, but with rubble walling it is virtually impossible to make a joint which is not detectable by eye. Sometimes a few of the stones forming the original quoins were left *in situ*, or the squaring off of an apse might be imperfectly

26 Chepstow, Mon. The west front of the Norman priory church survives to the point where the colour of the ashlar changes, just above the triple window. The conversion of the west front into a tower took place in 1705, following the collapse of the central tower in 1700. *Photo: author*

done, so that a small piece of curved wall may survive as a noticeable bulge. Even if the materials used were basically similar, rubble walling of different periods seldom matches: there may be different mixtures of stone, the mean size of the pieces will probably not be the same, nor will the coursing and method of laying. In fact the discerning eye should be able to pick out secondary work, including patching, blocking and refacing, in any wall of other than carefully jointed ashlar. In ashlar walls the differences between primary and secondary work may be more subtle, such as different sized blocks, varying colour tones and differential growth of lichen owing to variations in porosity. Work of more than one period should not be confused with different phases or stages within a single, continuous construction programme. Stage-breaks are discussed on pp. 126–7.

Much of what has just been said applies to alterations made to buildings not only in the horizontal but also in the vertical plane, generally the heightening of walls. The commonest place where such work is to be found is in towers, where stages have been added one upon another at different times. Furthermore, it is important to look at the tops of all walls, just below the eaves, to ascertain whether they have been raised. In numerous instances it will be observed that one or two feet of masonry or a whole clerestorey has been added, often in a character which is utterly different from that of the wall below. Thus it is not unusual to find an ashlar wall with a few rubble courses on top, or alternatively a rubble wall with a brickwork addition (figs 30, 36).

The raising of towers was a popular activity throughout the Middle Ages: sometimes the work was executed with great sensitivity, and it is now debatable whether a tower is of one or more periods; at other times it was done so insensitively that an eyesore resulted. A famous and often cited example of a sympathetic heightening, which Thomas Rickman used in 1819 to demonstrate changing architectural styles, is the Anglo-Saxon west tower at Barton-on-Humber (fig. 8). The lower part of the tower is of plastered rubble with gritstone quoins, while the later belfry stage is of chalk ashlar. A period of about a century probably separates the two builds. There is a somewhat greater time-gap, with correspondingly more obvious differences in the architecture, in the tower at Skipwith, Yorks., where a fifteenth-century belfry has been added to an Anglo-Saxon tower, itself of two builds. Many English cathedrals and great churches were originally provided with rather low towers, which were later doubled in height. None is more famous than the twin west towers of Wells Cathedral which were raised in c. 1380 and c. 1425 respectively (fig. 47); the central tower was also heightened c. 1315–25 and further modified c. 1440–80. A similar story could be told of the three towers at Lincoln Cathedral. In each case the stratification is clear.

As the Middle Ages progressed the desire to increase the heights of towers and to embellish their topmost parts spread throughout the country: the great churches had taken the lead and the small churches followed suit when they were able. Where an early, lofty tower already existed for some reason, the only addition might be a crenellated parapet and pinnacles: such was the case at St Mary Bishophill Junior, York, where there is a great Anglo-Saxon tower, probably itself of two builds, crowned by a modest medieval parapet.

In those areas of eastern England where building stone has always been in short supply, brick was used as a substitute from the mid-fourteenth century onwards. Thus additions or repairs to towers are readily discernible: for example, eighteenth-century brick belfries were added at Hagworthingham, Lincs., and Bradfield, Essex. In 1729 the top of the tower of St Mary-at-the-Walls, Colchester, was rebuilt in brick, after being demolished by cannon fire in the siege of 1648. These examples now appear very ugly, although they may originally have been masked with rendering. A rather unusual piece of architectural stratification is to be found at Chepstow, Mon., where the Norman west front of the priory church was adapted in 1705 to receive a neo-classical belfry (fig. 26). Externally the heightening is plainly visible, but internally the necessary alterations have introduced some archaeological enigmas. Another curiosity is to be seen at St Peter's, Northampton, where in the sixteenth century the Norman west tower was taken down, the nave shortened by one bay, and the tower rebuilt. The elaborate arch of the old west doorway was reset over a Tudor Gothic window.

Inserted and cutaway features

So far, we have mainly been concerned with walls and must now turn to the architectural features which are used by historians to 'date' those walls (p. 128). In the overwhelming majority of instances dating cannot be absolute but has to be argued on the basis of typological studies. In attempting a general understanding of the architectural history of a church it is essential to examine each part methodically, both inside and out, and to write notes which can be correlated after the complete examination. Begin, therefore, with the nave and chancel, which in many cases will be the earliest elements of the church, and then work towards the later components. Clearly, there is a certain amount of subjectivity in this process, but one has to begin somewhere and it seems logical for a superficial examination to try to look first at the earliest evidence and progress more-or-less in chronological order (but see also p. 16).

Each component part of the church should be examined wall by wall, and then considered as a whole. There is no reason why all the walls of a component should be of the same date and build, leaving aside the obvious effect of extensions or contractions: it may be that a wall leaned, bulged or suffered foundation movement and had to be taken down at some stage and rebuilt. Thus the north aisle at Backwell, Somerset, appears to be Victorian, but incorporating old stonework. This indeed is the case, but we also happen to know that G. E. Street faithfully reproduced the medieval original in all respects except for the dangerous outward lean which was the cause of the rebuild.

It is often said that an archaeological layer must date from the time of the latest (i.e. most recent) object in it, but while true in theory it is fallacious in practice. In the archaeology of a wall the exact opposite applies: the date of the wall must be that of the earliest *original* feature in it. The problems concerning the originality of architectural features are complex and are dealt with elsewhere (p. 128). In a superficial examination one has to assume that the earliest feature in a wall is likely either to date it correctly or to provide a *terminus ante quem* (i.e. the wall may be older than the earliest identifiable feature). Victorian antiquarianism did however give rise, not too infrequently, to the re-use of genuine medieval architectural features in new walls, or even in completely new buildings (see also p. 128). These cases are generally detectable without undue difficulty. But it must be added that occasionally a late

medieval builder respected an earlier feature (most commonly an elaborate doorway) and reset it in new work. A classic instance is the repositioning of a Norman doorway in a late medieval aisle, occasioned by the construction of an arcade in a nave wall where once the doorway was sited. The process of moving doorways into newly added aisles has continued down to modern times: the famous Norman doorway at South Cerney, Glos., was sited in its present position in 1862 when the south aisle was built. An early doorway might, rarely, be left in place and incorporated in a new aisle arcade: such is the case at Limpley Stoke, Somerset, where the Anglo-Saxon south doorway now forms part of an arcade built in the 1920s.

If the windows and doorways in a component part of a church are all architecturally similar and there is no evidence for earlier work, there is then a fairly high probability that that part is of one build. This applies even more strongly if there are symmetrically placed buttresses, plinths, string-courses and parapets, all forming part of a cohesive ensemble. If, on the other hand, the windows and doorways appear to be a jumble of varying styles and dates there is a strong probability that the walls of that component are older than most, or even all, of the features.

Inserted windows, doorways and arcades could destroy most of the evidence for original features but, fortunately for the archaeologist, a few traces of the early work usually survive. The main north and south doorways in the nave of an unaisled church tend on the whole to have been enlarged and rebuilt on the same spot. Just occasionally an old entrance may have been blocked up and a shift to one side may have taken place (e.g. Woolbeding, Sussex), especially if the nave was lengthened to the west. Windows are quite a different matter. Anglo-Saxon and early medieval churches had small windows, well spaced out and set high up in the walls. While logic might suggest that a new and greatly enlarged medieval window would be easiest constructed so as to engulf the earlier opening, this was not always the case. New windows were often set in relatively lower positions in walls and their spacing had to be adjusted to fit the physical constraints of the architectural frame and to achieve an aesthetically acceptable result.

It is therefore common to find that one or two early windows have survived completely intact,

27 White Notley, Essex. South wall of the Anglo-Saxon chancel. The original south-east quoin, doorway and one of two windows all survive as fragmentary 'fossil features' in this wall. The original design is thus fully reconstructable at a glance. *Photo: author*

although usually blocked, and that fragments of two or three more may be discerned by the careful observer, or may be revealed through archaeological investigation. Of course in some churches early windows have remained open and in use throughout the history of the building, but in most cases where refenestration has taken place such old openings as survived were blocked up and plastered over (fig. 35). Many of the Saxon and Norman windows which are visible in churches of mixed fenestration today were only discovered, opened and reglazed during Victorian and later restorations. A window or doorway which has been mutilated or partly cut away by later work is now not so much part of the architecture of the church, as it is an archaeological feature in the fabric. Redundant features were not meant to be seen and would have been covered by plaster or rendering when superseded.

The passion for stripping walls of their ancient coverings has led to the exposure of thousands of redundant features, detracting greatly from the architectonic quality of

buildings, but of course adding to their archaeological interest. A good example of this can be seen in the south chancel wall of the little church at White Notley, Essex, where the original south-east quoin, part of a south doorway and part of a window head—all constructed of reused Roman brick in the late Saxon period—have been rendered redundant and mutilated by 'improvements' of the thirteenth and fourteenth centuries (fig. 27). This is, incidentally, a good example of a doorway being resited for no apparent reason.

The enlargement of a church through the addition of aisles naturally gave rise to the destruction of windows and doorways in the sides of the nave, but the windows were often originally set so far from the ground that they were not wholly removed by the new arcades. Hence there are many instances where complete or fragmentary windows can be seen, usually from inside the church, in positions where it is obvious that they cannot have been of contemporary origin with the arcade. A notable example is St Nicholas', Leicester, where an inserted Norman arcade has cut away the sills of two Anglo-Saxon windows; here the destruction was minimal. At Tredington, Warks., the position is far more complex. In the north wall of the nave are four Anglo-Saxon

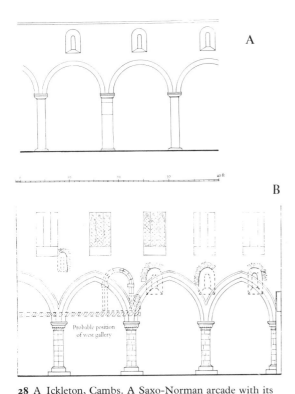

28 A Ickleton, Cambs. A Saxo-Norman arcade with its original clerestorey windows above
B Tredington, Warks. Fragmentary Anglo-Saxon windows and high-level doorway which clearly ante-date the insertion of the Transitional Norman arcade, making a formerly aisleless nave into an aisled one. Later in the medieval period the nave walls were heightened and the five large clerestorey windows inserted. *After Taylor and Taylor, 1965*

windows and a high-level doorway, all mutilated by the insertion of a Transitional Norman arcade (fig. 28B). The three easternmost windows form a series which clearly lit the nave, but the western window is smaller in size and set at a higher level. Between that and the other windows is the doorway, from which it is possible to deduce that there was, at a very early date, a western gallery. Access to the gallery was presumably via this doorway and an external staircase. Several churches preserve evidence in their walls for early western galleries with their own high-level windows and doorways: Deerhurst St Mary is another notable example. Even in the post-medieval period not all western galleries were approached from inside the church and the sites of external staircases may still be visible in the fabric. There is a clearly marked example of a blocked stair access in the south nave wall at Didmarton, Glos.

The earliest fabric in an aisled church may therefore be found to survive only above the arcades. The rules of stratification have again been broken. A fine example has been recorded at St Oswald's Priory, Gloucester, where small areas of Anglo-Saxon masonry of the first period survive above the north arcade. At the west end of the nave a thin column of original masonry connects one of these high-level survivals to the foundations, demonstrating the validity of the sequence (fig. 29).

A different situation obtains in those churches where high-level windows survive intact over arcades of contemporary date. Ickleton, Cambs., is a case in point. In the north wall of the nave is a Saxo-Norman arcade of four bays, with a round-headed window set symmetrically over each arch (fig. 28A). It is evident from the architectonic composition that the nave, as now seen, was provided with aisles and a clerestorey *ab initio*. Difficulty should not normally be experienced in deciding whether high-level windows are contemporary with an arcade or ante-date it. The position at Ickleton is slightly complicated by the fact that the original clerestorey windows are now entirely inside the church, because a later medieval clerestorey has been added on top of the earlier one, and the aisles raised externally.

Roofs and upper parts of churches

These areas are always the most difficult of access, but a great deal can be learned by looking carefully at timber roofs and the way in which they adjoin the masonry fabric. There are obviously several basic questions to be asked, apart from that of dating. Is the roof original to the walls on which it rests? Has it been modified or rebuilt? Has it been extended or reduced in sympathy with changes in the plan of the church?

The dating of timber roofs is a specialist matter, and reference should be made to the standard works (p. 33). Naturally, it is fundamental to determine whether a roof is ancient, Victorian Gothic in its entirety, or a rebuild using some old timbers. Inspection from ground level, aided by binoculars, can usually determine this point. If ancient, the relationship between the roof and the walls may next be considered. In cases where there is obviously a discrepancy between the dating of the roof and that of the walls the question of originality need not be dwelt upon, but if the

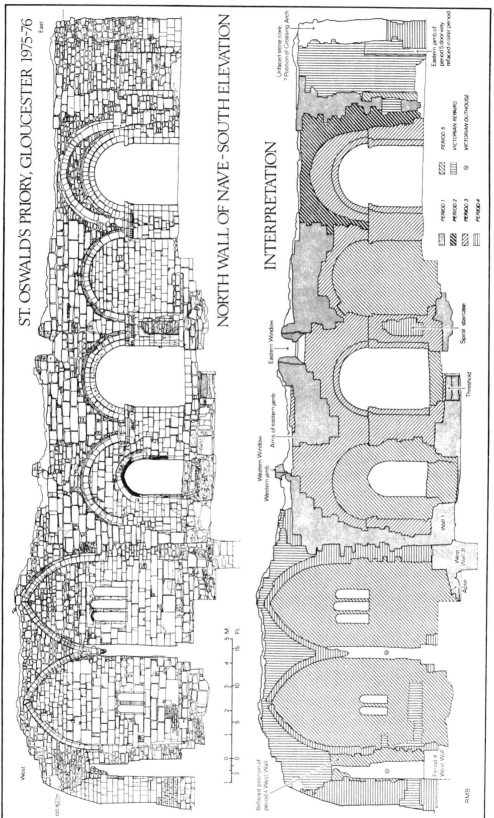

29 The ruined north arcade of St Oswald's Priory church, Gloucester: stone-by-stone elevation drawing and interpretation diagram prepared by Richard Bryant. Period 1, early 10th century Period 2, late 10th century Period 3, 12th century Period 4, 13th century Period 5, 16th century. *Drawing by Richard Bryant; after Heighway, 1978*

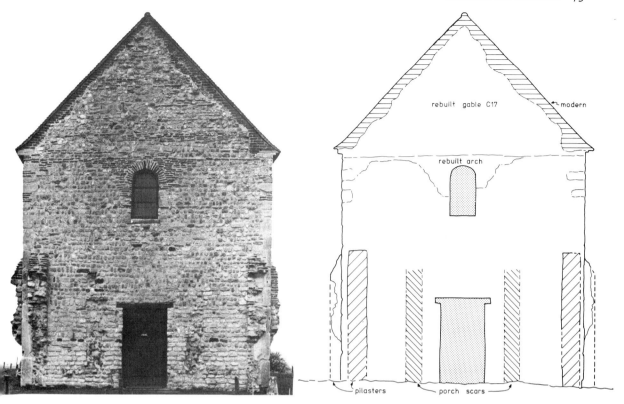

labels within the figure: rebuilt gable C17 · modern · rebuilt arch · pilasters · porch scars

30 The tell-tale evidence of scars and alien materials at St Peter's, Bradwell-on-Sea, Essex. This west elevation shows the remains of pilasters which have been robbed, scars where the Anglo-Saxon porch has been removed, infilling where the window head has been reconstructed, a rebuilt gable and modern repairs. *Photo: Jane Levitan*

roof and masonry appear to be broadly contemporary the finer points of detail should be examined. Traces of earlier roofs should be sought, such as redundant corbels and tie-beams, or wall-plates which have housed previous rafters. Unwanted tie-beams which were anchored in the masonry of walls were often left in place, or were sawn off flush, in order to avoid serious disruption of the fabric, and wall-plates are frequently found to be older than the trusses they support; if the plate is visible externally it can usually be ascertained whether there are housings for previous rafter feet. A wall-plate which is discontinuous, butt-jointed or misaligned on the wall top is suspect, and if the plate seems to disappear into the wall part-way along the chancel, the possibility that an apse has been deleted or squared off should be considered. If a change in roof construction or design, or simply a joint in a wall-plate, is found to coincide with a change in the character

of the masonry below, it is fairly safe to assume that the timberwork is of two periods. If those periods are not far separated in time the style of construction may be similar on both sides of the 'break'. In most cases where, say, a chancel has been lengthened, and where there is a clear structural break in the roof corresponding to the wall junction below, it may be assumed that the two roofs belong to the separate periods. Of course, the earlier part could be a Norman roof on a Saxon wall, or some similar composite arrangement. Two points will however be clear: that the earlier part of the roof will antedate the extension and that the roof on the extension will be contemporary with it. Any general re-roofing which takes place after an extension has been made will not respect the archaeological stratification of the walls.

We have already mentioned the common phenomenon of walls being heightened with a few courses of masonry or brick just below the eaves. In such instances the roof probably belongs to the period of heightening, and patently not to the original walls below (fig. 30). By extension, the same is true of a roof supported on a clerestorey which has been added to an earlier nave. Most ancient roofs on

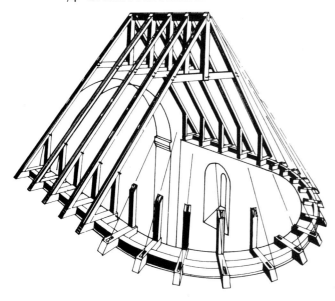

31 An isometric-perspective drawing of the Norman roof structure over the chancel apse at East Ham, Essex. A simple cutaway diagram of this kind illustrates clearly the relationship between principal structural members and is an essential component in a full set of drawings of an ancient roof. *After Hewett, 1974a*

late medieval clerestoreys are original, especially when the two components are intricately linked through the use of wall-posts, corbels, braces, hammerbeams, etc. Another hint which is useful in determining the date of a roof relative to certain parts of the church is the relationship of the trusses to architectural features, particularly arches. Roof trusses were often designed to 'frame' chancel and tower arches, and east and west windows, in an aesthetically pleasing manner. Thus if tie-beams, struts or braces impinge upon the mouldings of a chancel arch, or the truss is set asymmetrically over the arch, it is improbable that the two elements are of contemporary construction. The designing of roofs, especially those over complex buildings, was no haphazard business: the viewpoint from the floor of the church had always to be borne in mind. A great deal of care was, for example, put into the design of the Norman apse roof at East Ham, so that no structural members *appeared* to impinge on the semi-circular church arch when viewed from in the nave (fig. 31).

A church which has been reduced in some way will almost certainly display evidence for this in its ancient roofs. Irregularities in the bay structure—i.e. main divisions of the roof framing—should be examined. Thus if a roof is

$2\frac{1}{3}$ bays in length there is a likelihood that a $\frac{2}{3}$ bay, or $1\frac{2}{3}$ bays, have been removed, especially if the anomalous end bay is without a terminal truss or has one of a different kind from the rest. This phenomenon tends to occur at the west end of a church, where the nave may have been shortened or cut back for the construction of a tower (e.g. Buttsbury, Essex): the stratigraphical relationship between an incomplete roof and an inserted tower is important. Conversely, if an axial tower has been removed and the nave roof extended eastwards over the quire, the area of infilling should be evident unless total reroofing has taken place. Both these roof-tower relationships have been observed in the one church at Hadstock. The central tower fell in the thirteenth century and an inserted roof of that date, but conforming to the older style of the nave roof, can be seen over the crossing. Then, in the later fifteenth century a new tower was erected at the west end, at the same time shortening the nave slightly; a terminal truss must then have been removed. Thus at one end the nave roof was shown to be earlier than the fifteenth-century west tower, and at the other earlier than the thirteenth-century collapse of the central tower.

Finally on the subject of roofs, evidence should be sought for previous roof-lines above or below the present one, and at a greater or lesser pitch. Former 'weatherings' as they are called are usually seen as projecting strips of stone on the walls of towers. The purpose of these stone strips was to seal the joint between the vertical face of the tower and the lead or slates on the adjoining roof. If the present roof of the nave, or other limb, is low pitched and on the face of the tower there is a steeply pitched weathering, it is demonstrable that an entirely new roof has been constructed.

At Great Bedwyn, Wilts., two weathering lines on the west face of the central tower show that there has been, successively, a steeply pitched early medieval roof, a low-pitched late medieval roof, and the present roof of even lower pitch (fig. 32). On the north face of the tower is a steeply pitched weathering over the transept which, interestingly, does not relate to the present height of the walls. The east and west walls of the transept have evidently been slightly lowered at the time of reroofing. Yet another weathering, on the west fact of the north transept, shows that there was formerly a much narrower north aisle, also with a steeply pitched roof. Thus, simply by looking at the

32 Great Bedwyn, Wilts: former roof lines. The original steeply pitched roofs of the nave and north transept have left their marks on the tower; there has also been a previous low roof on the nave. Where the aisle abuts the transept traces of a former steep weathering are also visible. *From a nineteenth-century drawing*

evidence for previous roofs, we can reconstruct much of the form of Great Bedwyn church as it was in the Norman period (excepting the chancel).

Sometimes weatherings are to be found over chancel arches, hidden behind parapets, or on wall faces where there is now no structural component beneath. They thus provide clues to deleted transepts, aisles, porches, and so forth. At North Leigh, Oxon., there is a weathering high upon the west face of the west tower, showing that a major limb of this church has been demolished. In fact the tower was once axial and the entire nave to the west of it has been removed. Old roof lines can also occur inside churches, showing where roofs have been raised. The raising of the roof was usually due to the addition of a clerestorey, although it should be borne in mind that a weathering on a tower of early date need not be related to the present church. Thus the weathering on the east face of the tower at St Peter's, Barton-on-Humber, now inside the clerestorey, related to the roofing

of a Saxo-Norman nave of which there is now nothing standing above ground (fig. 13.2).

While roof-lines marked by projecting stone strips are readily recognizable, these are not the only form of weathering. Sometimes a roof was merely butted against a wall face with a simple lead flashing or a mortar fillet at the junction. If a chase (i.e. a slot) was cut into the wall face to receive the lead a permanent scar results: thus the north transept at Tewkesbury, Glos., is scarred with the former roof lines of several lean-to structures.

Summary—an example

In conclusion, it should be stressed that a large slice of the history of many churches can be extrapolated simply through the process of careful observation. Anyone who is interested and willing to acquire a basic knowledge of English architectural styles and building technology can apply the principles outlined in this chapter to virtually any historic church or monastic building in order to gain a greater insight into the history of that structure. We must not for one moment pretend that all eventualities have been covered here: every church is physically different and will present different problems to the investigator. It is

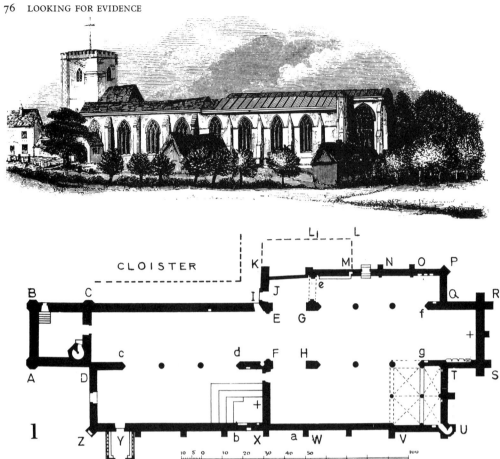

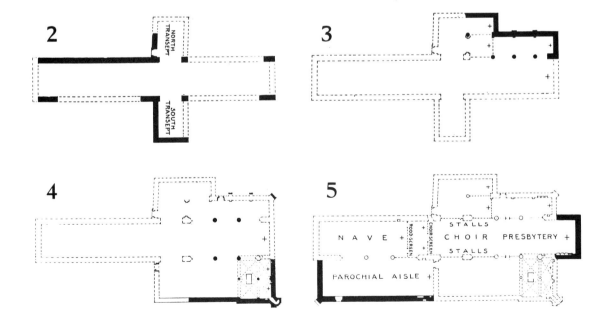

worth remembering that most of the architectural histories written for churches, cathedrals and monasteries over the past 150 years have been based on just this kind of study. Close scrutiny of the upper parts of the buildings has been possible in some instances, by making use of scaffolding which was erected to facilitate repairs, but in very few cases has expert archaeological investigation of the type which we are shortly to describe taken place.

An early example of the application of careful observation and reasoning, leading to the drawing out of a series of development plans, is Bond's work at Dorchester Abbey, Oxon. This was a model study at the time of its undertaking (1912), with evidence from the plan, the architectural ornament and documented history all being brought together (Bond, 1913, 254–69). This and several other examples discussed by Bond should be studied by students entering the field of archaeo-ecclesiology. It is well worth visiting the churches which he describes in order to compare the published exposition with the actual evidence. We will conclude this chapter with a précis of Bond's description of Dorchester Abbey, accompanied by his overall plan and development plans.

Let us go externally round the church (fig. 33). At the west is a tower, ABCD, which does not align with the nave, and is an afterthought; it was built in the time of Charles II. Walking east from C, we skirt a long wall, of which the lower portions at any rate are Norman work; a Norman string-course runs along it. There are traces also of the south walk of the cloister. At I is a blocked Gothic doorway and at J is another small doorway; both formerly led from the church into the cloister, I probably being used at some later period instead of J (dates to c. 1170). Further east are the windows, buttresses and doorway of c. 1280. Then from Q round to T

are three windows, not earlier than 1340. The masonry beneath the window at a is rude and differs from that to east and west; also a wall is seen breaking the roof-line above. At b, close to the ground, is an opening for access to a charnel house ('bone hole'). To the west is a fifteenth-century porch, Y.

Now we pass inside from the porch and find that the nave has a south aisle only, and at the east end of this aisle is a blank wall, pierced with a small doorway to the left. The altar is raised on a series of platforms to give headway to the charnel house below. The south aisle arcade appears to be of the mid-fourteenth century, and at each end the plan shows a deep respond, c and d. If we joined up the two responds we should have a south wall corresponding to the existing north wall of the nave. There is a Norman string-course on the side of the nave. In the nave is the Norman chancel arch, EF, which is pointed and has capitals of Transitional character (c. 1170).

Next we enter the chancel, which, has a narrow aisle to the north and a broad aisle to the south. At EG and HF are two rude semi-circular arches, said to be eleventh-century work. They may be early transept arches, but have been cut back in later times. From K to M there is much disturbed and modern masonry, and at e there has been opened up in the thickness of the wall a pier and capital of c. 1220; this pier must originally have had an arch to the north of it. Both aisles have arcades of three pointed arches resting on piers of the late thirteenth century, differing in design. The north arcade is of the same date as the windows, buttresses and doorway of the north aisle (c. 1280). The south aisle is in two parts, the eastern of which, TUV, is vaulted. The vault is a modern replacement. The western bays are narrower and unvaulted. The eastern arrangement probably accommodated two altars and a shrine. Finally, in the east bay of the chancel is a piscina and sedilia in the south wall.

The next thing is to collect and sort the chronological data which we have gathered, and to eliminate successively the work of each building period until we reach church No. 1. First we eliminate the seventeenth-century tower, next the fifteenth-century porch, Y. It follows that the church is in the main a work of the fourteenth and preceding centuries. Thirdly, we have, c. 1340, the extended sanctuary with its piscina and sedilia, QRST. Fourth comes the south nave aisle (evidently

33 Dorchester Abbey, Oxon. This church served both the abbey and the parish of Dorchester-on-Thames, and is on the site of an Anglo-Saxon cathedral; it is not therefore surprising that the fabric displays a complicated history. The engraving shows the church before 'restoration' in the last century, when its roofscape was complex, and there were various buildings in the churchyard. 1 The present plan of the church 2 The Norman plan reconstructed, showing in black those parts which are still extant 3 Early thirteenth-century additions of north chapels and chancel aisle 4 Later thirteenth-century addition of south chapels 5 Mid-fourteenth-century extension of chancel and addition of south nave aisle for parochial use. *After Bond, 1913* once the parochial nave, when the rest of the church was in monastic use) DFXZ (*c.* 1340). Fifth is the south chancel aisle (chapels) with a piscina (*c.* 1300). Sixth is the north aisle or chapel which appears to be *c.* 1280. Seventh, there is the arch G*e* and the pier *e* in the north wall (*c.* 1220). Finally, there is a good deal of Norman work, to which we have attributed the date *c.* 1170.

Out of this last we now proceed to construct the plan of church No. 1 (fig. 33.2). This shows the north wall and two pieces of the south wall of the nave (i.e. the responds at *c* and *d*). Two more responds at *f* and *g* are apparently the terminations of the side walls of a long chancel. The rude masonry we saw between W and X is probably the lower part of the end wall of a south transept: if so, FX is its west wall, On the other side of the church, in line with FX, is another bit of wall, EK, with a Norman doorway J. This will be part of the west wall of a north transept. The next thing is to restore from conjecture the missing portions of the Norman church. The result is a large cruciform church which probably had a central tower resting on the piers EFGH.

Now we come to church No. 2 (fig. 33.3). Make a fair copy of the previous plan and insert the pier and capital, *e*, and the vaulting shafts, N and O. The presence of *e* implies arches either side of it, one of which opened into a chapel, the other into the north chancel aisle. Walls LM and L₁L have actually been found in excavations outside the present church, and thus enable the reconstruction of the chapel. The vaulting shafts, N and O, are *in situ*, date to *c.* 1220 and must belong to wall MP. The wall can not therefore date to *c.* 1280, as the windows, buttresses and doorway would lead us to

suppose: they must be later insertions. Opposite each vaulting shaft there must once have been a pier (three in all), supporting an arcade cut into the Norman chancel wall. It will be noticed from the master plan (fig. 33.1) that the present north chancel arcade has only three bays, not four, and that its piers do not correspond with the vaulting shafts; hence the arcade has been rebuilt with broader arches.

Those new arches, dated *c.* 1280, belong on the next plan, to church No. 3 (fig. 33.4). There they are matched by another set on the south side, belonging to a new aisle and chapel. Presumably the new broad and lofty arches were constructed in the south wall of the chancel *c.* 1280, making this arm of the church appear lopsided: hence the north arcade (and the buttresses and windows of the aisle) were brought up to date. Then, *c.* 1340, the south nave aisle was added and the chancel (by this time worthy of the term presbytery) was extended by one bay eastwards: hence church No. 4 (fig. 33.5). Finally, the addition of the west tower and south porch, and the demolition of part of the north transept and adjoining chapel bring us to church No. 5, the present building.

I have greatly simplified Bond's logical, step-by-step account, especially in the later stages, but enough has been said to show the kind of evidence he was looking at, how he interpreted it, and how he was able to arrive at a series of development plans. Full archaeological investigation would undoubtedly show the picture as even more complex, and might possibly reveal fragments of the former Anglo-Saxon cathedral embedded somewhere in the Norman church.

6 Recording the Fabric: Aims and Methods

However hard we may look at a church, there is a limit to that which can be seen even with the experienced eye. The next step beyond superficial examination is detailed investigation, and that will normally involve an archaeological team and physical interference with the fabric of the church. While many of the well-established techniques of investigation, recording and interpretation, as employed by excavators, are applicable to church archaeology, they do not fulfil all the needs of the discipline, because it is a more complex subject than, say, prehistoric or Roman archaeology (at least in Britain). Techniques are constantly being developed and fresh approaches to the evidence adopted. In particular, the need to record, unite and interpret strands of evidence which may be hidden in roofs, encased in walls and buried in the ground—but which are inter-related and thus inseparable in reality—puts a considerable onus on the church archaeologist.

In this chapter we are concerned only with the study of evidence in the physical fabric of churches, which is normally above ground. The aims are similar to those discussed in the previous chapter—to discover the architectural history and development of the building—but the methods are more refined. For these we may use the term *investigation*, which connotes active work and probing, in contrast to *examination*, which we shall reserve for surface study. As with the making of surveys (Chapter 4), there are several levels of investigation. The most intense form would involve the total dismantling of the church, since the only way really to understand and record a building is to take it to pieces. That is seldom possible. At the opposite extreme an investigation need not involve any tampering with the fabric, although in practice it usually does.

Broadly, there are three sets of circumstances under which investigation may take place: first, for academic research, as at Brixworth, Deerhurst and Repton; secondly, in

conjunction with a restoration programme, as at Barton-on-Humber, Hadstock, Rivenhall, Little Somborne and Wells; and thirdly, in advance of, or in conjunction with, demolition. Fortunately, there have been few demolitions in recent years of churches with archaeologically complex fabrics, but it is a matter for concern that no detailed investigation has been mounted in response to such demolitions. A great deal could be learned from the systematic dismantling of a few medieval churches, and it is earnestly to be hoped that opportunities will be taken to conduct archaeological demolitions on doomed buildings in the future. In 1977 it was proposed that a fully controlled demolition should take place on the burnt-out shell of the Anglo-Saxon and medieval church at Alresford, Essex, when its intended destruction was announced but, happily for the church, it was given a last-minute reprieve and is now maintained as a ruin. Other medieval churches have been, and still are being, demolished without archaeological control. The purpose of an archaeological demolition would not merely be to learn more about a particular church, but also to provide a greater understanding of medieval regional building techniques, gang works, daily lifts, yearly breaks and scaffolding. We shall glimpse evidence relating to all of these in the examples discussed in this chapter.

Planning a church

It has already been stressed how important it is to have a good plan (p. 60), and there are three ways of producing one. The easiest is to take internal measurements, including as many diagonals as possible, and to plot these in order to arrive at a floor plan. The thickness of the walls is then added by taking measurements through doorways and windows. The second method is to establish a central base-line down the interior of the church from east to west, and to take measurements by triangulation and offsetting from this line. Again an internal ground plan is arrived at, to which the walls must be added. The third method, by far the most time consuming, is to lay out a metric grid within and around the church and to construct the plan by multiple offsetting.

The first method is quick and easy, requiring no more equipment than one 30 m. tape, but it is very inaccurate when applied to buildings which are complex or have irregularities in the plan. The second method requires a string baseline to be set up and securely anchored; if the church is transeptal a second line at right-angles to the first will need to be laid, and planning can be achieved using two 30 m. tapes. This method is more accurate than the first and enables arcade piers to be plotted by triangulation and the irregularities in wall alignments to be registered. Furnishings and fittings can also be plotted. In all, a comprehensive and reasonably accurate internal plan can be produced, to within a tolerance of $\pm$ 10cm., for an uncomplicated church.

The main disadvantage of this method, and the previous one, is that the exterior of the church cannot be plotted accurately in relation to the interior. A few measurements can be taken through doorways and through as many windows as are reasonably accessible from the ground. But these do little to help with the external planning of buttresses, stair turrets, towers and other complex projecting features; nor are irregularities in wall thicknesses easy to register. A small two-celled, unbuttressed church can be planned adequately by the second method or, if only a sketch plan is required, by the first method. Both are however useless for planning multi-cellular churches where some limbs project from the body and are approached through doorways or narrow arches.

The third method, the only way to cope with large or complex churches, requires the use of a theodolite or first-rate dumpy level and the establishment of grid points both inside and outside the building. If a serious piece of work is contemplated on a church it is well worth hiring or borrowing a theodolite and spending two or three days in setting out a proper grid, and at the same time fixing vertical datum points (p. 83). The basic aim in laying out a grid is to provide a series of fixed points on the ground which can be represented as the intersections of axes on a piece of graph paper (or, better, gridded plastic drawing film). The grid should be set out as squarely as possible to the body of the church and the axes provided with numerical values.

Thus a co-ordinate system is imposed on the building, which will have eastings and northings, like the Ordnance Survey's national grid for maps. There is however, no especial merit in trying to establish the OS national grid inside a church: it is very difficult to do accurately and in nine cases out of ten it will not be usefully aligned on the church anyway. Thus an independent grid is to be preferred, and two or more points relating to the national grid can be marked on the final plan. The procedure may now be discussed in relation to an example (fig. 34).

Laying out the grid should begin inside the church, working from an east-west base line which should run as nearly as possible along the central axis of the building. If there is a west doorway the axis must pass through it. This line, termed a 'northing', is given a value: in our example that is 450m. N. The first theodolite station (A) is then established on the line, opposite the south door of the church. If it is possible to establish a station from which site-lines may be obtained through both the north and south doorways this makes surveying much easier, but we cannot do that here because the doorways are offset. The first north-south line is then established, marking a grid point just outside the church (A1) and another well to the south (A2). This line, termed an 'easting', is also given a value: in our example 150m. E.

Henceforth, each theodolite station or grid point can be marked with its co-ordinates as it is established. Careful thought is needed before the first co-ordinate is given its value. The origin of the grid (i.e. the zero point of both axes) will be somewhere south-west of the church. It need not be a point which is ever established on the ground, but it must fall outside the area which is to be surveyed in order to ensure that all co-ordinates are positive. Thus if the ultimate intention is to survey the whole churchyard (p. 131) as well as the church itself, the origin of the grid must lie beyond the south-west corner of the churchyard. Look at a large-scale map of the area and estimate roughly where the origin needs to fall. A further point is important: northings and eastings should never duplicate the same values within the area to be surveyed, otherwise mistakes can be made by reversing co-ordinates. A reversed co-ordinate is easily spotted if the values of the eastings and northings are widely separated. Hence in our example point A was given the co-ordinate 150m. E by 450m. W, and nowhere in that

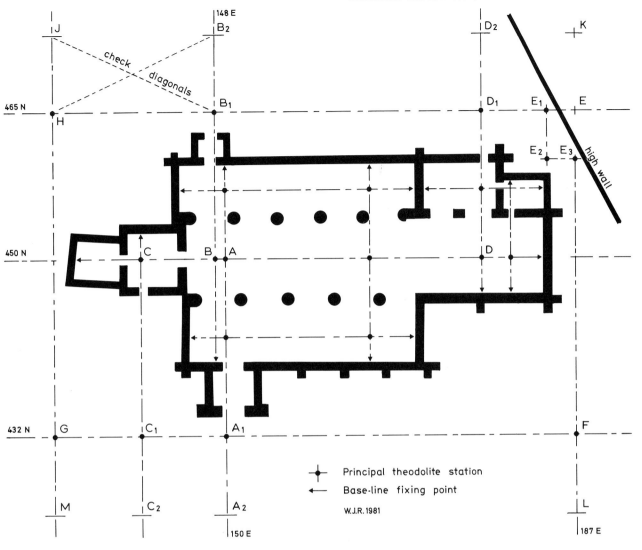

34 Diagram to illustrate the basic layout of a grid which enables a complex church to be planned in detail (St Peter's Church, Barton-on-Humber).

churchyard will co-ordinates run into negative values or be numerically similar.

The next stage is to establish theodolite stations opposite all other openings through which sightings can be taken (B, C, D), selecting round numbers on the base line wherever possible. Grid points B1, B2, C1, C2, D1, D2 are thereby established outside the church, providing stations which will be used for laying out the grid around the building. While a 'box' could be surveyed around the church using only points A1, B1, C1, D1 as the initial external stations, there is no means of making independent checks on right-angles. Hence the

advisability of creating an 'outer box' so that the accuracy of the grid can be checked as each part is laid out. Thus, for example, it is possible to check the diagonals of rectangle B1, B2, D1, D2 and to ascertain that it is not a parallelogram or a trapezium. If correct, it will confirm that B, B1, D, D1, is also a true rectangle, the diagonals of which cannot be measured.

Using all the external points so far established as stations, in turn, the corners of the two main boxes can be fixed, E, F, G, H and J, K, L, M. Finally, the whole grid is checked by setting up theodolite stations at the outermost corners in order to confirm angles, side lengths and diagonals. An error of no more than ± 2cm. should be expected around the perimeter of the outer box if reliable surveying equipment has been employed. It is, of course, possible to obtain a far higher degree of accuracy with electronic apparatus, but this is unnecessary; even an error of 10cm. over a distance of say 50m., is irrelevant in practical terms.

Obstacles such as tombs, trees and adjoining buildings may render it difficult to construct survey boxes around the church exactly as desired, in which case a certain amount of dog-legging and trigonometrical surveying may be required, which are fully explained in any elementary manual of surveying (a useful section will be found in Coles, 1972, 60–117). Thus in our example, points E and K lay beyond a high boundary wall and could not be established, so that the traverse at the east end of the church had to be closed via E1, E2, E3. After setting out the principal grid intersections, as many subsidiary lines may be put in as desired and, of course, the grid may be extended away from the church in all directions. In cases where excavation is envisaged, with the consequent loss of fixed points on floors and in the ground, all grid lines should be projected onto the church walls and marked there.

Once a comprehensive grid has been established, planning is easily and quickly achieved, using a 2m. boxwood rod (single fold only) and offsetting from the grid line. A tolerance of $\pm$ 0·5cm. should be achieved, enabling even very slight discrepancies in wall thickness and alignment to be registered clearly. Most medieval churches thus planned will be found to embody an amazing number of irregularities which were previously un-observed, but which are also vital archaeological clues. For a simple building a single plan may suffice, upon which the walls, windows and doorways can all be shown. In practice one usually plans the walls at ground level and then projects on the window openings, assuming that the walls rise vertically and are of constant thickness, excepting any offsets. If exceptional accuracy is required and the walls are battered or leaning, then separate plans at various levels may be made, but very sophisticated surveying techniques are required.

An architecturally complex church will require two or more plans. The first will be a ground plan showing everything up to and including window sill level (plinths, offsets, wall-benches, niches, recessed tombs, door-ways, etc.). The second plan will show everything above first window level (windows above doorways, string-courses, buttress tops,

roof corbels and vaulting). The third plan, in the case of an aisled church, will be at window sill level in the clerestorey (and will show the parapets of aisle roofs, high level openings, galleries, etc.). In a great church the third plan will be of the triforium, and the fourth of the clerestorey. Finally, a plan should be made of the roof, at wall-plate level, wherever possible.

There should be no difficulty in bringing the several plans 'into register', since the theodolite can be used to sight grid-lines up wall faces. It is gratifying that in most tall churches, where multi-level planning is required, the walls stand near-vertical. However, they seldom maintain a constant thickness from ground to roof, and there are usually offsets at each main constructional stage.

A few words are needed on planning scales. Architectural drawings in the past were prepared at scales of $\frac{1}{8}$in. to 1ft (1:96) and $\frac{1}{4}$in. to 1ft (1:48) and site plans tended to be at scales such as 48ft to 1in. (1:576). The multiplying factor was always twelve, nowadays it is ten. The normal scale for planning a church is 1:50, except in the instances of cathedrals and other great churches where 1:100 is adopted. A churchyard should be planned at 1:100 or, if very large, 1:200. In general, and within reason, it is better to make the initial survey at a large scale (perhaps occupying several drawn sheets), and then to reduce by one of the commercial photo-reduction methods, than to try to draw complex detail at a small scale. Frequently, one also needs plans at different scales for various uses. Wells Cathedral provides an example, where a new survey has recently been completed. The cathedral itself was planned in five parts, at 1:100; reductions to 1:200 are a convenient size for general use, and a reduction to 1:500 provides a useful key plan.

Drawing elevations of walls

An elevation drawing is essentially a plan of the surface of a wall, and therefore, the principles of planning may be applied to the vertical plane, although the practicalities differ. The first essential is to establish a site datum and to mark this at key points around the building, both internally and externally. Again, a little effort expended in surveying an adequate series of datum points will greatly facilitate later work. A theodolite is not essential for this task: a dumpy level and sopwith staff may be used. A base point for the site datum should be chosen which is unlikely to be displaced and which could easily be located again by later investigators. On many churches there is an Ordnance Survey bench mark close to the ground which may be a convenient datum. Otherwise use a fixed point such as a plinth, one end of a door step or the chancel step. The datum should be close to the ground, yet everywhere above ground and floor level. Site datum (SD) should be given a zero value: measurements above it will be positive and those below negative. The value of site datum should be recorded in terms of the Ordnance Datum thus: SD = 136·35m. AOD. But there is no point whatever in trying to record a church by relating every measurement to Ordnance Datum: this is cumbersome, involves a calculation with every measurement which is taken and proliferates errors. The use of a zero value site datum keeps figures in low numbers, speeds measurement and allows for the easy use of a scale rule for plotting. Values are quoted as zero (or datum) plus x metres, or zero minus y metres, thus: $0+2·45$m. (or SD$+2·45$m.), $0-0·97$m. (or SD$-0·97$m.). Virtually all measurements taken on the building will have positive values, and every measurement of depth in an excavation, if one is undertaken or contemplated, will have negative values.

By instituting a comprehensive grid and datum system it is possible to record a church three dimensionally with an ease and precision which could not be attained in any other way. Just as important is the fact that investigators of the future will be able to return to the building and relocate any recorded detail with ease. We may at present have the facility for drawing only the external elevations of a church, but at some future time the interior may be stripped of plaster and the opportunity arise for renewed work. A few months or a century may separate the two operations. That does not matter: the principle to uphold is that whatever record is made it should be comprehensive as far as it goes, reasonably accurate (with its limitations stated) and be precisely relocatable on the building. Any given point, wherever it is, above or below ground, has a unique three-dimensional co-ordinate value: thus a feature, however small (e.g. a blocked putlog hole, a mason's mark or a trace of medieval paint), can be recorded in such a way as to be readily traceable either on the building itself or on the drawings. Time and again one reads in old accounts observations such as, 'there is an unusual mason's mark on a stone near the west

end of the clerestorey'. Hours could be wasted searching for that detail, not even knowing whether it is inside or outside the building. Nowadays, a three-part co-ordinate would be used to locate that mark precisely. It is indeed curious that while the co-ordinate system has been in general use for two decades on competent excavations, it has very rarely been applied to the archaeology of buildings, where it is equally essential.

We may now turn briefly to the mechanics of making elevation drawings. A simple example may be used to demonstrate the principles and procedure (fig. 35). The site datum is set out near the base of the wall (using taut nylon cord), and one or two other principal lines are similarly marked at high levels, either by measurement from the datum or by optical siting (through a theodolite). In our example one principal line has been set out 4m. above datum. If the wall face is punctuated with buttresses, optical levelling cannot be avoided. Next the principal vertical divisions are set up. These will be lines projected up from the planning grid, which will already have been marked at the base of the wall (p. 80). The topmost points may either be fixed by plumbing or optical sighting; three principal verticals have been marked on our example. The elements of a grid have thus been established on the wall face and may be checked by measuring the diagonals. Assuming all is found to be correct, subsidiary vertical and horizontal grid lines may be marked at 1m. intervals, so that the wall is fully gridded.

Obviously, the grid must be securely fixed to the wall and the strings must remain taut: natural fibrous string is useless since it sags with changes in the weather. Horizontal strings need supporting with nails at intervals of not more than 2m., and vertical strings may need regular support too if they are likely to be bowed by the wind. It is a waste of time to try to insert nails at grid junctions since invariably there are stones in the way or loose patches of mortar which will not hold nails. So long as the anchorage and support nails are on their correct planes it does not matter where they are actually sited. Care must be exercised in driving nails into ancient walls: mutilation or a pin-cushion effect should not be incurred. Nails should never be driven into stones, but always into joints: masonry nails for cement pointing and wire nails for lime-mortar pointing. If a wall is being recorded in advance of repointing, the joints

35 Rivenhall, north wall of the chancel, stripped of rendering and ready for recording. Part of the string grid used to draw the wall is marked on the photograph. The solid lines (arrowed) represent the basic 5 metre grid, while the dotted lines mark some of the 1 metre and 0·5 metre subdivisions. *Photo: Gordon Ager*

should be raked out before the grid is set up. In some circumstances there may be objections to driving any nails into an ancient wall; this being so the grid will have to be marked with chalk, or a wooden framework erected to receive the nails. The latter needs a rigid scaffold to anchor it. In either case the magnitude of the task is great.

Finally, a word of warning is necessary on bubble levels. They should never be used for setting up principal horizontals, but are often necessary for the placing of short, subsidiary lines, for example around buttresses or into window splays. The line-level is the curse of archaeological surveying and has no place in church recording: it is fine in theory, but nearly always wrongly used in practice, with disastrous results. A line-level hung near the centre of a string 2m. or more in length will, by virtue of its own weight, deflect the line in such a way as to give a false impression of horizontality, even when one end of the line is

5cm. or more above the other. The builder's spirit level (0·5m. or 1m. in length) is, on the other hand, an indispensable tool if properly used. It is held under a taut line (never on top) so that it just touches but does not deflect the line. A short line can be set this way to an accuracy of a few millimetres, and even a string 5m. in length can be set to within a centimetre using a 1m. builder's level.

Once fully strung, the recording of an elevation can begin; as with all archaeological field drawings it is best done on clear tracing film mounted over a gridded background. The grid lines as set out on the wall are transferred to the drawing sheet and then the detail is filled in square by square. There are several methods of achieving this, depending upon the nature of the wall surface, the clarity of the joints between individual stones and the desired degree of accuracy. A wall of regular ashlar is the easiest to draw since a 1m. rod can be used to measure the position of each joint in relation to the nearest grid line. Plot all the horizontal joints first, then the vertical. A rubble wall is infinitely more time consuming to draw and an aid such as a planning-frame is needed for accurate work. This is a lightweight frame 1m. square with a string or wire grid attached at 20cm. intervals; it

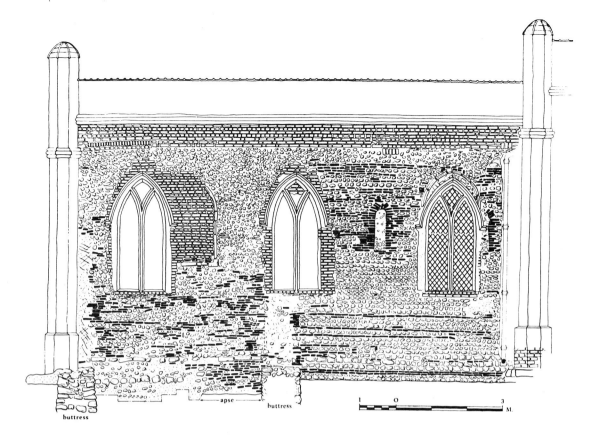

buttress apse buttress

1 O 3
M.

36 A stone-by-stone drawing of the wall shown in fig.
35. This was drawn working from ladders. The materials
shown in solid black are reused Roman bricks, whose
significant distribution in the wall is thus highlighted.
Drawn by Daryl Fowler and Mary Haynes

can be hung onto the wall over each strung-out
square in turn. These 20cm. units are small
enough to enable a draghtsman to draw the
average rubble wall face without the need to
take many additional measurements. A hand-
tape is used for these and for measuring small
inclusions, bricks and details of mouldings.

There should be no need to take two-
dimensional measurements to every corner of
every stone. If a wall is laboriously plotted in this
way the drawing will usually have a 'wooden'
appearance and look as unattractive as a child's
game of join-the-dots. Nor need we be misled
into thinking that copious measurement is a
prerequisite of accuracy. Only in exceptional
circumstances can accuracy to within less than
1cm. be seriously called for. Few stones have
sharply defined edges, while flints and pebbles
are so rounded as to have no edges. Even the
scraping away of a little mortar between two
stones can shift apparent edges by several
centimetres, and unless constant care is
maintained with the use of a hand-tape parallax

errors of 1cm. or more will be a regular feature.
It is easy to become obsessed by accuracy and
work at too close a range, a case of not seeing the
wall for the stones. The draughtsman should
stand about a metre away from the wall face and
always look squarely at the stones which he is
drawing. If he cannot look at a 20cm. square and
estimate to within 1cm. the position of each
stone, he is the wrong person for the job, and no
amount of laborious measurement is likely to
improve the accuracy or aesthetic quality of his
drawn record.

There is nothing sacrosanct about gridding a
wall in 1m. squares: if it is complex, or there are
numerous obstructions, it may be well to
employ 0·5m. squares and work with a smaller
planning frame. At Rivenhall, rectangles of 1m.
by 0·5m. were used (fig. 35). Where
architectural features such as windows and
string-courses occur in a wall these should be
drawn first and the rubble filled in around. To a
certain extent the gridding arrangements will be
affected by the intended scale of the drawing.
Two scales are used: 1:20 is employed for most
work, and 1:50 for very large elevations (e.g. of
cathedrals), where the individual stones are
usually of considerable size. Architectural
mouldings of average size and walls of small

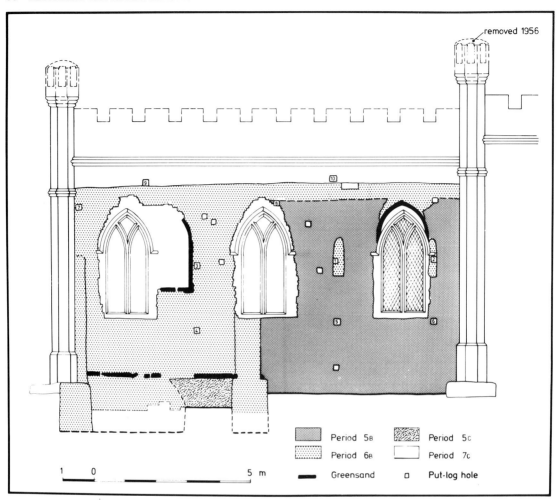

37 An interpretation diagram to illustrate the constructional phases in the wall shown in figs. 35–6 *Drawn by Kirsty Rodwell*

rubble cannot be satisfactorily drawn at 1:50, and when attempted the results are usually crude and lacking in detail.

Very few church walls can be drawn from ground level or a step-ladder, so that means of access to higher parts have necessarily to be provided. A proper scaffold is ideal, but the cost of erection is such that it can seldom be put up solely for the promotion of research. Every year scaffolding is erected upon thousands of churches for repair purposes, but seldom is the opportunity taken to record the walls at the same time. However the advent of the portable scaffold-tower has meant that access to eaves level of the average parish church is now a relatively simple matter. If the ground around the church walls is so uneven or encumbered that a tower cannot be erected the third

alternative of drawing from ladders may be considered. This is difficult and very tiring and is only to be recommended in exceptional circumstances. The north side of Rivenhall church was drawn by that means (fig. 36; Rodwell and Rodwell, 1976, fig. 18).

Photogrammetric recording and related methods

When doing penance on a scaffold we are constantly asked why we do not draw from photographs or use photogrammetry or rectified photography. It may therefore be helpful at this stage to take a short excursus into these forms of recording, to explain their uses and limitations. First, we may consider photography, for which see also pp. 101–4. The plane of the film must be parallel to that of the subject being recorded, and the camera must be sited far enough away from the wall for the whole of the required image to occupy the central half of the image area, in order to avoid excessive distortion around the margins. In practice, this means using a scaffold-tower and working at such a distance from the wall that much of the finer detail does not register on the film. Enlargement to a scale of 1:20 is usually impracticable and a satisfactory drawing cannot generally be made. If one simply wishes to produce an outline drawing of a building without showing archaeological detail (which we shall discuss shortly), a long distance shot taken with a plate camera will be capable of sufficient enlargement to do this. The elevations of the gates at Portchester Castle, Hants., were drawn that way (compare the detail registered on the drawing of the watergate, Cunliffe, 1976, fig. 8, with that on the drawings of the much taller landgate, Cunliffe, 1977, fig. 10). Regardless of the technical problems, as like as not the church photographer will be unable to set up his camera exactly where he requires it, or his subject will be partly obscured by trees and tombstones.

In contrast to the problems of overall photography to aid drawing, it is possible to take photographs of each 0·5m. square or 1m. square on a gridded wall, to print them at 1:20 and to trace off the detail contained within each grid unit. But to take scores of photographs (avoiding scaffold poles and all other obstructions), to print them with perfect stone by stone joins on all edges, and finally to trace the outline as required is no quicker or cheaper than doing the job properly.

Next, we should mention rectified photography. This is basically a quick method used by architects for obtaining photographic elevations of buildings upon which instructions to contractors can be marked. A photograph is taken square-on to the elevation, with a ranging pole to provide a scale. The negative is then converted into a positive transparency on plastic drawing film at whatever scale is required. One can write or draw in ink on the positive and produce any number of dyeline copies at the same scale. Obviously, one could photograph a church elevation, take a positive print at 1:50 and make a line tracing from that. This is a very quick and inexpensive method of producing elevation drawings, which are adequate for some purposes but not for a detailed record.

Thirdly, there is the sophisticated and accurate, but very expensive, process known as photogrammetry. The principle upon which it operates is that stereoscopic pairs of photographs are taken, from the ground (no scaffolding needed); these are then fed into a computerized plotting machine which will correct all distortions and allow the information recorded on the film to be plotted in various ways, including a stone by stone drawing or a contour plan. Furthermore, by photogrammetry all unevenesses in a wall face can be reduced to a single, accurate plane and the face of a projection such as a buttress transposed onto that plane. In all other forms of photographic plotting projections will appear out of scale, if not actually out of focus.

Photogrammetry is extremely accurate, but is prohibitively expensive if it has to be charged to an archaeological research budget. The cost of producing photogrammetric elevation drawings of even a very small church will run into thousands of pounds. Apart from the cost, there are other limitations. Any blind areas of the photographs (e.g. behind trees, tombs, drainpipes and laterally projecting buttresses) still have to be drawn manually and added to the master copy. The plotting machine can only cope with detail which is visibly registered on the photographs. If all the joints between stones are clearly visible a perfect drawing will be obtained, but if the joints are smeared with mortar or are so fine as to be invisible except at very close range, or if there is a film of lichen over the stone surface, the plot-out is bound to be incomplete. Where the circumstances are ideal, a photogrammetric elevation drawing will provide the most accurate result and save innumerable man-hours on the scaffold. The east end of Deerhurst church (Addyman and Morris, 1976, front cover) and the east face of the tower at Barton-on-Humber have for example been drawn photogrammetrically for archaeological study.

A combination of photogrammetry and photography was employed to draw the very complex eastern elevation of the cloister at Wells. The main outlines of the wall and its numerous features, including all ashlar work, were plotted photogrammetrically (fig. 38), providing a reliable matrix onto which the rubble and minor details could be plotted from close-range photographs. As an aid to the plotting of rubble from photographs, small groups of stones were outlined on the photogrammetric plan at convenient intervals.

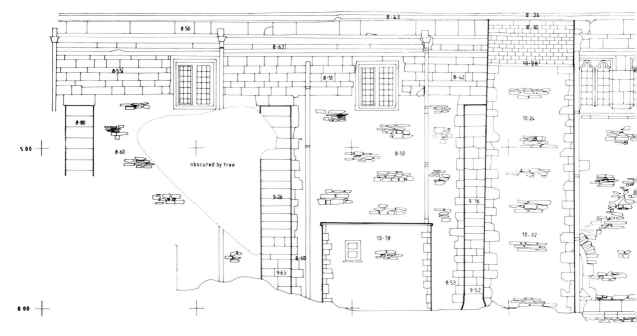

38 Photogrammetric elevation drawing of the east side of the cloisters at Wells. All ashlar work and samples of rubble walling have been plotted: the remainder could be filled in from photographs or measurements taken from the ground. The 5 metre grid is keyed into the excavation grid so that the foundations, plinths and other buried details can be added at a later stage.
Courtesy of The North East London Polytechnic

This is a very satisfactory approach for combining the best of both techniques.

Photogrammetry is being used increasingly by architects, ecclesiastical and secular. These commercially produced surveys, often with stone by stone coverage, are of inestimable value to the archaeologist, but are simply lost, if not actually destroyed, once the jobs for which they were commissioned have been completed. One of the most intricate photogrammetric elevation drawings ever produced of an ecclesiastical building must be that of the west front of Wells Cathedral. There are 49 separate architectural faces to that front and the task of drawing that, accurately, by hand from the scaffolding could never have been contemplated. Although the elevations are plotted at a scale of 1:100, the building is so massive that every stone is nevertheless visible. Without this survey, archaeological recording would have been impracticable.

Let us return now to the examination of the elevations of a church. The production of a drawing at 1:20 with every stone delineated is no end in itself: much more recording remains

to be done. Multiple prints of the completed elevation, at full size, are made and taken back to the church to be used as base-plans for recording information under various headings, such as geology, construction and modification. First, under geology, we record with the aid of a colour-coded key all the stone types present in the building. In the highland zone of Britain a church may be built entirely of one stone type, but over the greater part of England most churches will embody two or three distinct materials. Not all of these need be stone: brick and tile are commonly found in churches in the south-east, especially in areas where good building stone is in short supply.

In the London area re-used Roman brick and tile are abundant, as evidenced in St Albans Abbey, while in East Anglia medieval bricks appear in churches from the twelfth century onwards, and over large parts of eastern England post-medieval brickwork is common. Different colour codes should be used for different periods of brick and tile. Curiosities must never be overlooked simply because the recorder does not know what they are; a numbered key to these should be provided, supported by co-ordinates. In churches in Essex I have for example recorded alien materials, such as fragments of Roman quern of Rhenish lava, millstone grit and puddingstone. There are often pieces of timber and metal embedded in walls, and these all need recording, however large or small, as does coal,

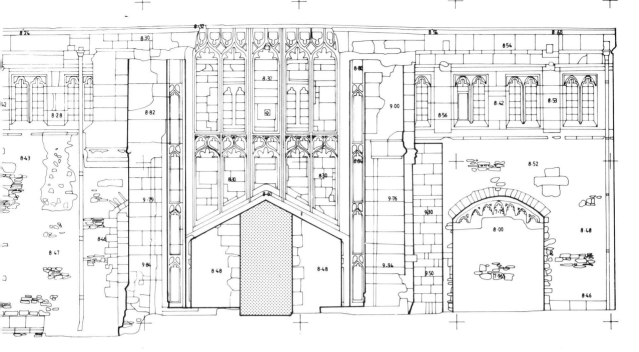

clinker, slag, kiln waste and pottery.

When graphically recorded, it is surprising how differences in the use of various building materials immediately begin to suggest constructional phases and alterations which have entirely escaped attention hitherto (fig. 29). The colour coding of materials also has the effect of highlighting differences in stone-laying techniques and the relative widths of mortar joints. Equally important is the coding of materials which are geologically similar but visually different.. Thus a church built of gritstone may have had its materials drawn from different quarries at different times and thus present a range of colours and textures. Flint, too, comes in several colours, principally brown and white-grey; and bands of brown flint were sometimes used decoratively in churches which were basically constructed of white flints.

After materials, we must consider constructional matters. The most obvious features to look for are the putlog holes left by former scaffolding; they will generally have been blocked, perhaps with an alien material which is readily spotted. Alternatively, putlog holes may be recognized by a characteristic grouping of stones. In a rubble wall ashlar blocks may be placed either side of a putlog and capped by a thin flat slab; indeed all use of ashlar in rubble walls is of potential interest. Dressed stonework, by definition, should exhibit tool marks: the nature and direction of these need to be recorded. Thus symbols should

be used to indicate the various forms of dressing (adze, chisel, claw, etc.) with the direction of working indicated on the drawing. If the tooling runs in an unbroken line from one ashlar to the next the dressing must have been done *in situ* and is therefore quite likely not to be original, but a re-dressing; and several different forms of tooling in a single wall will be indicative either of work of more than one period or of the reuse of previously worked stones.

An important but almost totally neglected aspect of church recording is the subject of building-lifts and gang breaks. A building-lift is the amount by which a wall is raised in one day's work. A gang break is the change, seen either horizontally or vertically, between the work of one group of masons and another. Seasonal breaks can also be recognized in some walls, where one building campaign ended and the next started. These are the kinds of detail which the observant draughtsman will notice while he is drawing the wall face and which can later be fully explored and recorded on copies of the elevation (p. 126).

Under the heading of modification will be recorded all those features or areas of walling which do not belong to the original or principal period represented in the elevation drawing. Thus there may be blocked openings where windows, doors and niches have formerly existed (fig. 27). There may be blockings were joists or other members have been set into a wall and later removed (or may still be in place with

39 Perspective axonometric drawing of the free-standing medieval timber belfry inside the church at Stanford Rivers, Essex. This illustration shows not only the articulation between structural timbers, but also the belfry's relationship to the west end of the church. *After Hewett, 1974a*

intrusive packing material around them). Windows, doorways or arcades may have been cut into a wall, disrupting the original fabric, leaving the tell-tale signs of scars, fractured stones and intrusive packing (fig. 29). We have already mentioned the heightening of walls (p. 68) and the actual joint, not just the general change of materials, should be found and recorded. Rubble walls are notoriously liable to bulging, with the consequence that sections of facing may need rebuilding from time to time. These refaced areas will differ from the original and can be recorded separately. Buildings of ashlar (or those with ashlar dressings to openings, quoins, etc.) suffer from differential stone decay, with the result that some blocks may crumble. They have to be cut out and

replaced during restoration. The replacement can never be a perfect match with its weathered neighbours, and it can therefore be detected. Thus we must seek to record precisely how much of a window, for example, is medieval and how much Victorian, and indeed whether the whole ensemble is original to the wall in which it lies or whether it has been inserted.

In conclusion, the study and drawing of an elevation is not just a matter of acquiring a pleasing picture of a wall—a photograph will serve that purpose—or of spending weeks on a scaffold measuring and drawing because it is good for the soul: it is the process of deciphering a piece of archaeological stratification, of looking at it through enquiring eyes, stone by stone and joint by joint. To stand and stare at a wall in the hope of 'seeing something' is futile and at best will only result in the recognition of the most obvious features. There is no substitute for prolonged acquaintance through the eyes and the pencil. In principle, one aims to draw all ancient wall surfaces, both internal and external. In practice, if a wall is completely obscured by plaster or rendering, or has had its facing largely replaced it is not usually drawn unless it contains architectural features of distinction. The assimilation and interpretation of the data recorded in elevations will be further discussed in Chapter 10.

Drawing sections through buildings

A section drawing is the representation of a vertical slice cut through a building, or layers in the soil, to show the nature of construction or stratification on that plane. While in excavation a section can literally be cut through strata, and drawn and photographed with ease, the same is not true when dealing with standing structures. Unless obtained during demolition, a building cannot have a section cut through it for the purposes of illustration. The section is therefore a notional phenomenon and the drawing which is prepared is really a composite profile around the fabric: it cannot for example illustrate the composition of wall cores because these are not visible. Sections are just as important as plans and elevations and together they form a trio which demonstrates the stratigraphical relationships between the components and how the several parts of a building are articulated. Sections are by far the most difficult element of the record to achieve with accuracy, owing to the need to take

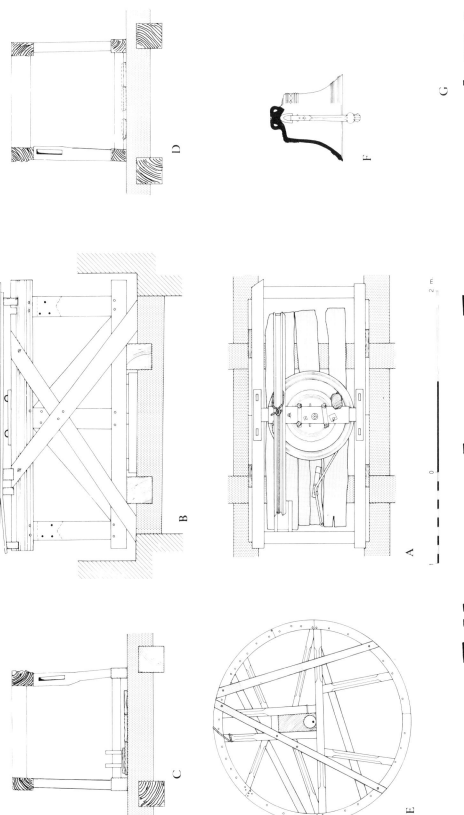

T. MEARS OF LONDON FECIT 1823

G

40 Drawings of an eighteenth-century bell-frame, assembled with timbers from a medieval one

A Plan of complete assembly, including the bell and its mountings

B East elevation of the frame (omitting bell and wheel), showing redundant mortices and peg holes

C South elevation as in B

D North elevation, as in B

E The bell-wheel, with secondary repair straps shaded

F Section and elevation of the bell

G Inscription and sample of the decoration on the bell (ten times scale) *Drawn by Kirsty Rodwell*

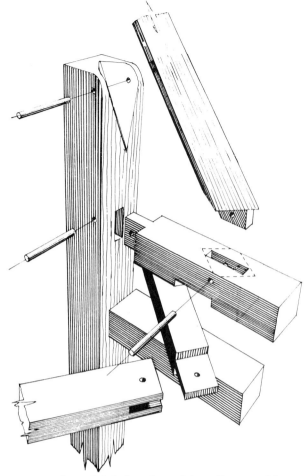

41 An exploded view of one of the wall-posts and its components in the tower roof at Sompting, Sussex. Every joint and peg-hole is clearly illustrated. *After Hewett, 1978*

measurements across large voids and through solid walls. Sections are drawn along and at right-angles to the axes of a church; they are positioned with care to show salient features and to pass through the centres of openings. A section which passes obliquely through a wall or just clips the edge of an archway is useless, since the dimensions shown will be architecturally meaningless; and whenever possible sections should be taken on or parallel to grid lines.

One of the most important sections through a church is that through its long axis (east-west). It is logical for this to fall on the first grid line to be laid out (p. 80). The next section will be a north-south one which passes centrally through the principal lateral doorway of the nave. Thirdly, a section across the width of the chancel is required. That, in the case of a simple church, completes the three fundamental sections. If the building is transeptal a north-

south line should be taken through the centre of the crossing, embracing the central tower if there is one. Ideally, one should take east-west sections across the transepts too. A western tower will appear on the main axial section of the church, but if the structure of the tower is irregular a north-south section might also be drawn.

Not unnaturally, the sections through a major church, with triforium, clerestorey and flying buttresses will be a labour of great magnitude and it must be admitted straightaway that the majority of such sections are schematic. The task of producing a truly surveyed section which will register minor irregularities is monumental and cannot be done without highly sophisticated equipment, and the additional information gained will seldom justify the cost. Hence in practice when drawing a section through a cathedral one may have to assume that the major walls are in plumb. But that is no excuse for the slapdash treatment of small buildings. They can be measured properly from ladders or scaffolding, and their walls will frequently be neither in plumb nor parallel faced. Walls which may appear to lean outwards were in fact sometimes deliberately battered, to counteract the illusion of converging verticals inside a tall narrow church. Moreover changes in the thickness of a wall above an arcade are often indicative of a clerestorey heightening.

A church with a clerestorey is naturally more complex than one without and drawing the higher parts of the nave will be difficult, if not impossible, without scaffolding. There is however the advantage that many clerestoreyed churches have low-pitched roofs edged by parapets, so that access by ladder, first to the aisles and then to the nave, is straightforward. Unless roof or window repairs are in progress enabling measurements to be taken from the outside to the inside of the building, it is inevitable that the section drawings must be composite. The corollary is that they will be less accurate than the plan and elevations, but they are still a vital part of the total record. The enthusiastic recorder will adopt all sorts of ingenious devices for obtaining measurements to places which he cannot reach (cf. Taylor, 1975).

There are two types of section. The first merely shows a slice through the building, registering only those features or parts of features which happen to fall on the face of that slice: it is really a profile taken around the walls. The second type cuts a building through a notional line and everything to one side is removed. The draughtsman then views the cut face square-on and draws what he sees. Not only does he see a section through the solid fabric, but also an internal elevation of those parts beyond the section-line. This is called a sectional view (fig. 20). Both types of section have their place in church archaeology. Sections are always drawn at the same scale as the plans to which they relate; the position of each section and the direction of viewing is marked on the plan. Sometimes it is desirable to draw a 'staggered' section: that is one which is not in a single plane, but has some part offset. The reason for this is to show on a single drawing features which are not in the same plane. Thus, for example, a section through the nave at Barton-on-Humber could not pass through both the north and south doorways (fig. 34). If it were deemed necessary to illustrate both doorways it could be achieved by setting back the southern part of the section 2·5m. behind the northern. The offset would be made at the crossing point of the longitudinal axis.

Recording roofs, vaults and structural timberwork

Timber roofs have been badly neglected by archaeologists, perhaps owing to the difficulties of access; but they are a major element in church buildings and need to be integrated with the drawn record. They call for special treatment and techniques of presentation, on account of their multi-dimensional character. A straightforward plan—either looking down from above or upwards from underneath—is not very intelligible or useful in most instances. But the relationship between the roof-members and the plan of the church must not be neglected (p. 73), and the positions of tie-beams should be indicated, in broken lines, on a plan. If a plan is made at parapet or clerestorey level it should show not only the positions of tie-beams but also corbels and any other supports.

Few roofs respond well to representation through elevation drawings from the exterior, but for some an internal elevation of one or more bays can be useful, viewed from below at right-angles to the roof slope. This applies mainly to fully framed roofs of the late medieval period, which may have decorated side-purlins, wind-braces or ornamental bosses. The most

important form of record, which should be prepared for every timber roof is the sectional elevation, normally included on the main section drawings of the church. The elevation of a principal truss will be drawn on a cross-section of the building and a separate illustration, set on its own to one side, will be required if the subsidiary trusses differ from the principals. The longitudinal section of a church should be taken not to the tops of the walls, but to the ridge line, and will therefore show sections of tie-beams and collars and a full elevation of the bay structure of the roof, together with every rafter (fig. 20). For all but the simplest of roofs another figure is required to illustrate its three-dimensional form: an axonometric or isometric view, partly cutaway to show the structure more clearly. If the timbers have been recorded fully it is worth preparing the drawing to scale so that all measurements of length are true. If, however, the roof cannot be comprehensively measured, a well proportioned isometric perspective drawing will suffice. Perspective drawings are aesthetically more pleasing than isometric and axonometric views, but they are not technically accurate and cannot be used for scaling measurements (unless the perspective is mathematically calculated). One of these forms of bird's-eye view is essential to show all the members which make up on bay of a roof and their articulation with one another. It is virtually impossible to illustrate a really complex roof, such as that over an apse, by any other means (fig. 31). The same applies to those roofs where there is a change of truss type or period of construction part-way along the building, or where there have been complicated repairs or modifications. Needless to say, it is not sufficient to record only the original form of the roof and to omit later works. One drawing may be needed to illustrate the timbering now extant, and another to show a reconstruction of the original arrangement.

Next to main-span roofs, tower and belfry framing constitutes the second significant class of structural timberwork. The material for consideration is divisible into two groups: free-standing timber frames and those which are integral with masonry. The free-standing structures mainly comprise western belfries which may lie outside or inside the masonry shell of the nave. Normally a sectional elevation of a belfry will appear on the longitudinal section through the church, but if the timber framing is complex it will merit a separate set of drawings either at a scale of 1:50 or perhaps 1:20. A full elevation of one side and an axial section at right-angles to this will serve, together with a plan or two, to provide the basic record. But again, this needs to be augmented with a three-dimensional drawing (fig. 39). The study of external timber belfries, internal frames which project above roof level, and timber spires is greatly facilitated when the cladding has been removed for reasons of repair.

Structural timbers embedded in, or supported by, the masonry of towers survive in large numbers from the Middle Ages. They are divisible into four groups. First, lanterns and spires, which are recorded in the same way as free-standing belfries. Secondly, simple tower roofs, which are dealt with in the same way as main-span roofs. Thirdly, floor frames of which plans may be made at the various levels. Fourthly, bell-frames and their associated supporting timbers. Bell-frames and cages can usually be treated as separate structural entities within towers and belfries. They are often complex and of several periods of construction, so that plans, sections, elevations and three-dimensional views are required for an adequate record (fig. 40).

Although relatively uncommon, other free-standing timber structures are associated with some churches and need to be recorded as though they were individual buildings; for example, bell-cages at ground level (as at East Bergholt, Suffolk), priests' houses, framed porches and ancient lych-gates.

So far, we have said nothing about mouldings on timber, or carpenters' joints. Both are of vital importance for dating and the study of regional styles of carpentry. Profiles through mouldings should be drawn full-size, as with stone mouldings (pp. 97–9); and each joint type should be illustrated by an exploded or cutaway view so that its components and method of fastening are clearly understood (fig. 41). Special attention needs to be paid to the hidden parts of a joint to ascertain, for instance, whether it contains secret notches. The internal workings of timber joints in a repetitive construction such as a single-period roof can usually be ascertained by careful examination of broken and badly fitting joints. Otherwise, engineers' feeler gauges will have to be used to probe for invisible components. Joints on structural carpentry are normally drawn at 1:2 or 1:4.

Access to timberwork inside towers and spires is not usually difficult with the aid of ladders, and the same applies to roofs on churches of no great height. Nor is it difficult to record a roof when there is a suspended ceiling or vault below it. Obviously, in cases where a ceiling is attached directly to the underside of the rafters recording is impossible, except from the exterior at a time when the roof is stripped for recovering.

Stone vaulting is not very common in parish churches, although it was ubiquitous in the great and monastic churches of the Middle Ages. It is not therefore often met with as a recording problem, but where it does exist, or where there is evidence of former vaulting, it needs to be recorded. First, the positions of vaulting shafts will be shown on plans, and so will the positions of ribs (in broken lines), indicating at a glance the overall pattern of vaulting in a church (fig. 10). In a great church the entire interior may be vaulted, in a lesser building it may be in the aisles alone and in an elaborate parish church side chapels, porches and the lowest stage of the tower might on occasion carry vaults (fig. 33.1). Internal elevation drawings will show the springers and the scars where vaults may once have been. Details of the construction of a vault will appear on the sections through the church, and a special plan of the vaulting viewed from below should be drawn to illustrate at least one bay. The full setting out of a Gothic vault in the form of a set of working drawings is a complex task, the art of which virtually died out with the Victorian restorers. It is generally reckoned that there is no more than a handful of architects of the older generation alive in Britain who have the practical knowledge to set out correctly a Gothic vault. The recording of such structures cannot therefore be embarked upon lightly.

Recording architectural features

There are three aspects to this task. First, most features are recorded in plan and elevation in the principal drawings, as discussed earlier in this chapter. Secondly, individual plans and sections should be made of each feature (or a sample of a group), with every stone or timber component shown clearly (fig. 42). Features of large proportions, like arcades and great doorways, should be drawn at a scale of 1:20, but smaller doorways, windows, tomb recesses and sedilia should be at 1:10. Thirdly, there is the record of moulding profiles, which should

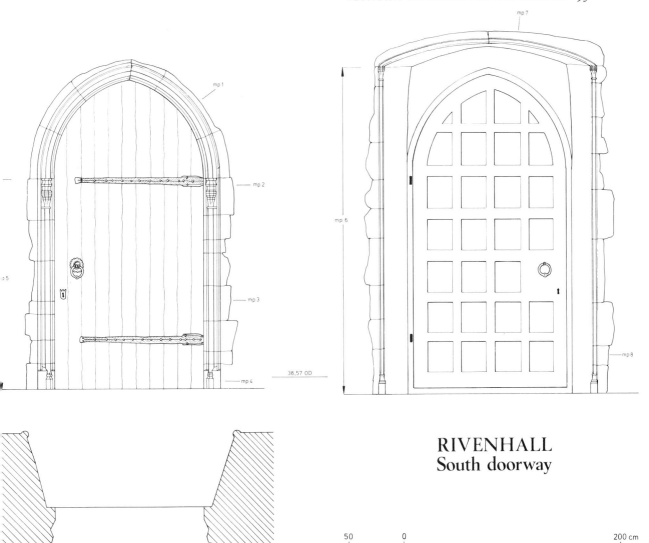

RIVENHALL
South doorway

50   0   200 cm

42 Recording a simple medieval doorway by means of external and internal elevations and a plan of the opening at threshold level. The positions of the eight drawn moulding-profiles are indicated, six of these being cross-sections; the remaining two are long vertical sections through the capitals and bases of the decorative shafts attached to the front and rear arches. The door itself is modern and has not been drawn in detail. *Drawn by Kirsty Rodwell*

be prepared at full size, unless the material under study is both of large dimensions and elementary form. It is simply not possible to record a complicated curvilinear moulding at other than full size with a hope of anything approaching accuracy.

It might be asked why there is a need to produce drawings of, say, a window both in its wall and on its own. The two records serve different purposes. Elevation drawings demonstrate composition and relationship and, when published as figures, have of necessity to be reduced to a considerable degree. A feature drawing, on the other hand, should be a full working drawing: that means enough details given for a mason or carpenter to take scaled measurements and to make the item without the need for supplementary instructions. The feature drawing may well include a sectional plan and other details in addition to a true elevation. It may also bear annotations, and when published will not be reduced to a high degree. Feature drawings can also be used to illustrate repairs and modifications, by various shading techniques; and of course fragmentary features can be reconstructed (fig. 43). None of this is possible on a main elelvation drawing without cluttering or obscuring it.

The scale of a detail drawing will not usually be the same as that of the elevation: thus in a great church if the walls were drawn at 1:50 the features would be at 1:20, and in an average church the scales would be 1:20 and 1:10 respectively. Obviously, one does not draw the same detail twice, at different scales: it is normally recorded at the larger scale required and then a reduced photographic copy made to match precisely the smaller scale. By this method much finer detail and an enhanced aesthetic quality at the smaller scale is obtained. There is a basic rule in architectural and archaeological recording and drawing: always prepare illustrations at as large a scale as is reasonably possible, photo-reducing to smaller sizes as required. Reductions can be made mechanically, using gridded overlays or proportional dividers, but this is slow and tedious and the resultant product may be of rather coarse appearance. If photographic reduction is not within the means of the recorder he should try to gain access to a drawing office which possesses an optical enlarging/reducing machine. Although care is necessary in its use, to avoid excessive errors through optical distortion, this instrument is an invaluable aid to the archaeological draughtsman: it allows for a drawing to be enlarged or reduced to any desired degree (up to a factor of five or even eight times), with the image being traced from a screen.

The process adopted for drawing a feature will depend upon its size and complexity. A large feature, such as an arcade, a main doorway or a great east window, can be drawn at least in outline from the temporary grid set up on the wall face for elevation drawing (p. 83). A small feature, such as an Anglo-Saxon window, is easiest drawn with the aid of a planning-frame suspended on the wall.

It is all too easy to make the task of drawing, say, a complicated traceried window a great labour and to find that the end-product is neither beautiful nor accurate. It is surprising how much error is introduced, mainly through parallax, when drawing details like the recessed parts of an arch or tracery; all too easily a component such as a mullion, which in reality is parallel sided and regular, becomes distorted

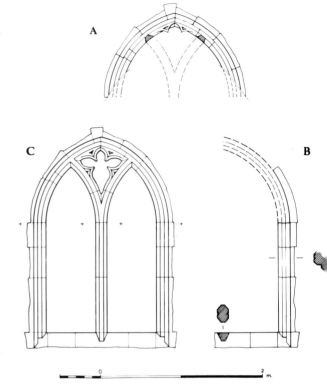

43 A simple exercise in the reconstruction of a fourteenth-century window from fragmentary evidence. A and B are fragments of two identical windows surviving in the wall shown in figs. 35–6. C shows a reconstruction of one window; the centres for the curvature of the lancet heads have been calculated and are marked by crosses. The cross-section of the central mullion is drawn from a fragment found during excavation below one of the windows.

and ungainly on the drawing. Cartographic disasters of this kind must be avoided. Parallax errors are seldom consistent, with the result that a centimetre's error on one measurement will be visually exaggerated by an opposing error on another measurement. Basic inaccuracies of this nature are compounded by more subtle problems such as deciding where to take a measurement on a moulding of rounded form. Measurements taken to mouldings with sharp arrises (edges) are straightforward until one comes to a damaged part and an estimation has to be made.

This brings us to the heart of architectural recording: should we draw the feature precisely as it now is, or should we draw it as it was obviously intended to be? There is no hard-and-fast rule, and in an ideal world we should do both. In reality a compromise has to be adopted. With very skilful draughtsmanship it is possible to show every crack and flaw in masonry without detracting from the overall intelligibility of the drawing: nineteenth-century architects exelled in this kind of presentation. But now it is no longer economically viable to draw in this way, and it is virtually a lost art. Plain outline drawings of features, to take the opposite extreme, are unsatisfactory and fail to convey an adequate impression of the character of the masonry. Even a small amount of shading, line thickening, etc., can instil sufficient life into a drawing to enhance its value both technically and aesthetically, so that in practice one ignores the minor cracks, chips and irregularities and concentrates mainly, but not exclusively, on making an intelligible representation of the feature. Where there is real doubt as to the form of a decayed or incomplete detail broken lines should be used to indicate the uncertainty. The same convention is used where a reconstruction is offered.

The greatest difficulty is encountered with Gothic arches and window tracery. Originally, all curves would have been set out with compasses from a series of geometrically interrelated centre-points (fig. 44). In the process of translating the master mason's design into stone (or the master carpenter's into wood) minor errors may well have crept in with the result that the finished product may not have been geometrically perfect. That imperfection may not be sufficient to notice on casual inspection, but will show up when drawing starts. There may be added complications through the physical distortion of the feature. Distortion may occur if an arch settles during construction, perhaps through the premature removal of centring. The displacement of stones often occurred through later settlement and cracking and through disruptions caused during repairs and rebuilds. Whatever the cause of the problem, it needs to be recorded and understood, and it naturally follows that the draughtsman cannot use compasses to set out the basic geometry of the feature.

There can be no question of 'correcting' a distorted feature in a main elevation drawing, since to do this compensations would have to be made in the masonry surrounding the feature, and a falsified record would result. On the other hand, there is nothing wrong with correcting a feature drawing, so that compasses can be used for the setting out, providing two conditions are satisfied. First, the cause and extent of the

distortion must be understood, and they must clearly be accidental; that is to say a round-headed arch which has been taken down and rebuilt in pointed style should not be corrected to its earlier form. Secondly, it must be stated on the drawing that is is a geometrical correction and not a precise record of the feature as it now appears.

The process of re-establishing the pattern of centre points for striking the arcs which are fundamental to a traceried window has to be done by trial and error using such measurements of curvature as can be taken from the window itself. The geometry of tracery has been well explored in various manuals (e.g. Brandon and Brandon, 1874), to which reference should be made before drawing begins.

The discussion of features has so far concentrated on recording in the vertical plane: when plans and sections are drawn temporary datum lines have to be established and measurements taken by offsetting, which brings us onto drawing profiles and sections of mouldings. Here again there are great difficulties in taking measurements which, when plotted, provide anything like a presentable drawing of the moulding, owing to the relatively small scale of the subject and the critical angles and curvatures involved. The planning of a Gothic window is best done in two stages: the first on site, the second in the drawing office. On site the straight lines forming the sill, the glazing grooves and ashlar joints can be drawn without difficulty. So too can the flat faces of the mullions and jambs. Next, a full-size moulding profile should be recorded, which can later be reduced to the required scale, by photographic or optical means, and the details filled in on the plan.

Drawing a moulding profile is an exacting task which must be conscientiously tackled. Mouldings are critical evidence for dating and for schools of masons: sketched and roughly measured profiles are useless. A full-size profile of every different moulding in a church should be drawn. There are several ways of achieving this. The simplest is of course to trace the profile from an exposed cross-section, but this is only possible when loose stones are being studied or when features are dissected during restoration. Normally a 'template former' has to be used. There is unfortunately only a limited range of these on the market. The gadget comprises a spring-loaded clamp which holds a

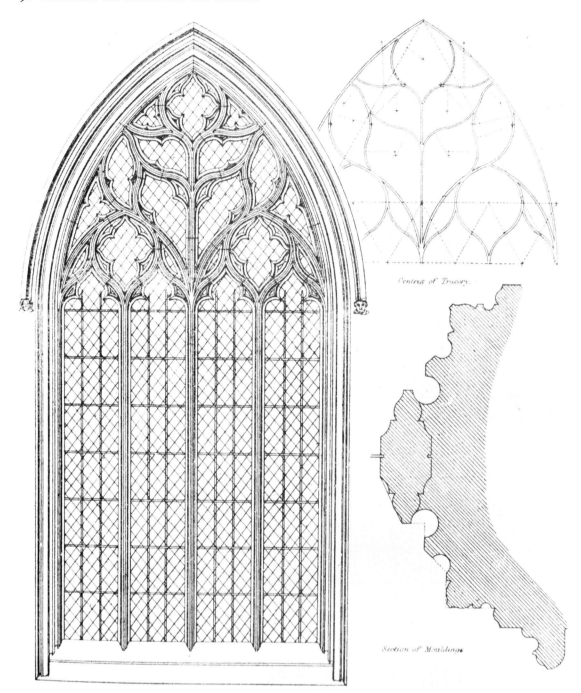

Centres of Tracery.

Section of Mouldings

44 A set of drawings to illustrate the tracery of a
decorated window at Sleaford, Lincs.: the full elevation,
a diagram of the geometry of the tracery and a profile of
the mouldings used on the jambs and mullions. *After
Brandon and Brandon, 1874*

bank of small steel rods or thin brass shims.
When the former is pressed against a moulding
the ends of the pins are bedded around the

profile, taking up its contour. The former is
then placed on a sheet of paper and the profile
traced. Template formers can only encompass
about 15cm. of moulding cross-section at one
time, and therefore several separate profiles
have to be taken to make up the complete
outline of a large moulding. In order to obtain a
proper register between individual parts of a

profile, overlapping impressions must be taken. When the composite profile has been drawn checks should be made, using calipers or direct measurements, of distances between defined angles, diameters of rolls, etc.

If it is envisaged that a recorder will need to draw hundreds of profiles it may be worthwhile to commission an engineer to make a large template former which will encompass 30cm. or even 50cm. of profile at a time. In a large instrument of this kind the feelers are made of aluminium or plastic-laminate strips. It has been objected by some pedants that the template former is not absolutely accurate and that in taking multiple impressions of a large moulding there is room for error. This is true, but equally it is true that the use of a former allows a moulding to drawn in a quarter of the time taken by manual measurements. It also certainly gives a more accurate result than most recorders would otherwise be able to achieve: only very sophisticated means of measurement can improve on it. Unless the shims are very thin the former will not be able to register sharp angles with precision, and it cannot of course reach into re-entrant curves. But these are very minor limitations which can be corrected whilst producing a fair copy of the moulding profile. This, it must be stressed, should be done on site and not as a retrospective exercise. If one wants to make doubly sure that the drawn profile is correct, it is simple enough to cut out a negative profile in cardboard and try it for a fit against the actual moulding.

The other alternative for drawing a moulding is to take a large number of linear measurements and angles and to reconstruct the profile geometrically. This is tedious and is not guaranteed to result in an accurate drawing, especially if there is any imperfection in the cutting of the moulding. It is more useful to make a good profile drawing with a template former, check it, and then reconstruct the geometry on the drawing. This way it should be possible to ascertain whether the architect's theoretical profile and the mason's product are in agreement (for handbooks of mouldings, see Paley, 1845 and Sharpe, 1871). All full-size drawings of mouldings, whether of timber or stone, should be retained and deposited in one of the archives where 'mouldings banks' are held, and reductions should be published, normally at a scale of 1:4. The importance of moulding records to architectural history has been ably demonstrated through recent studies such as those by Dr Richard Morris (Morris I, 1978; 1979) and Dr Eileen Roberts (Roberts, 1977; 1979).

Special problems of architectural sculpture

A fundamental difference exists between architectural mouldings and their associated ornament, and sculpture: the former is repetitive, while the latter is unique. Thus one may draw a representative profile of a moulding and sample of the ball-flower ornament around an arch, extrapolating from the better preserved parts to reconstruct those which have been lost. But this cannot be done with sculpture, where any damaged or missing part is lost for ever, and no amount of effort can re-create it unless old illustrations or other forms of reliable evidence are to hand. I am referring here mainly to outdoor sculptures which form part of the fabric of a building but, by extension, these remarks could be applied to free-standing works of art and monumental effigies.

By far the commonest forms of architectural sculpture are the moulded label-stops (or drip-stones), found in pairs flanking arched openings, and gargoyles. Less common are sculptured friezes and capitals, crucifixions, armorial bearings and statuary, but they are nonetheless far from scarce, as the vast arrays of figure sculpture on the west fronts of some great churches and cathedrals remind us. Not every ecclesiastical archaeologist will be faced with the problems of recording such buildings, but there are few parish churches which do not possess at least a few label-stops. The importance of these little figures, as the surviving representatives of the lesser medieval sculptor's art, has been largely overlooked, and they are disappearing rapidly through decay and 'restoration'. They all need recording, mainly by photography in carefully selected lights. Normally two or three views of a gargoyle or label-stop are sufficient to record its salient features, together with written details.

Many of the finest later medieval sculptures are to be found high up on towers and parapets, where they are not normally accessible for close-up photography; tele-photo photography from the ground is not an adequate alternative and should only be employed where access to the subject is impossible. Whenever scaffolding is erected and close access is attainable, sculptured detail should be fully recorded

because the opportunity may not arise again for fifty years or more—by which time further deterioration will have taken place (fig. 45). All architectural sculpture is worthy of record, whether it is medieval or Victorian. Indeed, in some cases Victorian additions and replacements have now weathered to such an extent that they are not immediately recognizable; but close inspection will usually determine the point, especially in respect of human figures: rarely does a Victorian face pass for a medieval one. Amateur cleaning of sculptures to improve photography should not normally be attempted, unless a contractor is about to hasten their destruction with a high-pressure water hose or sand-blasting equipment. In general, medieval stone carving will survive longer if left uncleaned than if incompetently tampered with. When a piece of sculpture is to be replaced by a new stone the original work should always be recorded, however dilapidated, and a note should be made of the name of the carver of the new piece, together with date of fixing and the source of inspiration for the work; i.e. whether it was an attempt to re-create the old, whether it was copied from another church, or taken from a picture in a book. It is important to remember that the work of today is the archaeology of tomorrow, and if we fail to pay due attention to modern restorations, and to Victorian ones, we shall be causing unnecessary gaps in the historical record for future generations.

Major figure sculptures present different kinds of problems for the recorder in terms of scale, accessibility and condition. Indoor sculptures are less problematic, for access is seldom really difficult, lighting can be arranged (p. 103) and weathering will not have taken place. Outdoor sculptures are generally set high up on towers and in gables where nothing can be done to make a record without proper scaffolding. Each figure will stand in its own niche, which may also be highly ornamented, and thus the whole forms an ensemble. The niche and its surrounding ornament can be treated, as far as possible, as an architectural feature, with plans, sections, elevations and

45 Full-sized figure of a mid-thirteenth-century knight in armour set high up on the west front of Wells Cathedral. Details of this figure, its condition, surviving paint traces, etc., could only be recorded when scaffolding was erected for restoration works. This opportunity for study may not be repeated for perhaps 100 years. *Photo: Jerry Sampson. Copyright Dean and Chapter of Wells*

moulding profiles being prepared in the usual way, but the recording of the figure itself can best be achieved through a combination of photographs, sketches and notes. The same applies to other forms of free-expression sculpture, such as spandrels, tympana, corbels and foliate capitals. Originally, the figures, and probably much of the associated architectural ornament, would have been covered with a thin coat of plaster or lime, to form a 'ground', upon which polychrome painting and gold leaf were applied. Medieval sculpture was rarely intended to be seen as stone, either indoors or outdoors. The west fronts of great buildings such as Exeter, Lincoln and Wells cathedrals, Southwell Minster and Bath Abbey were meant to be colourful spectacles. Traces of that colouring survives today and it is the archaeologist's task to seek them out and record them, both before and during any cleaning, conservation or restoration processes which may be applied.

An indispensable aid to all detailed sculpture recording is a simple drawn outline, or 'base-map', which can quickly be produced from photographs. A square-on frontal photograph is taken to show the whole piece and a print is made at a convenient size (usually 10 × 8in.). This then forms the base for a tracing, in ink, of the outline and main features of the sculpture (fig. 46). Multiple photocopies can be made of this drawing, each being used to record a particular class of information: paint traces; old repairs; areas of surface decay; metal fittings, cramps and dowels; and all new repairs, as they are effected. Base-maps can be annotated, coloured and used as a key to close-up photography. Some of England's more important medieval sculpture has, fortunately, been photographed during restoration works in the past and it is now very instructive to be able to compare photographs which may span a century or more, and to learn something about the rate of stone decay and loss of evidence in modern times. At Wells Cathedral many of the 297 surviving medieval figure-sculptures, as well as other details on the west front, were first photographed in 1870, then in 1904, and again in the late 1970s. Through a combination of photography, photogrammetry, drawings and written records it should eventually be possible to achieve a thorough understanding of how that west front was designed, built, modified and restored, a continuous process spanning some centuries.

renewed 1870   repaired 1980

46 Outline drawing of a medieval tympanum, prepared as a 'base-map' for recording the condition of the sculpture and conservation treatment. *Copyright Dean and Chapter of Wells*

The photographic record

It is self-evident that photography is an indispensable aid to almost every aspect of recording, but it has been sadly abused and misunderstood. Photography may be part of a record, or used as a means to an end (e.g. to help with the production of a drawing), but seldom is it suitable as the only form of record. It will be useful to introduce some aspects of photography in church recording.

First, a few words must be said on the problems of photographing three-dimensional rectilinear subjects, like towers, since they are susceptible to unfortunate distortions which are not so apparent through the view-finder as they are on the actual photograph. Thus if there are major vertical elements in the picture, such as a tower or a view through an arch, the camera should be held with the film in the same plane, in order to ensure that vertical lines on the subject also appear upright on the image. As soon as the camera is tilted, usually to gain more coverage, vertical lines will appear to converge towards the centre-top of the picture. The greater the tilt, the worse is the effect of converging parallels. Photographs which suffer from perspective distortion are ungainly and jarring to the eye. There are several ways of overcoming the problem. If possible, avoid

47 The importance of perspective control
Right A photograph taken with a standard wide-angle lens and the camera tilted to reach the apex of the building. The entire image tapers towards the top, appears to lean backwards and is aesthetically displeasing
Left The same photograph taken with a 28mm. perspective-control lens and the camera held with a horizontal line of vision. *Photos: author*

tilting the camera, and to gain height use a ladder, a builder's trestle or a lightweight scaffold tower. The last mentioned is an extremely useful asset for all aspects of drawing, photography and general access in smaller churches. A light tubular steel tower 5m. to 8m. in height, with a base about 1·5m. square, is inexpensive, can be carried in the average estate car and can be erected in five minutes.

Ground level photography of tall subjects is possible with special equipment, but the cost of that equipment is beyond the reach of most archaeologists. Nothing takes a better picture than a large-format plate-camera, and this is normally fitted with a device known as a 'rising front' which will correct converging parallels. The disadvantages of a plate-camera, apart from the high purchase price, are that it is cumbersome and slow to use, the cost of film is considerable for monochrome and prohibitive for colour, and it does not make convenient transparencies. Today, the use of the 35mm. single-lens-reflex camera has become so widespread that it must be accepted as the norm for all but the most ardently professional of photographers.

Two camera bodies—one for colour transparencies, the other for monochrome negatives—and a selection of interchangeable lenses are generally required. Fortunately, there is no longer an objection to the use of the 35mm. camera for architectural photography on the grounds that it does not have the facility of the rising front. A lens is now available which embodies a shift mechanism, termed a 'perspective-control lens'. It is expensive but is a virtual necessity (fig. 47). The versatility of the perspective-control lens is enormous and has advantages over the traditional rising front since it has many applications apart from reaching the high parts of buildings. The lens can be rotated so that the rising front effect can be turned downwards ('falling front'), laterally or diagonally. These movements allow perspectively controlled photography into excavations, tombs and situations where the subject is below the level of the camera. The lens permits views over parapets and other places where the photographer may not be able to reach sufficiently far to obtain the shot that he desires. The perspective-control lens is also useful for obtaining unencumbered photographs behind trees and scaffold-poles which would obstruct the view through a normal lens.

We may now turn to the various kinds of photographic record required in church archaeology. First, there are the general shots which show the form of the building, its interior and its surroundings. Next there are what may be termed subject shots: that is those which show an element in the architectural composition, such as a tower or the interior of a chapel. Thirdly, there are the square-on views of a wall, which approximate to a dimensionally correct record of part of the building. The wall must obviously be in a single plane, and photographs of this kind should normally include a ranging pole or other graduated scale, which must also be sited on the viewing plane and square to the camera. Drawings of limited accuracy and usefulness can be made from such photographs (p. 87). Fourthly, come the detailed, square-on shots of features in a church, such as windows and doorways, and the even closer views of intricate details like carved spandrels, inscriptions, traceried panels and wall paintings.

Photographs of all of these can be used as the bases for drawings, provided that there is not too much depth-of-field to the subject, or as aids to filling in the details of a piece of carved ornament on a feature which has otherwise been recorded on a measured drawing (e.g. a tympanum over a doorway). While one can make measured drawings of regular ornament such as chevrons on an arch, or traceried panelling and ironwork on a door, it is well nigh impossible to produce a true measured drawing of, say, foliage carving. Given proper lighting, a photograph may constitute the best record of that particular aspect. But if the carving is part of a capital which is integral to an arch that has been measured and drawn, then the carving must also appear on that drawing. If the recorder is a good artist he will be able to sketch the detail freehand, within the measured confines of the capital; but if he lacks artistic skill he will produce a better result by tracing the foliage from a scaled photograph. Sculptured detail, especially when defaced, decayed or impossibly sited for proper illumination, is often best recorded by the complementary methods of photography and drawing. The photograph will convey the general 'feel' of the subject and show its condition while the drawing will bring out details which are hard to capture on film. Fifthly and finally, a range of oblique photographs is necessary to record sculpture, small features and details which are essentially three-dimensional in form and which are not susceptible to illustration by conventional plans and elevations, such as statuary, carved finials and *objets d'art*.

Photography inside churches, particularly when using colour film, can be a nightmare. Undoubtedly flash-light provides the best form of illumination for colour photography, but there are so many imponderables that it cannot be recommended without caution. First, if large spaces have to be illuminated, very high powered and expensive flash equipment is needed: the results can be superb, as demonstrated at York Minster (Phillips, 1976), but there the cost of the operation was regarded as immaterial. Secondly, flash photography, other than in the hands of the most experienced, is unpredictable in its results. Unless several flash units are employed simultaneously the subject is usually 'flattened' and there are problems with light spots and shadows.

Tungsten lighting may be used with monochrome photography, perhaps coupled with a long exposure, to produce fully controlled results at insignificant cost. But indoor colour photography with artificial lighting is far more difficult. If there is good natural light in the building it is better to use this than any other form, even if a fairly long exposure is required. However, exposures in excess of $\frac{1}{8}$ sec. produce progressively greener shades on most colour films. Bright sunlight, on the other hand, is useless for all kinds of indoor photography, owing to the strong shafts of cross-light which it introduces. If sunlight passes through coloured glass windows, or even 'clear' glass of the Victorian pale yellowish-green type, the colour composition is wrecked. Photo-flood lights and a blue filter can be used for indoor colour photography with reasonable success. Ordinary tungsten lights produce a reddish-yellow result on coloured film, even when a blue filter is used; and flourescent lights turn the colour to a ghastly green. It is however possible to obtain flourescent tubes which are 'colour matching'. In summary, indoor church photography, especially in colour, is not a subject for the inexperienced photographer to tackle without expert advice on the spot if colour correctness is deemed important.

We may conclude this chapter with a few words on the subject of photographic scales. In general and oblique views there is often little point in having a measuring scale in the picture, but a different situation obtains for elevational views, square-on shots of detail and even general shots of sculptures. It is a basic rule of archaeological photography, universally obser-ved on excavations, that a photographic scale is included in every picture. By contrast scales are virtually unknown in photographs taken by architectural historians and art historians. This endemic laxity needs rectification. A graduated scale of standard dimensions must always be provided in a photograph which might be used for the extraction of measurements or as a basis for tracing. It also helps the person who is not familiar with a building or monument to register its size from a photograph if a scale is included. Likewise the appreciation of sculpture is enhanced by a knowledge of its true size.

Some would argue that a photographic scale is an obtrusion on the aesthetics of a picture, and that is certainly true in some circumstances. But if the purpose of taking the photograph is to provide a permanent record, its value is greatly impaired if the scale is unknown. It is not sufficient to rely on some extraneous object, such as a brick or a chair, which happens to appear in the photograph, to provide an approximate order of scale. Even worse is the deliberate inclusion of oddmenta to provide scale, like a coin, a match box, a hymn book or the photographer's foot. Every effort should be made to exclude all debris from a photograph and to place a scale in an unobtrusive position.

The scale must obviously lie on the same general plane as the object being photographed. It must also be parallel to the plane of the film and squarely aligned. A ranging pole which leans drunkenly across a picture or which is too large for the subject it accompanies attracts the eye and ruins the photograph. Whenever convenient, the scale should be put close to one of the margins of the frame so that it may be trimmed off during printing if it is unwanted. An alternative is to take one shot with a scale and another without. Either way, both the needs of the record and aesthetics of pure art photography are satisfied. It is now normal to use metric scales, and a useful complement is a pair of 2m. ranging poles, a 0·5m. rod and small scales of 5cm. and 30cm.

I hope that it has been shown in this chapter that the detailed recording of ecclesiastical buildings is a worthwhile and stimulating task, albeit difficult at times. We have only skimmed the surface of the practical hints on recording, but it would be inappropriate to launch into more detailed discussion here. The main point to emphasize about fabric recording is that it can be completely non-destructive and can be carried out on a variety of levels, as determined by the recorder. Enough should have been said to enable the potential recorder to assess his resources and energies in relation to the project in hand, and to choose a realistic level of operation.

7 Church Excavations

The interior of a church, below floor level, is an intensely complex archaeological site, the potential value of which has not always been adequately appreciated by historians or even archaeologists. The average parish church has stood on the same spot for about one thousand years and the space enclosed by its walls has been the scene of more human activity than any other comparable area of ground in the parish. The potential for the encapsulation of a rich haul of historic evidence could not be higher. Of course, circumstances vary, and a church in a busy town will have seen more activity than a rural one.

What is there to find?

There are two aspects to the buried evidence in churches: the additive and the destructive. The former is the process of accumulating evidence, such as the laying of new floors, one on top of another. The second is the process of removing evidence which has previously accumulated, as in the lowering of floor levels or the digging of graves. New features which are agents of destruction—graves are the commonest—are at the same time fresh capsules of evidence. It is therefore misleading to speak of all the archaeological evidence as 'destroyed' by grave digging. This is nonsense: one form of evidence has been replaced by another. It is only when the interior of a church has literally been shovelled out and the material carted away that the buried archaeology can be said to have been destroyed.

Throughout the Middle Ages archaeological deposits were steadily accumulating inside churches; this often meant that when new floors were laid the tell-tale evidence for the positions of internal furnishings was preserved, although hidden from view. Destruction began in a big way towards the end of the seventeenth century when burial vaults became fashionable. Their popularity increased throughout the eighteenth century and down to the mid-nineteenth. The wealthier the inhabitants of the parish, the more devastation they wrought to the medieval levels inside the church. In a great town church like Bath Abbey the modern floor is simply a skin over a vast honeycomb of post-medieval vaults. Churches in rural areas were not greatly affected by vault construction, and their medieval floor levels remained intact until the advent of Victorian re-ordering. The great wave of church reflooring and repewing which took place in the second half of the last century was thoroughly destructive. Over the centuries ground level inside churches had risen, often by 0·5m. or more since the twelfth century, obscuring the bases of pillars and reducing the heights of doorways. The Victorian desire to make everything neat and correct led to the levelling of church interiors, with the result that archaeological deposits were cleared away wholesale. Many restoration accounts refer to the lowering of floors to the 'original level'. For example at Stow, Lincs., 'before the nineteenth-century restoration the floor of the church had been raised above its present level, and a great part of the impressive plinths, which support the crossing, had been hidden beneath the floor', (Taylor and Taylor, 1965, 590). In this particular instance the debris from a disastrous but archaeologically important fire in the church lay on the Norman floor level and was cleared away with no more than a passing mention.

Thus the underfloor archaeology of ancient churches will vary according to circumstances. In few cases will nothing remain: in many town churches the evidence will be largely of post-medieval date, but elsewhere it will span many centuries. Today a new wave of church reflooring is sweeping the country, and with it further destruction of the buried history of these buildings. The amount of evidence which can be recovered from merely watching reflooring operations is strictly limited. Contractors always assure the enquiring archaeologist that they found nothing except bones and 'made-ground'. Likewise, the historically minded incumbent who looks down holes and hopes to see the Anglo-Saxon predecessor of his church is always disappointed, because the remains are never preserved in the form in which he expects to see them. He might comment that just 'a few loose stones' turned up. Expressions of this kind ring alarm bells in the minds of archaeologists, because all 'made-ground' must, by definition, be deliberately deposited and therefore of archaeological interest, and references to 'loose stones' almost invariably mean that the fragmentary foundations of some ancient wall have been torn up without being appreciated for what they were.

The upshot of all this is that the buried archaeology of a church can only be studied and interpreted through skilled excavation on a scale large enough to yield useful dividends. In every instance where such conditions have been fulfilled valuable results have been obtained. In some instances the results have been truly remarkable and far beyond expectations. There are two critical factors. First, the excavation must be conducted in a competent manner, under the direction of a person who is not just a skilled excavator but is also an archaeo-ecclesiologist. So much can be missed by simply not knowing what to look for in the ground. Secondly, the area available for excavation must be of worthwhile size, or the results are almost bound to be thoroughly misleading. To excavate a trench covering two or three square metres is not merely futile but positively harmful. It seldom does more than result in the destruction of precious but fragmentary deposits in the name of research. There is no such thing as a 'typical section' through the deposits in a church, and it is fatuous to speak of 'sampling' them. In the average parish church one could excavate half a dozen 1m.-square trial holes at random and learn little or nothing about the history of the building and the site, and even the excavation of two dozen such areas would run the risk of providing no more than a deceptively incomplete story.

Even when a relatively large proportion of the interior of a church is available for excavation, such as one quarter of the nave, or a whole transept or aisle, the results obtainable from the investigation can be very variable, owing to localized conditions. Many medieval churches were not built on level ground and the site may or may not have been terraced as part of the construction works. It was evidently common for floors to slope, either across the church, or along its length. New floors perpetuated these slopes, although there was a tendency as the centuries passed for the lower areas to fill up to a greater degree. The floors at Wharram Percy sloped to the east, and excavation revealed a considerable build-up of levels in the chancel, but at the west end everything had been sliced away in order to level a relatively recent floor. At Hadstock excavation has shown that the floors sloped in two directions: the west end of the nave was nearly 0·5m. higher than the east end, and the floor of the south transept was in the region of 0·8m. higher than that of the north. The tilt must have been readily visible, but nobody worried about it until 1884 when a grand reflooring took place. The interior of the church was dug out to a constant level. Hence over the western and southern parts of the nave and in the south transept all medieval and post-medieval floors were removed and even the surface of the natural clay was scarped away to a level below the bases of the walls, while in the north transept some twenty archaeological layers were left intact, covering the whole range of the church's history from the later Saxon period to post-medieval times, fig. 48 (Rodwell, 1976). By good fortune, the small trial excavation of 1973 was undertaken in the north transept. The results were completely baffling, but on the strength of the very survival of ancient deposits here a full-scale excavation of the interior was mounted in 1974. Had the trial excavation been sited in the south transept, absolutely nothing would have been found except the truncated surface of the natural clay immediately below the Victorian floor. Hadstock church would not then have been investigated and its interesting history would have remained undeciphered.

A similar story can be told of the much larger and more complex town church of St Peter's, Barton-on-Humber, also built on ground which sloped to the north. The floor of the large, early twelfth-century nave must have been canted from south to north, the effect of which would have become more noticeable when aisles were added. The pillar bases of the north arcade are set 0·6m. lower than those of the south arcade, relative to the horizontal; and the overall slope from aisle to aisle must have been nearly one metre. This bothered nobody—not even the paviers who laid medieval tile floors—until the new Victorian benches were installed. As at

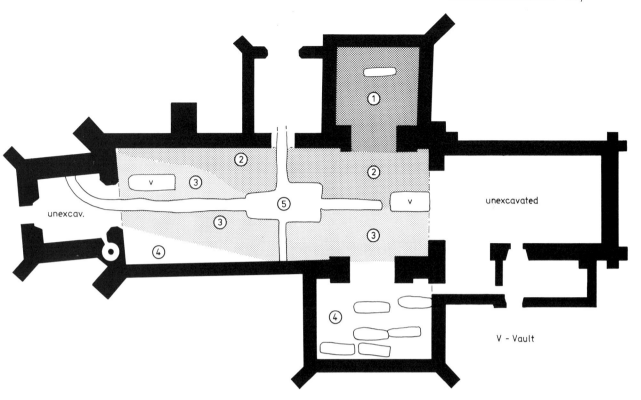

48 Hadstock: the survival of archaeological deposits inside the church, schematically represented
1 All floor levels preserved intact
2 Anglo-Saxon floors only survive, with no overlying deposits
3 No surviving floor levels, but a pre-church buried soil remains, which elsewhere underlies the floors
4 No archaeological layers extant; only the exposed surface of the natural boulder clay
5 Nineteenth-century features dug through all deposits, into the natural clay (heating chamber and ducts in the nave, two brick vaults and several graves)

Hadstock, the interior of the church was scarped so that all ancient floor levels in the south aisle were erased. On the south side of the nave only early medieval floors survived, but on the north side there were later ones too; and in the north aisle the post-medieval floors were entirely intact.

It was only through total excavation of the nave and aisles in 1979–80 that all the various levels could be inter-related and tied to building phases. Another salutary lesson learned from that investigation was that the weathering line of a former roof, now visible at the west end of the nave, on the east face of the tower, does not belong to any part of the standing building but to a hitherto unknown eleventh-century apsidal church which lies beneath the nave floor (fig. 49). The foundations of that church are fragmentary in places and 50 per cent or more of the interior of St Peter's could have been excavated without discovering the Saxo-Norman building. That omission would have resulted in a radically different history of the church being written. The corollary of this is worth bearing in mind: no matter how badly the early archaeological deposits seem to have been cut about by post-medieval graves, vaults and heating ducts, it is most unlikely that every trace of any substantial phase of building will have been wholly eradicated.

These examples could be multiplied many times over, and they all point the same moral—that large-scale meticulous excavation, coupled with structural study, is the only satisfactory way to tackle the interior of an ancient church, if one wants to be sure that the results are a true reflection of the history of that building. It is not my intention here to provide a manual on church excavation, but simply to outline some of the general and particular classes of evidence which derive from such work. Careful excavation and recording techniques which are capable of adaptation to church archaeology are discussed by Barker (1977) and Hirst (1976).

Types of evidence

There are four basic categories of evidence to be found in church excavations. First, there is the structural development of the building; secondly, the associated 'works features'; thirdly, the remains of floors, furnishings and fittings; and fourthly, the burials. The first three categories will now be examined in turn, while the discussion of burials is reserved for Chapter 9. Not all the investigations cited relate to excavations inside standing churches: some of the buildings mentioned are ruins, while others have long since been demolished and have been 'rediscovered'.

1 Development of the plan
One of the most remarkable achievements of post-war church archaeology has been the elucidation of the complex development plans of relatively minor buildings. Few of the parish churches so far investigated have been found to have simple structural histories, and in this chapter we are considering only the plan, not all the successive phases which may be enshrined in the superstructure. In most cases churches prove to have had simple beginnings, becoming more complex as time passed. Small timber chapels, single or double-celled, were the first recognizable religious buildings at Wharram Percy, Yorks., Thetford St Michael, Norfolk, Burnham, Lincs., Rivenhall and Asheldham, Essex. At Wharram and Thetford the timber churches were encased by the later stone buildings (Hurst, 1976; Wilson, 1971, 130); at Burnham the post-built chapel lay under the later chancel (Coppack, 1978); at Rivenhall the stone church was built to the west of its timber predecessor (Rodwell and Rodwell, 1973) and at Asheldham to the south (Drury and Rodwell, 1978). At Nazeingbury, Essex, a pair of wooden churches has been found without a stone-built successor (Huggins, 1978) and at Potterne, Wilts., a cruciform timber church had its stone replacement on a nearby site (Davey, 1964). In all these instances our knowledge of the Anglo-Saxon timber churches has been derived exclusively from excavation, representing a considerable academic advance, especially since only one wooden church of that period survives

49 Indoor excavation. Foundations of a previously unknown apsidal Saxo-Norman church revealed through the total excavation of the interior of St Peter's Church, Barton-on-Humber, in 1980. For the plan see fig. 13. *Photo: author. Crown copyright*

in Britain, at Greensted-juxta-Ongar, Essex (Christie, Olsen and Taylor, 1979).

As might be expected, the majority of the early stone-built churches were also of simple form, having one or two cells: excavated examples include Wharram Percy, Burnham, Thetford and Rivenhall, already mentioned, together with St Mary Tanner Street and St Pancras, Winchester, Bargham, Sussex, St Nicholas Shambles, London and Raunds, Northants. Other buildings, also of simple form, have been found to include an eastern apse as a primary feature: e.g. St Chad, Barrow-on-Humber, St Paul-in-the-Bail, Lincoln, St Bride, London, St Benedict, Norwich and probably St Nicholas, Angmering, Sussex. In all cases these early churches were so completely destroyed by later rebuildings or so thoroughly engulfed that they were wholly unrecognizable until excavation took place. Sometimes the plan of a simple church could rapidly change in a manner which now seems to us so illogical that it is difficult to envisage the process of evolution. At Asheldham, for example, a fourteenth-century two-celled church with western tower superseded a three-celled Norman building with an axial tower over the chancel and an apsidal sanctuary. Excavation has traced the steps by which this change took place (fig. 50).

Excavation of the Old Minster, Winchester, has shown that this began life as a cruciform church, as did the minster at Hadstock, while the small urban parish church of St Pancras, Winchester, had transepts added at a very early stage in its development. More common than the addition of transepts was that of aisles. St Pancras' church also received these and at Wharram Percy aisles were variously added and deleted. We have already discussed aisles, their addition, enlargement and subtraction, in relation to standing churches (pp. 63–6) and here it will suffice to note that excavations at several sites have demonstrated the same kind of sequence. Great churches, basically those of monastic and minster status, developed amazingly complex plans. We know very little about these in general terms, but excavations on several key sites, such as the Old Minster at Winchester, St Augustine's Abbey at Canterbury, and Glastonbury Abbey, have shown that each is unique. These, and simple churches like St Mary's, Deerhurst, and Brixworth, are characterized by a multiplicity of inter-linked chambers, the development of

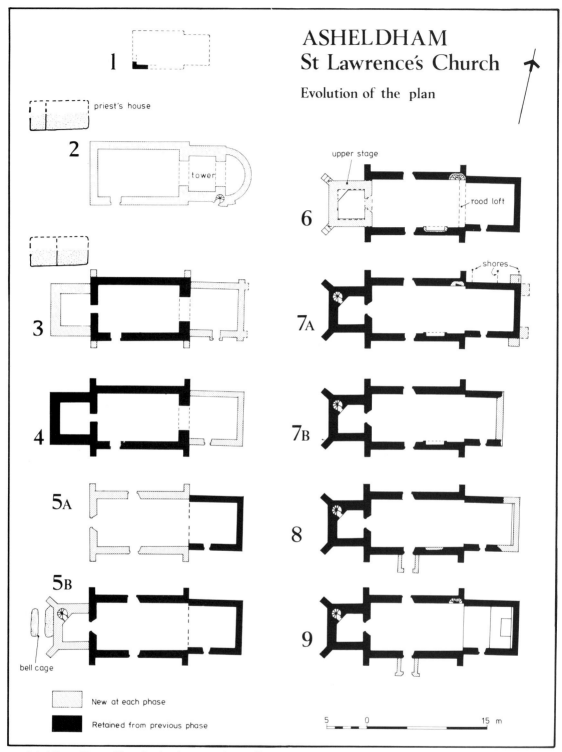

ASHELDHAM
St Lawrence's Church

Evolution of the plan

1

priest's house

2

tower

upper stage

rood loft

6

3

shores

7A

4

7B

5A

8

5B

bell cage

9

New at each phase

Retained from previous phase

5   0   15 m

50 Asheldham, Essex. Here the development of a small rural church of proprietary origin, and now redundant, with no visible features earlier than the fourteenth century, was studied through 'rescue' excavation during its conversion to a new use. The church's structural history was not as simple as it first appeared: 1 Anglo-Saxon (timber) 2 Norman 3 13th century 4 Early 14th century 5 Mid-14th century 6 Late 14th century 7 15th–16th century 8 18th century 9 19th century. *After Drury and Rodwell, 1978*

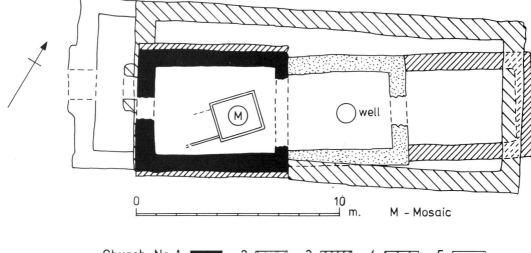

Church No. 1 ■■■■ 2 ▦ 3 ▨ 4 ◇◇ 5 ▭

51 St Helen-on-the-Walls, York. The development of a simple church, in five stages, from Anglo-Saxon to late medieval. The siting of the first church, in the suburbs of Roman York, is evocative of interest, especially since a mosaic medallion depicting a female head, and belonging to an underlying Roman building, lay where the first altar should have stood. The door was probably in the west end, and a well formed an eastern focus. When the church was extended in the second period the well would have lain beneath the altar. *After Magilton, 1980*

which only excavation can elucidate.

While excavations have revealed that there are many permutations for church development—and no two buildings so far investigated are quite alike—several basic enlargement trends are discernible which agree with the architectural evidence recorded in standing churches. By no means all churches were extended to the four points of the compass, but most have at least received an enlargement of the chancel. The processes of expansion were usually logical, with just one component of the building being demolished at a time: this not only allowed the church to remain in use for worship but also ensured that the inflow of funds and the building programme were kept in step. There was often no need to pull down an old part or breach a wall until the new addition was well advanced. Thus a square-ended chancel extension could be built around an apse, or an aisle could be widened without the need to tear away a large area of walling before there was something to close the gap. The ways in which new parts were wrapped around old are often discernible in excavated plans. Just occasionally—perhaps as the result of a

disastrous fire or foundation failure—a church was completely levelled and new one built on the same site, without making use of the earlier foundations: such was the case at Raunds, Northants, fig. 64 (Boddington, 1980).

Most commonly the extension of a church took place in such a way as to respect the position of the chancel arch: at Wharram Percy and at St Pancras, Winchester, despite the multiplicity of changes which took place, the one consistent feature of the plan was the chancel arch. The original arch was not maintained throughout, but its site remained constant. The sanctity of the division between nave and chancel may have been partially responsible for maintaining the location of the arch, but much more important was the practical consideration that the two parts of a parish church were usually the responsibility of different persons or institutions. The parishioners were responsible for the upkeep of the nave, while the rector (whether in the person of an incumbent, or an institution) had to maintain the chancel. Minsters and monastic churches were not troubled, at least initially, by this divided responsibility for the fabric, which may provide a clue to the status of early churches whose history is uncertain and where rebuildings have not respected the site of the chancel arch. The excavations at St Peter's, Barton-on-Humber, have shown that the chancel arch is now in its fourth position (fig. 13). The fine axial tower was obviously considered the most important feature of the church and all extensions took place to the east of it. The same is true at Wootton, Surrey, where excavation has confirmed that the original nave, which lay to the west of the axial tower, has been demolished and the body of the church is now on the east side. At St Helen-on-the-Walls, York, the chancel arch was resited on at least one occasion, and the whole axis of the church shifted slightly, fig. 51 (Magilton, 1980).

It is perhaps worth mentioning that the development of the plan of a church does not manifest itself simply by recording the positions of foundations hidden beneath the floor: the task of disentangling walls and trying to date the various periods of work is slow and painstaking. Every junction between walls and foundations needs to be examined carefully to ascertain the constuctional sequence. There may be straight joints or obvious differences in materials, but early foundations, in particular, often look deceptively uniform even when they are not contemporaneous. Foundations of rammed chalk or banded hoggin (clay, sand and gravel mixture) were common throughout the Saxon and Norman periods, and in some areas down to the end of the Middle Ages. These materials can often knit together over the centuries: consideration has to be given to factors such as width, depth and profile of foundation trench, nature and coarseness of the filling material, thickness and continuity of layering, degree of compaction, and so on. It is straightforward to dissect and examine redundant foundations, but care has to be exercised when tampering with those which still support major walls. Unless access can be obtained to all buried foundations and at least most of the junctions examined in detail it is not easy to propose a developmental sequence with confidence: almost without exception, phases of work will be overlooked and the history of the church oversimplified. While nobody wishes to generate complexities where they do not exist, it is of fundamental importance to demonstrate that two foundations are contemporary, not to assume that they are. Some excavators have regrettably assumed contemporaneity 'because there is no evidence that they are of different dates', even when foundations are visibly of non-uniform construction. This has led to simplistic conclusions and some curious monstrosities being proposed as single-period buildings. St Nicholas, Angmering, Sussex, is a likely example of this (Bedwin, 1975). The contemporaneity of adjoining or non-adjoining foundations must be demonstrated by positive argument if an association between them is to be claimed. Where the critical evidence is missing, this fact can only be reported, and followed by an informed discussion.

Excavation on the site of a ruined or demolished church can encompass remains both inside and outside the latest shell, but when a standing church is under investigation it is often not possible to excavate on both sides of its walls simultaneously. A reflooring programme may present the opportunity for internal excavation, or a drainage operation may be preceded by external excavation. Those were the circumstances under which Hadstock and Rivenhall churches, respectively, were excavated. Since the latter is a simple church which has not been subjected to changes in width it is probable that the true development of the plan has been ascertained through external excavation only. Extensive restoration works carried out at Little Somborne enabled excavation to take place both inside and outside the church, as well as the recording of the fabric, providing an exceptionally complete picture.

It is naturally more reassuring to be able to examine foundations from both sides to ascertain whether they present a uniform appearance. Usually they do, but there are instances where a foundation has been widened by trenching along one side and adding new material, to give extra support to a rebuilt superstructure. This happened at Hadstock, where the hoggin foundations of the quire were thickened for the construction of the central tower; and at Wells the Saxon Lady Chapel was enlarged slightly by building new foundations exactly around the old ones.

That brings us to one of the great difficulties of church archaeology: how to determine whether a wall is contemporary with the foundation upon which it rests. Again, there have been widespread assumptions by archaeologists, on the basis of 'no evidence to the contrary'. One cannot help wondering what evidence they were looking for and how they decided positively on its absence. The relationship between every wall and its foundations is so important that it requires careful investigation and discussion. If a wall is not contemporary with its foundation, and if this fact is not elucidated, it is likely that one or more phases in the history of the church will be overlooked. This might only be unfortunate, and not disastrous; but usually it is the latter, in terms of chronology. Foundations can be centuries older than the walls which rest upon them and if this fact is not ascertained the basic chronology of the site will have been falsified. One of the main causes of the late dating applied to a number of churches is the failure to recognize reused foundations.

There is also a growing recognition of the reuse in churches of Roman foundations, and in some cases entire or part buildings of Roman origin. The lower parts of the north wall of St Helen's, Colchester are Roman and St Nicholas' church in the same town was also on Roman foundations (Rodwell and Rodwell, 1977). In Canterbury the north wall of St Mary Northgate rests directly on the crenellations of the Roman city wall. Excavations on the site of the church of St Helen-on-the-Walls, York has shown how it grew up over a Roman town-house, fig. 51 (Magilton, 1980); and the south aisle of Aldborough church, Yorks., rests on a line of large gritstone blocks which are certainly of Roman origin and may be *in situ*. At Silchester, Hants., Lullingstone, Kent, and probably Ancaster, Lincs., Anglo-Saxon churches rose from the foundations of Roman temples. Many more examples of certain and probable structural connections between Roman and later buildings could be cited. In some instances the distinction between Roman and later walling is easy to see: the Roman mortar may be pink and the Saxon yellow. Unfortunately, that is not a universally applicable rule, since Roman builders also commonly used cream and yellow mortars, while Saxon and Norman builders occasionally made pink mortar in imitation of the Roman (e.g. at Ickleton, Cambs., and Farnham, Yorks.). So the distinctions begin to fade away. Likewise, unmortared foundations were used in the Roman period and for a millennium thereafter. To confuse the issue even further, different mortars were sometimes consciously used in foundations from those in the walls, even when they were certainly contemporary. The Roman villa under Rivenhall church had yellow mortar in its foundations and pink in the walls, while Bishop Stillington's chapel at Wells, built in the period 1477–86, used pink mortar for the foundations and white for the walls. In some ways these obvious mortar changes are easier to grapple with than the indistinct ones which are liable to be passed over without detection.

The internal excavation at Asheldham church provides a timely reminder of the most difficult pitfall to avoid—the correct association of a mortared wall with an unmortared foundation. For about two-thirds of their circuit the fourteenth-century walls of the nave rest directly upon a hoggin foundation and, had only a parial investigation taken place, it would have been claimed that the nave was first built at that time. However, the true situation was revealed near the east end of the north wall where one or two courses of masonry of a different character and build were sandwiched between the fourteenth-century wall and the foundation. The mortars used in the two periods of walling differed slightly in colour. Close scrutiny of the junction between the standing wall and the foundation around other parts of the nave revealed small patches and trails of the early mortar which had previously escaped notice. Evidently this was a case where the Norman nave was dismantled down to foundation level and rebuilt. Had those ephemeral traces of the early work not been recorded the development of Asheldham church would have been outlined in a rather different way and the plans would not have made good architectural sense (Drury and Rodwell, 1978).

The alignment of a wall upon its foundation is another area of difficulty, since it does not follow that a well aligned wall is necessarily contemporary with what is below, or that a misaligned one is later. Each case needs to be examined on its merits. As a crude generalization it may be said that there was a tendency in the Saxon and Norman periods to set out foundations with reasonable care and to raise walls squarely upon them. In the later medieval period, however, the opposite became the norm: broad foundations were formed with little attention being paid to consistency of width, straightness of edges and right-angled corners. The walls proper were then laid out with care on this irregular base.

2 *Site works and builders' evidence*

Churches did not spring up as a result of divine command; nor were they erected by the clergy between offices. They were built—like castles, town walls and manor houses—by gangs of workmen brought in for the task and superintended by the architect, who was usually the master mason. We must therefore envisage a church and its surroundings as a medieval building site at times when new works were in hand. Between digging the foundations and applying the final coat of paint, several years, or even decades, may have elapsed, scores of men will have been employed on the project and many activities will have taken place which could leave archaeologically detectable traces in the ground. Some of these will be inside the building, others outside.

The first and most obvious process to look for is that of scaffolding. Of one thing we can be sure: no masonry church was ever built without scaffolding. Unless a completely free-standing scaffold was erected (like the modern tower scaffolds) it will have left anchoring marks in the walls or the ground, or both. Cantilevered scaffolds were well known in the Middle Ages and these will only leave evidence in the walls. This usually takes the form of putlog holes which pass right through the thickness of the wall. When the job was done and the scaffold was struck (taken down) the putlogs were sawn off flush with the wall faces if they could not be pulled out. A length of Saxon putlog was found embedded in a wall at St Mary's church, Deerhurst, and decayed wood fragments have been recovered from a putlog hole in the clerestory at Brixworth, Northants., and there dated to the early tenth century (Parsons, 1980).

The available evidence suggests that it was common in church building to erect a conventional scaffold of vertical poles and horizontal putlogs and runners, all tied together with rope. This practice continued until the advent of tubular metal scaffolding in the present century. The lower ends of the poles were set into postholes in the ground and the inner ends of the putlogs were embedded in the masonry of the wall as building proceeded. Medieval walls had normally to be built from both sides simultaneously: thus scaffolding was required inside and outside the building. Long putlogs could be used, passing right through the wall and serving both scaffolds; alternatively separate putlogs could be set in from either side. The advantage of the latter arrangement was that the putlogs were recoverable at the end of the job: they could be wriggled and pulled out of the wall, rather than sawn off. Both arrangements were in use in medieval England. When a putlog hole in a wall is unblocked for archaeological investigation it is readily apparent whether it held a through timber or a stopped one.

Putlog holes, especially those on the interior faces of walls, were carefully blocked with stones and plastered over (p. 89), but externally they were often left open, or at least

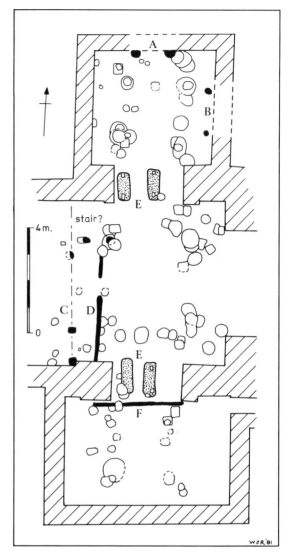

52 Evidence for timber structures in church floors. This plan shows all the postholes and timber-slots in the crossing and transepts at Hadstock, representing both the scaffolding erected by successive generations of builders, and the ground fixings of furnishings:
A postholes for Anglo-Saxon internal doorcase
B postholes for architrave associated with opening into former transeptal chapel   C postholes for supporting rood screen and loft   D slot for a timber screen
EE two pairs of short slots for timbers probably associated with a bell-cote, after the fall of the central tower   F slot for timber screen in south transept.

were reopened, to receive scaffolding again on subsequent occasions. Nowadays these holes are blocked up to prevent birds from nesting in them, but many an old photograph or engraving shows a church wall peppered with putlog holes. The original putlog holes in a wall will be more or less evenly spaced and in rows, both

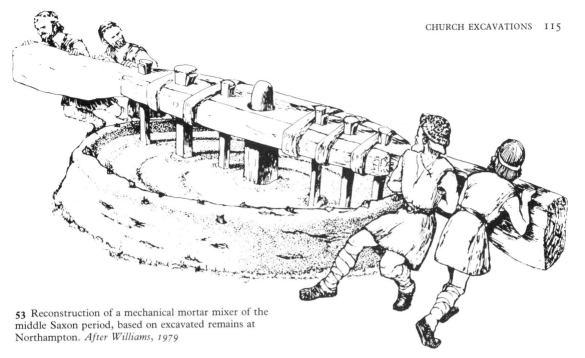

53 Reconstruction of a mechanical mortar mixer of the middle Saxon period, based on excavated remains at Northampton. *After Williams, 1979*

horizontally and vertically. Each 'lift' will be about 1·5m. or a little more, and the putlogs will have projected from the wall face by a similar or slightly greater distance. At the end of each vertical row of putlogs will have been a pole, and there in the ground below should be a posthole. If for any reason, such as the presence of a foundation or pavement, a posthole could not be dug, the foot of the pole would be anchored in a barrel of sand (note scaffolding in fig. 87). Ancient timber scaffolding poles and putlogs could be circular or squarish in section and sometimes both types were used in combination. Careful excavation of postholes and putlog-holes can determine the precise forms of timber used. If a putlog or post was set directly in contact with wet mortar the 'cast' thus provided can be used to examine the grain of the timber and ascertain whether the bark had been removed before use.

Excavations inside churches commonly reveal scores of postholes, some of which can be linked with the original scaffolding, while others will have belonged to secondary periods of work (e.g. when the church was reroofed, or new windows inserted; fig. 52). Secondary scaffolds erected internally did not necessarily have their putlogs tied into the wall cores because stability could be obtained by wedging across the church or against piers. Therefore every internal posthole does not have to have a counterpart in an adjacent wall. Once a scaffold pole had been removed, the hole was filled in

and covered by the next floor. It is therefore readily apparent that where there are multiple floor levels containing and sealing multiple postholes, the opportunity exists to reconstruct the various scaffolding schemes which have been employed in the building and to relate those to observed phases of work. Thus through the stratigraphic connection of scaffolding it may be possible to show which floor was in use at the time of heightening a tower or putting a new roof on an aisle. The study of external scaffolding arrangements is generally difficult, owing to the thorough destruction of all but recent postholes by grave digging.

Medieval walls, especially those built of rubble, required vast quantities of lime mortar to bind the masonry together. Lime is best stored for a while before use, in a large pit or in a building above ground; and it is interesting to note that part of the north transept of Stow Church, Lincs., was formerly screened off and known as 'the lime house'. The preparation of mortar had to take place on site and may be evidenced by hollows in which puddling and mixing was undertaken. This was normally done by hand, and it was therefore a remarkable discovery when three mechanical mortar mixers of the middle Saxon period were found near the east end of St Peter's Church, Northampton (Williams, 1979). Each mixer comprised a circular basin in the ground, bounded by a wattle kerb; a central post supported a horizontal beam, from which several paddles projected. The beam was rotated, like a capstan, using human or animal power (fig. 53), and the paddles churned the mix.

As the masons raised a wall they would constantly be dropping small quantities of mortar and stone chippings. These bedded down against the base of the wall and formed a path-like feature, known as a construction layer, which should be readily identifiable during excavation. The layer will be at its thickest adjacent to the wall and will gradually tail off into the general horizon of builders' trample across the site. In a church which has seen many periods of building activity there will probably be several construction and trample levels interspersed with true floor surfaces. The relationship of walls and foundations to these layers and any finds of datable objects in them are critical to the correct interpretation of the history of the church.

Most churches incorporate some ashlar work (dressed freestone) for quoins, door jambs, arcades and the like, and many buildings in good stone-bearing districts are constructed wholly of ashlar. The dressing of blocks and cutting of mouldings was done on a bench by a mason. He might be working inside the church or, more likely, in a temporary shed, known as a 'lodge'. As he dressed stones to shape he generated a considerable quantity of waste chippings and dust which was trampled into the ground and soon a compact layer, or 'working floor', developed. Traces of these working floors, or redeposited debris from them, are often encountered during excavation. At Wells Cathedral the site of the medieval masons' yard has been excavated and found to comprise a build up of more than a metre of stone dust; on top of this two masons' workshops of the late fifteenth century were found. They had been erected for the ten-year project of building Bishop Stillington's Lady Chapel (fig. 54).

The activities of the church carpenter, although no less important than those of the mason, scarcely survive in the buried archaeological record. Carpenters had to make the scaffolding, prepare the centring for the erection of each arch, and construct roofs, spires, galleries, screens, doors and so on. Occasionally carpenters' shavings and offcuts have survived through being embedded in the mortar dropped by the masons. The carpenter had also to erect shoring and build cranes to hoist heavy materials to the higher parts of buildings. He therefore contributed to the rash

of holes and other marks in the floor of the church. The excavator may find curiously angled 'dents' and canted postholes in church floors which are the evidence for props and shores for short-lived functions in the constructional process.

The debris of metalworkers' activities survives better in the ground than that of woodworkers. While nails and iron fittings were doubtless produced by the local blacksmith at his forge, the plumber did all his work on site, usually inside the church. Invariably one finds lead-melting hearths in parish churches, while cathedrals and monasteries usually had special areas set aside for metalworking. Thus at Salisbury a space between the south aisle and the cloister was a permanent workshop and was called the Plumbery. At Barton-on-Humber the former Saxon baptistery at the west end of St Peter's Church became a plumbery in the medieval period. A doorway was knocked through the west wall to gain access from outside and sand was brought in and spread on the ground to form a casting floor. A casting box and about twenty lead-melting hearths of the twelfth to fourteenth centuries have been excavated at Barton.

Medieval churches, particularly those with complex roof arrangements, required a vast amount of lead which had to be prepared on site. Sheet lead was required for roof coverings, spires, ridges, flashings and spouts, while H-shaped cames were needed for glazing windows. The plumber had no qualms about setting up hearths inside a church where sparks might easily ignite inflammable materials. Lead casting had to be undertaken indoors, not just to avoid bad weather, but to prevent winds from cooling the melt too quickly, or cracking would result.

The smoke, fumes and fire risk generated by the plumber's activities in a church were probably exceeded by those of the bell-founder when he arrived on site. Until little more than a decade ago almost nothing was known of Saxon and medieval bell-founding in England from archaeological evidence. But lately there has been a rash of discoveries of bell furnaces in and beside churches. A bell-foundry dated to c. 980 has been excavated at Winchester, inside the Old Minster (Biddle, 1965, 254); and another of similar date inside the west end of Hadstock church. The latter comprised an oval furnace pit, c. 4·2 by 2·1m., and two circular casting pits nearby (Rodwell, 1976). Other recent

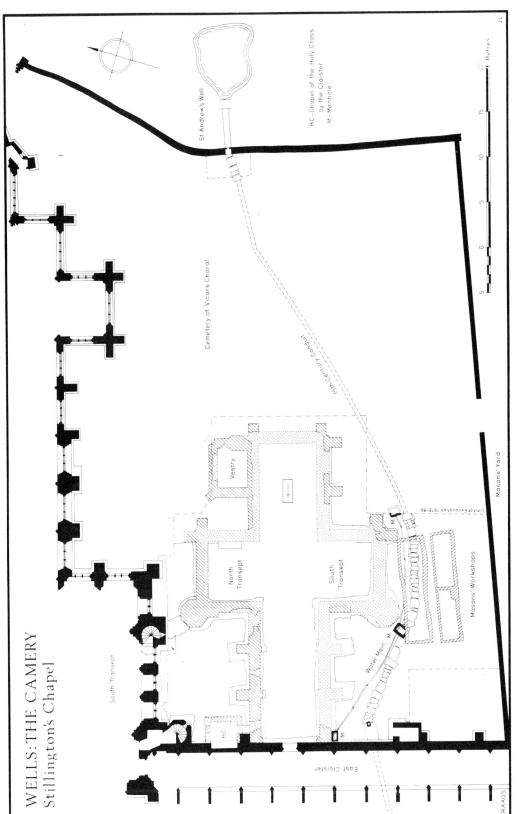

WELLS: THE CAMERY
Stillington's Chapel

South Transept

Cemetery of Vicars Choral

St Andrew's Well

HC – Chapel of the Holy Cross
by the Cloister
M – Manhole

North Transept

Vestry

South Transept

15th-Century Conduit

Limit of Excavation 1978-80

Masons' Workshops

Masons' Yard

Water Main M

East Cloister

HC

M

M

CRAAGS

JL

Metres

54 The plan of Bishop Stillington's chantry chapel, built 1477. Immediately to the south lay a pair of masons' workshops which were in use for the ten years that it took to build the chapel. The workshops were established on the edge of the masons' yard which has been sited here since the thirteenth century. Notice how the early medieval conduit which carried water westwards from St Andrew's Holy Well had to be realigned in an arc to the south in order to be clear of the foundations of the new chapel. *Drawn by Jane Levitan. Copyright C.R.A.A.G.S*

55 Integration of evidence above and below ground:
Excavation in progress on Bishop Stillington's Chapel at
Wells. In the foreground are the foundations of the
eastern arm and north transept of the chapel; in the
background is the east cloister wall against which the
chapel was built. Here, there are many tell-tale scars
which hint at the form of the chapel's superstructure.
For the plan see fig. 54 and for the elevation of the
cloister see fig. 38. *Photo: author. Copyright
C.R.A.A.G.S.*

excavations have located bell-foundries inside
churches at Wharram Percy, the palace chapel
at Cheddar, St Oswald's Priory, Gloucester,
and St Peter's, Barton-on-Humber. At this last
site there were two foundries, a Norman one in
the nave and a late medieval one in the base of
the tower. A brick-built furnace chamber which
would have accommodated several crucibles of
bell metal was also constructed in the base of the
tower. Although the tower had been gutted by
fire in the medieval period it does not seem to
have been an event contemporary with either of
the known bell-casting operations. Until the

rise of post-medieval urban bell-foundries it
was customary to cast bells on site, close to the
tower in which they were to be hung.

Amongst the documented bell-foundries
which await discovery in churches are those
recorded at Kirkby Malzeard, Yorks., and St
Albans Abbey. Long after the establishment of
centres of bell-founding some great bells were
still cast on site owing to the difficulties of
transport. Such was the case at Lincoln in 1610,
Canterbury in 1762 and Wells in 1877, where
the great bells were cast in their respective
cathedral closes.

Amongst the other artists and craftsmen
called to work at a church was the glazier, who,
together with the plumber, had to fabricate the
windows. The remains of glazing waste are
occasionally encountered during excavations;
more commonly one finds the debris of smashed
windows embedded in floors and trodden into
the ground outside churches. The most
important haul ever recovered by excavation is

from the Northumbrian monastic site at Jarrow, which has yielded hundreds of pieces of coloured glass of the middle Saxon period (cf. Cramp, 1970).

3 *Floors, furnishings and fittings*

A floor in a church may refer to many different things. Since the mid-nineteenth century the majority of churches have had their floors relaid using paving bricks, glazed tiles and timber decking under the pews. Prior to this, floors of earth, stone paving or bricks were the norm. In those areas where natural stone was readily available for paving this has remained the traditional flooring material for centuries. Otherwise, materials varied according to availability, local preferences and, of course, affluence. Likewise, the number of times a floor was repaired or relaid over the course of centuries will have depended upon many variables, not least of which was durability. Straw was often used as a covering for rough earth floors. The renewal of a floor normally took the form of laying new material on top of the existing, thereby creating a series of 'levels'. Each level may, after being worn by the passage of feet and compressed by later overburdens, be no more than a few millimetres in thickness; and it is normal to find that one thousand years of flooring may occupy a total thickness of only 30–50cm. On the other hand, in certain towns and cities, such as London, York and Oxford, where there has been a considerable accumulation of archaeological deposits and where some churches have been demolished and totally rebuilt (e.g. after the Fire of London in 1666), 1·5m. or more may separate the earliest floor levels from the latest. Relatively speaking, deep stratification of this kind in churches is rare, and is generally well punctured by post-medieval vaults.

Churches in most parts of England acquired a partial flooring in glazed ceramic tiles in the thirteenth, fourteenth or fifteenth century. Only in monasteries and great churches was the tile cover likely to have been extensive: elsewhere tiling tended to be restricted to the sanctuary of the church, to side chapels and perhaps areas around important graves. Tiled floors, where subjected to regular foot traffic, could become badly worn in less than a century, with the consequent need for relaying. Thus one tile pavement is sometimes found on top of another. Alternatively, the least worn tiles might be salvaged and reset, together with some new ones. As encaustic tile fragments became irreparably worn, and at the same time passed out of fashion, they were often covered by floors of earth or timber.

Thus excavation inside a church usually reveals a hotchpotch of floors of many different dates and materials. There may be no areas of medieval pavement *in situ*, but it is rare for an excavation to fail to yield fragments of encaustic tiles, demonstrating the former presence of such floors. If tiles are found in a mortar bedding, study of their surface condition and the joints between them can ascertain whether they have been reset. In untiled areas floors will have been of stone, earth, sand, mortar, chalk, clay, stone dust or brick, according to local conditions. All of these materials were susceptible to wear and would need frequent maintenance; obviously the degree of wear will have varied in accordance with the use the floor received. This is an important indicator for the archaeologist since, by recording the wear patterns on ancient floors, he can tell something of the movement of people inside the church. It is, for example, possible to suggest which doorways were in most frequent use, where there were once doorways which are now gone (fig. 56), and where there were screens, benches and other obstructions to walking. By examining the wear patterns around the sites of altars and fonts it is sometimes possible to indicate the movements of the priest.

It goes without saying that large areas of intact flooring need to be examined in order to recognize and elucidate patterns of human movement inside a church. These patterns will themselves have changed from period to period, as the building developed and as liturgical practice evolved; therefore the archaeologist must make careful plans and contour surveys of each floor level as he peels it off to reveal the next. When floors have been extensively worn and patched, or when they are very fragmentary, owing to later disturbances, it can be very difficult to disentangle the true number of phases represented and to relate these to the constructional history of the church. Again, the prerequisite is systematic investigation on a large scale. Layers of significant material interleaved between the floors—such as builders' construction levels or debris from a fire—may provide fixed points in the chronological development of the church. Those points may be precisely known from documentary references to building work or to a

56 Hadstock: patterns of floor use. This view into the north transept shows an early medieval chalk floor through which a central passage has been worn by foot traffic. This observation led to the discovery of a blocked Saxon doorway in the wall at the top of the picture. The circular holes in the floor are settings for medieval scaffold poles *Photo: Donald Stewart*

fire, or they may only be approximately fixed on the basis of architectural or archaeological evidence.

Architectural dating is based on 'style' associations and typology, and archaeological dating mainly uses objects recovered from the ground. Neither is of course precise and both can be open to margins of error which range from a few years to several centuries. Items found in excavation are hardly ever intrinsically datable and must therefore depend upon architectural or art historical style-dating: e.g. fragments of moulded stone, decorated window glass, painted wall plaster or encaustic tiles.

Domestic debris, such as pottery, is seldom found in churches except in the sparsest quantity, and nevertheless still depends on typology for its dating. One might have thought that coins—the most precisely datable class of artefact—would be recovered in some numbers from church excavations, but this is not the case. No wholly convincing explanation has yet been advanced for the remarkably small number of coins found in British churches, compared to those on the Continent. In Scandinavia, for example, it is normal to find 500 or more coins during a major excavation in a church, whereas in England a total of ten coins and jettons from one church is not considered unusual. They are of very little use to the archaeologist in such circumstances: first, the majority of medieval jettons cannot be closely dated and, secondly, a single coin from a layer may not be taken as a reliable indicator of date. If securely stratified, the coin merely gives a *terminus post quem* for the floor or layer upon or in which it sits. Conversely, there are plenty of opportunities for small objects like coins to find their way down to layers of much earlier date. Rodents were frequent burrowers in churches, particularly into graves, and their activities have caused the movement of small objects in the soil, not just by a few centimetres but by distances of up to a metre. In dry weather earthen floors are susceptible to cracking, especially if doors are left open and there is a strong air current through the building; cracks in floors facilitate the downward movement of small objects. Here, however, one of the bonuses of indoor excavation may be appreciated and exploited: the very crisp definition of floor and soil layers enables the archaeologist to detect and record animal burrows and cracks with relative ease (but this is not usually possible in grave fills), and displaced objects should not therefore falsify the record to the same extent as they do on outdoor sites (p. 140). The reason for crisp definition of archaeological layers inside churches is simple: there is no disturbance caused by roots, worms, ploughing and natural leaching. The visual difference between archaeological deposits inside a church and those outside is most striking.

Next we must consider furnishings and fittings insofar as they affect floors. Timber pews were not introduced into English churches until the later Middle Ages, and even then they were not common at first. The positions of pews are easily detected in floors since early examples were often affixed to sleeper beams which were trenched into the ground for stability. Benches placed alongside walls seem sometimes to have taken the form of large baulks of timber which rested on the ground and against which the floors abutted; alternatively benches could be made of planks supported on short posts which were sunk into the floor. Many large churches had stone wall-benches, and sometimes further benches between the aisle arcades too. Although the benches themselves were often removed in post-medieval times, their foundations can be located by excavation and the scars remaining from their attachment to the walls detected with a keen eye.

Medieval churches were frequently sub-divided into several cells or functional areas by traceried screens. Great churches had their principal screens built of stone and many of

these survive today; in lesser churches the medium was generally timber, but there are some notable exceptions such as the stone chancel screens at Stebbing and Great Bardfield, Essex. In south-west England there was a late medieval vogue for translating timber screen designs into stone: e.g. Totnes, Devon. The quire in a cruciform church would be screened on all four sides, and in an aisled building sections of the aisles would be demarcated for side chapels and chantries. Some town churches, where chantries abounded, even had the nave partially screened off to provide a series of cubicles. In archaeological terms, floors will have been cut by narrow foundations, slots or postholes where screens were anchored to the ground, and there will also be channels and sockets cut into pillars and walls at points where screens were fixed in the vertical plane (fig. 52). Through a combined study of the excavated evidence and the standing structure it should be possible to determine not only the positions of screens but also their height and the size of the major openings through them. If fragments of ornamented stone or timber survive architectural reconstructions may also be attempted. Floors will be found to abut screen slots and will only show signs of wear at points of access through these barriers. Frequently a change of flooring material occurred at screened divisions: thus the floor of the church may have been of earth, while inside a chapel it was of crushed chalk, and there might have been a tiled threshold or step at the point of entry.

Most side chapels in parish churches and cathedrals were used for the burial of important or wealthy persons, particularly if chantries were founded there. Sometimes a grave was simply marked in the floor by a patch of glazed tiles; others had an incised or sculptured slab, or an indent containing a brass, while the richest graves were marked by table tombs or great monumental erections with canopies and iron railings. Although much of this splendid funerary art was destroyed during and after the Reformation, fragments, from which recon-structions can be attempted, are usually found embedded in contemporary floors or in the backfilling of looted graves. Thus at Wells Cathedral Bishop Stillington's grave was looted and his tomb and chantry chapel destroyed in 1552, but excavations in 1980 rediscovered the site of his grave, together with fragments of the great painted and gilded stone tomb canopy. A similar exercise of reconstruction, providing some idea of the decorative schemes depicted in stained glass windows, can be attempted by collecting the fragments which excavators find lying on floors, where they fell during acts of puritanical vandalism.

We have left until last the two most important liturgical furnishings in a church, namely the altar (or altars) and the font. The former positions of these can often be determined by excavation, providing a valuable insight into the liturgical planning of a church, perhaps at several periods in its history. In an important paper on the position of the altar in Anglo-Saxon churches, Dr H. M. Taylor (1973) has shown, largely using archaeological evidence, that in early buildings the altar stood west of the chancel arch, and that in the late Saxon period it tended to be sited just inside the chancel (that is east of the arch). In the medieval period the high altar was often in the centre of the chancel, or towards the east end, but not against the east wall as has been the practice in the last few centuries. Archaeologically, the site of the altar may be recognized as a rectangular plinth or rubble foundations or, at Barton-on-Humber, as a pair of small foundations marking the north and south ends. There the altar was in the centre of the tiny tenth-century chancel and was apparently backed by a screen on the east side. Beneath the foundations lay a pair of important graves; the same arrangement seems to have obtained in a middle Saxon timber church as Nazeingbury, Essex (Huggins, 1978). At Winchester and Reculver excavation has shown that the seventh-century altar lay to the west of the chancel arch in both cases. At the former four postholes were recorded in the floor, indicating that a canopy or *ciborium* stood over the altar (Taylor 1973, figs. 1 and 2). Excavation on the site of the old Lady Chapel at Wells Cathedral has shown that the thirteenth-century high altar stood two-thirds of the way towards the east end. Subsidiary altars, placed in side chapels and aisles, were often sited on stone plinths attached to the east wall or even housed in specially built recesses, as in the north transept at Stow, Lincs.

Even when the foundations of an early altar have not survived in a church, owing to later disturbances, it may be possible to ascertain its location from the condition of surrounding floors, the disposition of 'satellite' graves, or the location of a reliquary. Some altars were built with chambers inside them, into which holy relics could be put, while others were sited over crypts, as at Repton or Ripon. Yet a third alternative was to bury a collection of relics in a pit as a kind of foundation deposit before the altar was constructed. A relic pit of this kind has been found beneath the altar in the Saxon chancel at Barton-on-Humber, and at St Mark's, Lincoln, a trench beneath the altar may have been dug to receive relics (Colyer, 1976). At St Nicholas', Colchester, a deep shaft was found under the presumed site of the late Saxon altar.

While the positions of early altars must often now be lost beyond recall as a result of intensive grave digging in the chancels of many churches, the same does not apply to the sites of fonts. The font was traditionally placed towards the west end of the church, close to the principal door. There is generally much less disturbance at the west end of a church than at the east and the font may, in any case, have remained more or less on the same spot for many centuries. Again, wear patterns in floors can help, but much more definite is the identification of the font drain. This normally took the form of a soakaway pit, filled with gravel or rubble, immediately beneath the font. No less than five successive font positions have been traced in St Peter's, Barton-on-Humber (fig. 13), while in St Pancras', Winchester, there were two. The first was placed axially just inside the west door of the church, but the inconvenience of this orthodox position is probably reflected in the second siting, when the font was moved to one side, so that it lay on the left of the west door as one entered (Biddle, 1975, fig. 16). Excavation at Hadstock showed that the Norman font had probably once been centrally placed near the west door, but was later shifted to the right. Excavations on the site of the old church at Potterne, Wilts., located a baptistery with an indent in the floor to receive a lead font basin. The tenth-century basin still survives and is now in the medieval church (Davey, 1964).

Excavation of the fabric

Excavation is not a process which has to be conducted below floor or ground level: anything which comprises a series of superimposed layers can be dissected by excavational techniques—stones in a wall, layers of paint on a mural, or wrappings on a mummy. We have already mentioned some of the factors which contribute to stratification in standing walls, such as new walls erected on old foundations (p. 112), the insertion of arcades into old walls (p. 69) and the heightening of wall tops in association with reroofing (p. 68). Here it only remains to draw these various threads together and to provide some additional hints on the techniques of investigation and recording.

Assuming that the archaeologist is not able to demolish the building by excavation (p. 79), his activities are likely to be limited to relatively shallow probings into one or both faces of its standing walls, and will normally be undertaken in connection with a restoration programme. If plaster or rendering is to be stripped this should be tackled archaeologically if possible, or at least supervised closely. Although external rendering may appear to be fairly modern, there may well be concealed beneath the surface traces of medieval lime plasters which should be retained *in situ* for recording. The stripping of internal plaster is an even more delicate task since, whatever the *apparent* date of the material currently being removed, there will almost certainly be older plasters underneath. These might be very extensive, or confined to traces in odd corners, around monuments, behind pew ends, etc. Even when it is known that a church was replastered during a Victorian restoration it must not be dismissed as wholly without interest, since old plaster and paintings continue to turn up in most unpromising places.

While Victorian and later cement renders, internal or external, can be removed carefully but without qualms, all hair-plasters and other wall coverings need the most careful scrutiny and recording. It is not generally appreciated just how much archaeological evidence can be derived from such unedifying material as seemingly plain plaster. It is all too easy, in a fit of enthusiasm, to hack off 'modern' plaster without recording it and subsequently to realize that it must have contained evidence which would have helped in reconstructing the pre-Victorian history of the church.

First, wall surfaces should be photographed and drawn, even if only in a summary fashion, before *anything* is removed. The purpose of this is to record cracks, bulges and patching in the plaster; time and again we find that these apparently trivial details in modern wall finishes reflect or conceal ancient features which are not always detectable once the plaster has been stripped. Let us take Rivenhall as an example. When the church was remodelled in

1838–9 it was totally replastered internally (except behind one or two large wall monuments which were not dismantled, and thereby concealed a mural painting), and when a second restoration took place in 1878 some repairs to the wall plaster were necessitated by alterations to the furnishings. In the later restoration the eighteenth-century western gallery and box pews were all ejected in accordance with the fashion of the period. Since, however, these and other furnishings were *in situ* when the 1839 replastering took place their silhouettes were preserved in the plaster, for in 1878 only the defective areas were made good. Although no illustration of the gallery has survived, it is possible fully to reconstruct its general form from what are now just slight irregularities in plain plastered walls: its elevation above floor level, height of front panelling, projection from the west wall and site of access stairs are all plainly visible, yet remained unnoticed until 1978.

The removal of pre-Victorian plasters should not be undertaken lightly, and whenever possible they should be considered *in situ*, regardless of whether they bear painted decoration. It is inexcusable to strip large areas of ancient plaster to satisfy antiquarian curiosity. The older the plaster the more 'features' it will have in it, and when destruction is unavoidable the surface should be drawn and the various patches and layers of which the plaster is composed excavated stratigraphically. Thus it is possible to examine relationships between wall surfaces and architectural features such as windows, doorways, piscinae, sedilia, floor joists and tie-beams, helping to establish relative sequences of construction, alteration and insertion of features.

Before leaving the subject of plaster, a few words must be said on painting. The majority of medieval churches were decorated with wall paintings, which will often have been concealed by limewash in the sixteenth and seventeenth centuries. New paintings, in the form of black-letter texts, sometimes accompanied by polychrome borders, may have been applied over the limewash, only themselves to be smothered when tastes changed again. It must therefore be remembered that there is a high probability that *any* ancient wall plaster will still bear traces of painted decoration (for an introduction to church painting see Rouse, 1971 and Croome, 1959). There are specialized techniques for the 'excavation' of paint layers which need to be applied before ancient plaster is removed. Furthermore, the search needs to be thorough because large areas of plain limewashed plaster may originally have lain between individual mural scenes or texts. Where superimposed paints are found to exist these have to be uncovered and recorded stratigraphically if removal is necessary. Only under exceptional circumstances is it permissible to remove or destroy an ancient painting, however fragmentary.

Paint, like plaster, is an archaeologically valuable layer which can be used to establish stratigraphical links between separate parts of a church or features within a single wall. Furthermore, paintings can often be dated within reasonably close margins on art-historical grounds and therefore have a contribution to make to archaeologically-based chronologies. Victorian wall paintings, although often crude and simple, were occasionally created in full medieval-style splendour; fine examples are to be found at Little Braxted and Foxearth, both in Essex. The lateness of their date does not exempt them from proper archaeological recording.

The inter-linking of painted decoration with architectural stratification can sometimes be complex, as at Breamore, Hants., where Mr Clive Rouse cleaned the medieval murals in the upper chamber of the south porch in 1980. In places there were at least three superimposed paint layers on the Anglo-Saxon carved stone crucifixion which is built into the south wall of the nave, over the main entrance (fig. 57). The first layer is probably Saxon in date and represents decoration on the sculpture belonging to a period prior to its erection on the nave wall. The second paint layer runs over the sculpture and surrounding plaster, passing behind the porch walls where they abut the nave, and is therefore *outdoor* decoration ante-dating the construction of the upper chamber of the porch. The final painting is a landscape scene which was applied in the sixteenth century to decorate the chamber over the porch, and is thus found on all four walls and on the crucifixion. Hence at Breamore the interpretation of paint layers, and the plasters upon which they lay, was instrumental in disentangling the history of the Anglo-Saxon rood sculpture.

Although churches were normally plastered, both internally and externally, in the Middle Ages, there were periods and geographical areas where the natural stone was permitted to show, sometimes for decorative effects (p. 89). Close examination may reveal that masonry was simply limewashed and painted, perhaps only with red lines in imitation of ashlar jointing, without a plaster layer intervening. In most cases walls which are now devoid of plaster will have had the joints between the stones pointed with cement or mortar within the past century or thereabouts. After recording the types and extent of the pointing materials, these may be removed with a raking-out chisel to reveal the mortars which actually bind the fabric of the wall. It is at this stage, when walls are fully stripped down, that stone by stone drawings and photography should ideally take place (pp. 82–6.

We have already dealt with the recording of stone types, constructional details, and so forth, on the drawn elevations (pp. 88–9); a further copy of each prepared drawing should be used for recording mortars. This is a task which requires some practice before an 'eye' for subtle differences can be developed. The aim is to record every change which can be perceived in the mortars. Small brushes, spatulae and probing tools are useful for cleaning out masonry joints and excavating pockets of mortar. It is easier to detect mortar changes in walls composed of small rubble than in ashlar work: these changes are divisible into three groups. First, overtly different types of mortar indicating different periods of work, for example: a well defined horizontal joint associated with the heightening of a wall, a vertical joint marking the junction of walls of two periods, or an irregular joint around the masonry of an inserted window. The greater the lapse of time between the two phases, the more radically different the mortars may well appear. In a single church there may, for example, be broad divisions on the following lines: Saxon and Norman mortar, yellow and sandy; early medieval, white and gritty; late medieval, cream with chalk lumps; post-medieval, grey with ashes and coal specks; Victorian, pink imitation 'Roman cement'.

57 Breamore, Hants., the defaced Anglo-Saxon rood sculpture made available for close study for the first time in 1980 when the conservation of the wall paintings around it was undertaken. This figure has been the subject of much discussion in the past, and the major questions concerning its physical history and relationship to the church have now been answered through archaeological study. *Photo: author*

58 A mortar joint of double thickness in the rubble-built tower at Hadstock, indicating a seasonal break. The joint is not horizontal, but rises to clear the apex of the nave roof. *Photo: Gordon Ager*

Secondly, there are mortar changes which are not immediately obvious, but which can be detected and followed more or less consistently when sought. In such cases there is usually little difference in colour or texture between the two mortars, especially when dry, but a 'break' is nevertheless present. If the joint is vertical then two periods of work are almost certainly represented, but if it is horizontal it is more difficult to decide whether the joint is indicative of separate acts of construction or merely short pauses within a single building programme. If the former obtains, there is likely to be confirmatory evidence of other kinds that two periods of work are in question: there may be different materials, or stones of smaller size, or other techniques of stone laying involved. If, however, there are no differences between the masonry above and below the joint, it may be that only a pause or seasonal break is represented.

In building rubble walls it was common practice to cap the uncompleted work with a thin spread of mortar at the end of a season, in order to reduce water penetration into the core; a temporary 'coping' of thatch was also provided for protection during the winter months. When building recommenced the thatch was removed, a bed of fresh mortar laid and the next course of stones set. Since the previous spread of mortar had had time to harden before the second was laid a clear joint between the two is usually perceptible and, more significantly, the joint will be of double thickness here. With patience and careful probing traces of the straw or reeds used for the temporary thatched coping may be found in the joint, a detail which has been recorded in the towers at Hadstock (fig. 58) and Barton-on-Humber. At the latter a fragment of the handle of a wicker-work basket was also trapped in the joint.

The third type of mortar joint, the most difficult to detect, is the break between each day's work. There is usually no visible difference between the mortars, unless the mix used on one occasion was aberrant in some way (e.g. the lime was badly burnt or contaminated with charcoal). The joint is usually detectable as the finest of hairline cracks running horizontally across the tops of mortar fillings between adjacent stones. The joint is no more than a short-lived drying-out line, which may be emphasized by salts migrating to the exposed surface of the mortar, causing a very slight discoloration (a brownish tinge). Furthermore, careful excavation with a dental probe may enable the upper layer of mortar to be scaped away to reveal the previously exposed surface of the lower layer.

These daily lifts in the masonry may coincide with levelling courses (of tiles or flat stones) and will generally be found at intervals of 20–50cm. in rubble walls. In East Anglia, where small flints were the principal building material in the medieval period, walls were often raised with the aid of shuttering and regular lifts, each of about 30cm. (one foot), can be detected. The uniform results achieved by this method of construction stand in sharp contrast to 'heap' building, as seen in some Anglo-Saxon churches. In parts of Brixworth and Barton-on-Humber churches rubble masonry was laid with little attempt to form courses and we can clearly see how several masons worked on the scaffold side by side. Each man built a 'heap' of walling without regard to what his colleagues were doing. From time to time the tops of the heaps were levelled off and a fresh start made (fig. 59). Even in walls where coursing was practised there was a marked tendency for masons to tilt the courses out of the horizontal as they worked over the curve of an arch or the pitch of a roof. This phenomenon of 'cambered coursing' is a good indicator of the contemporaneity of a wall with the arch it contains (figs 58, 59).

Quite apart from mortar studies, it is not usually difficult to detect breaks in the construction of ashlar walling. For obvious reasons, the mason will try to obtain stones of the same height for a single course. This presents few problems in new work, but when joining onto old walling or partially completed work there are always difficulties in sorting one's stock of ready-prepared ashlars to achieve a perfect tie up with every course. In practice one is lucky if two courses out of five tie together neatly, and points of junction between old and new work are therefore characterized by 'stepped' joints, one stone having to be cut to lap partly over another.

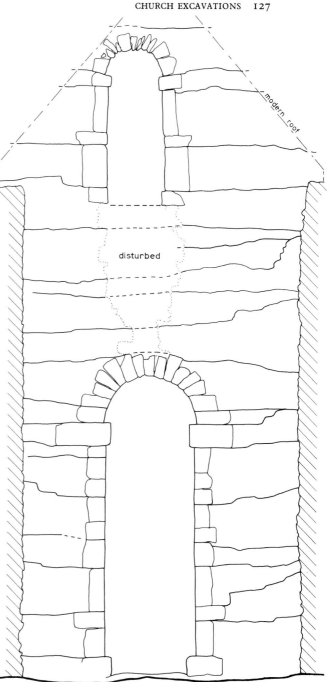

59 Interpretation diagram of the building lifts in the wall between the baptistery and the tower of St Peter's, Barton-on-Humber. Although this building is of 'random rubble' construction, it is not difficult to establish how it was erected. Typical features of this kind of work are: the coincidence of some lifts with joints in the ashlar dressings; the 'humping' of the lift which incorporates the major arch; and the stepping up of the courses towards the outer walls (especially evident here on the right), owing to the corners having been built up first. *Crown copyright*

Finally, we must return to the matter of inserted features. The general principles for their understanding have been outlined (pp. 68–71), and the investigation of mortars and masonry coursing will normally provide a categoric answer to the question of contemporaneity of build. But there still remains the problem of the actual ages of the component parts: a new window may be inserted into an old wall, an old window may be inserted into an old wall, or an old window may be built into new work. Failure to recognize these possible permutations regularly leads to disastrously incorrect interpretations. Let us examine each proposition in turn.

When a new window (arcade, doorway, piscina or any other feature) is inserted into an existing wall an aperture slightly larger than the required size has to be cut and the gap made good afterwards. Thus if a matching series of fifteenth-century clerestorey windows appears in a Saxon wall (cf. Tredington, fig. 28B) it is reasonable to suppose that the masonry of the windows was newly fashioned for the purpose. On the other hand, a single feature inserted into a wall, and not known to be part of a scheme of refurbishment, cannot automatically be claimed as providing an architectural 'date' for the alteration. That feature might have been salvaged from elsewhere and be centuries old at the time of its insertion. Hadstock provides a case in point. The nave is late Anglo-Saxon and the palmette-decorated north doorway has long been regarded as a primary architectural feature, while the south doorway is early thirteenth-century in style and has always been accepted as an insertion. Archaeological excavation into the fabric of the walls in 1974 showed that everything was not as straightforward as it appeared, and both doorways were insertions of the thirteenth-century in places where no doorways had previously existed. Further study of the north doorway indicated that it was in fact a medieval reconstruction, using masonry from not one, but two, almost identical Saxon doorways which had been brought from elsewhere in the church.

This brings us to the third relationship between features of different dates, the re-use of old elements in new work. The antiquarian aspect of architectural salvage has been noted (p. 69), and the appearance of fine Norman doorways in the Victorian aisles at Stanstead Mountfitchet, Essex, is unlikely to cause confusion, notwithstanding the fact that archaeological stratification would suggest, incorrectly, their apparent contemporaneity (i.e. the doorways are entirely constructed with the same mortar as is used for the building of the aisles). Although we may brush aside architectural amalgams of this kind as inconsequential, that is not the end of the argument. Take Taunton priory gatehouse, for instance: excavation and structural study have shown this to belong to the early sixteenth century, yet in one gable-end there is a pair of windows with plate tracery of the thirteenth century. These are integral to the fabric of the gatehouse and can only be explained in terms of architectural salvage (Leach, forthcoming).

A second example in this category is worth mentioning for the unexpected results yielded through fabric excavation. It is at Hadstock again. The fourteenth-century south transept replaces an Anglo-Saxon *porticus* and the archway which provides access from the crossing has been accepted as Saxon up to impost level, while the pointed arch is assignable to the thirteenth century. The responds rise from four-tiered plinths of which the lower two orders are more elaborately moulded than the upper pair (fig. 60). When the archway was thoroughly cleaned for study, the limewash and plaster removed and the joints between the ashlars excavated, an unexpected sight was revealed. First, it was evident that the plinth blocks belonged to two different periods, with the lower pair on each side probably being re-used Roman stones from a major building. Secondly, the stones which comprised the upper pair of plinths were jumbled and certainly not in their original positions, or in some instances even in the correct plinth course (the topmost plinth being less deep than the one below it). Thirdly, it was clear from a study of the mortar that the entire archway, from ground to apex, was a reconstruction of the thirteenth-century. The chaotic jointing between the incorrectly reassembled stones was masked with generous pointing and an overall coat of limewash upon which false joints were outlined with red paint (fig. 61).

Excavation into the fabric of walls regularly reveals re-dressed and re-arranged stonework, and patently much information awaits recovery through this form of investigation. It was common practice to cut new mouldings onto the plain 'back' faces of old stones, and then to reset them so that original mouldings, tooling and

13th-century

Anglo-Saxon
reset

Roman?
reused

60 Hadstock, *c.* 1920. South transept arch, showing the
use of masonry of different periods, assembled into its
present form in the thirteenth century. Prior to the
'excavation' of the masonry joints of this arch in 1974, it
was believed simply to be of two periods, both *in situ*.
For details of the stepped plinth on the left, see fig. 61.
Photo: National Monuments Record. Crown copyright

61 Detail of one of the stepped plinths of the south transept arch at Hadstock, after removal of limewash and excavation of masonry joints. This shows clearly how the whole plinth is a makeshift reconstruction, using battered mouldings and wide mortar joints. All the other plinths in the crossing of the church revealed similar evidence upon investigation; a radical re-interpretation of the architectural history of this part of the building is now required. *Photo: Gordon Ager*

painted decoration were embedded in the fabric of the wall.

In this chapter we have only examined some of the more obvious classes of information which can be derived from church excavation. But enough has been said to demonstrate that no ancient church can be fully understood and its history properly expounded without large-scale meticulous excavation, not just internally but also against the external wall faces, and into the cores of the walls themselves. Clearly, this is something which can only rarely be achieved, but when it is the results are usually of more than passing interest. No matter how thoroughly the visible fabric is studied, a full understanding of the structure, methods of building, modifications and liturgical use cannot be approached without the hidden evidence from below the floors and in the walls.

8 Churchyard Archaeology

Churchyards vary enormously in shape, area and relationship to the church. Some are circular, some rectilinear, and some wholly irregular; the area enclosed may range from a tiny fraction of the traditional 'God's Acre' to three acres or more; and the church itself may lie centrally, to one side, or in a corner. Occasionally, the church and graveyard may not even be contiguous, as at St John's, Bristol, or St Runwald's, Colchester, where the two elements are well separated. At the other extreme, there can be two churches in one churchyard, as at Swaffham Prior, Cambs.

The modern concept of the churchyard is a plot of land filled with graves and dotted with memorial stones, but there is much more to it than that and the surface features seldom constitute more than the tip of the iceberg. There are three principal aspects to churchyard archaeology: first, recording the visible evidence; secondly, the excavation of the remains beneath the turf; and, thirdly, the interpretation of relationships between the churchyard, the church and the surrounding topography. In exploring these aspects, we should remember that the term 'churchyard' and 'graveyard' (or 'cemetery') are not entirely interchangeable: we have already noted that some graveyards do not contain their related churches, and conversely some churchyards were not used for burial. The important Norman church as Stoke Orchard, Glos., for example, has a medium-sized churchyard, but no burials were made here before the mid-nineteenth century because the building was technically only a chapel-of-ease in the parish of Bishops Cleeve. In all, churchyards and graveyards, and their associated functions, are a much neglected subject of study, but are nevertheless crucial to ecclesiastical history and archaeology.

The visible evidence

As always, the first essential to proper study is the production of an accurate, scaled plan. This is a task which involves basic archaeological surveying, and can be linked with the planning of the church (p. 79). For most purposes a plan at 1:200 scale will suffice, but a larger scale will be required (1:100 or 1:50) if excavation or other detailed work is contemplated. First, one records the outline of the yard, then the position of the church and any other buildings, followed by the plotting of paths, trees, earthworks and general landscape features. Finally, the monuments and grave mounds themselves are planned.

When recording boundaries careful attention must be paid to banks, ditches, kinks in hedgerows, changes in walling materials or alignments, and evidence for former entrances, since these are all clues to the history of the churchyard as an enclosure. If there is a substantial and abrupt fall in ground level from the yard to the adjoining property or road, the boundary at this point is probably very ancient; the same holds true if the boundary is marked by a large ditch and bank crowned with old trees. Conversely, a simple fence or modest hawthorn hedge which is not sited over a noticeable earthwork is unlikely to be of great age and may be associated with a relatively modern churchyard extension. The stumps of felled trees should always be examined and recorded, since their annual rings can be counted to ascertain a date of planting.

Within the churchyard, earthworks and traces of former boundaries may be clearly visible, and these often help to distinguish the ancient core of the yard from later enlargements; some levelling of the old boundary will have taken place. By no means all

RIVENHALL
Earthworks

62 Simple hachured plan of the earthworks around Rivenhall church. The present graveyard, ABCD, contains a large earthwork platform (site of Roman villa), while to the north is the late Saxon churchyard boundary and beyond that a platform upon which the middle Saxon hall may have stood. The old quarry is probably also of Anglo-Saxon or earlier origin

earthworks in churchyards are related to boundaries: some may belong to traces of former secular structures or pre-Christian funerary monuments. For example, Rivenhall churchyard is dominated by a triangular platform which silhouettes the Roman villa building that once stood here (fig. 62), while in the old churchyard at Taplow, Bucks., a circular mound 25m. across marks the site of a rich Anglo-Saxon burial of the seventh century. In fact mounds—some of which are certainly tumuli—are not uncommon in churchyards. Sometimes the mount itself is the central feature of the churchyard, as at Wickham St Paul, Essex, and the church, being set to one side, appears to be a secondary feature. But in many instances the church stands on a slight eminence within the yard, as at Kirk Hammerton, Yorks., and it is impossible to decide without proper excavation whether a natural feature of the landscape has been utilized or whether the mound is man-made. The church at Tidenham, Glos., stands on a terrace cut into the hillside, and to the south of the nave the fall of the land is punctuated by a great mound which is most unlikely to be of natural origin. Excavation at Barton-on-Humber has demonstrated that St. Peter's church was erected on a much earlier, artificial mound about one metre in height.

Elementary   recording   of   churchyard

earthworks may be accomplished with a hachured plan (fig. 62), while a more accurate and informative record can be achieved with a contoured plan (for techniques of earthwork surveying, see Taylor, 1974, ch. 3 or Aston and Rowley, 1974, ch. 2). Unless exceptional detail is required there is no need to record each modern grave mound as an earthwork: a symbol will suffice, but it is however important to show the grave alignment correctly. The same applies to the recording of tombstones. Normally two points will be measured for the positioning of a grave mound or a headstone, and four points for a table tomb or other substantial monument (for details, see Jones, 1976).

The recording of grave positions is most expeditiously   achieved   by   setting   out temporary   base-lines   between   rows   and planning by triangulation or offsetting. When correctly planned, it is interesting to observe how graves and tombs are seldom aligned on a true east-west axis, as theoretically they should be, but will normally be influenced by the nearest dominant topographical feature. Thus graves close to the church will follow its alignment (whether liturgically correct or not), while those near to paths or boundaries will reflect their influence. This phenomenon has been well illustrated by a survey of the surviving tombstones in Deerhurst churchyard (Rahtz, 1978), and excavation can show the influences that determined orientation in ancient graves which are no longer marked on the surface (p. 135; and fig. 63).

Finally, on the subject of planning, trees and shrubs are as much a part of the man-made landscape of churchyards, as are the structures and monuments. Yew trees, for example, have been an important feature of churchyards for many centuries (Cornish, 1946), yet we know very little about their real significance and effectively nothing about the reasons for the siting of individual trees. Some yews might perhaps have been planted as markers for important graves, others seem to perpetuate the lines of lost boundaries. In the eighteenth century the deliberate planting of churchyards began, often with nothing more than a simple arrangement of elms, but sometimes more ambitious and semi-formal schemes were planted by landscape gardeners. They caused the introduction of exotic trees such as cedars and cypresses, and the cult of topiary: there is no finer example of the latter than in Painswick churchyard, Glos. Even in a modest village like

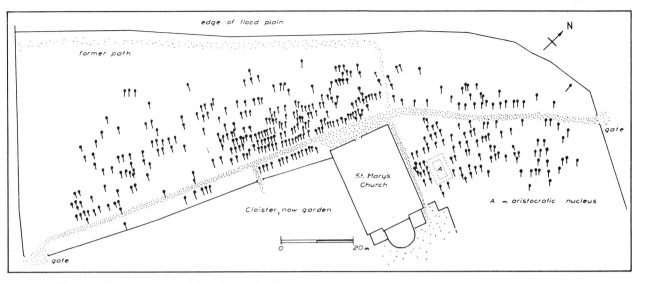

63 Plan of St Mary's churchyard, Deerhurst, showing the diverse alignments of post-medieval graves; note the influence of boundaries and paths. *After Rahtz, 1978*

64 Raunds: outline plan of the two superimposed Anglo-Saxon churches and their associated cemetery, as excavated in 1979. Graves on the eastern edge of the cemetery were clearly related to a boundary, and the two 'blank' patches, A and B, on the plan suggest the presence of structures or other features reflecting the layout of the site. Point A, in particular, would be a possible location for a churchyard cross. *After Boddington, 1980*

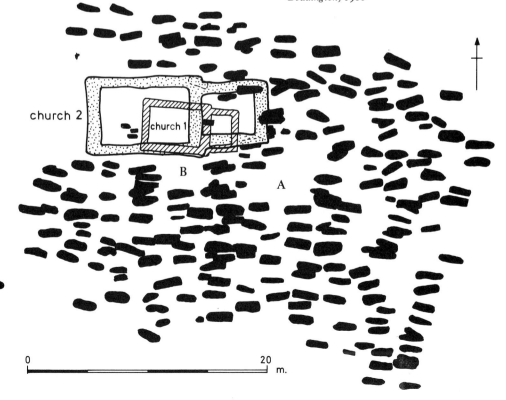

Rivenhall the hand of the landscape architect can be seen in the churchyard. It was probably Humphrey Repton who bordered the churchyard with impressive elms at the same time as he was landscaping Rivenhall Park in 1791, and when his son J. A. Repton remodelled the church in 1838–9 he completed the ensemble of planting yews, cedars, cypresses and Spanish oaks in a formal and mathematically planned arrangement (fig. 66).

When surveying churchyards it is well to examine all stonework carefully, since an amazing number of interesting discoveries may be made. It is common to find ancient carved stones in boundary walls, and even complete features which have been removed from the church and re-assembled, such as the Anglo-Saxon doorway at Heysham, Lancs., or the Saxo-Norman doorway at Tackley, Oxon. At St Nicholas' church, Leicester, various sections of Roman column adorn the graveyard and at Stow, Lincs., large blocks of stone which must be derived from a Roman public building lie amongst the tombs.

Churchyard excavation

Cemeteries of medieval and later date are not usually considered as places of interest for the archaeologist to excavate, and in the past exceptions have only been made where Roman villas or other monumental remains are known to lie beneath the sepulchral horizon as, for instance, in the old churchyard at Woodchester, Glos. Regrettably the burials were merely regarded as a nuisance and were shovelled out unceremoniously. But the archaeology of the Christian cemetery is a subject in its own right, and one about which we are woefully ignorant (Rahtz, 1976b).

Graveyards are complex archaeological sites, stratified both vertically and horizontally, and the average cemetery which has been in use for a millennium or so probably contains the remains of some 10,000 corpses. It is not therefore surprising that most ancient graveyards have one to two metres of accumulated 'grave earth' above the natural subsoil: burial and consequent decay are the processes which give rise to the common phenomenon of elevated churchyards. At no time, even down to the present day, have grave-diggers respected interments of the past, and they normally hack through them without the slightest concern. This naturally means that many ancient burials

have been destroyed, the bones now simply loose in the topsoil and in the backfills of later graves. These bones are however worthy of collection since they can sometimes be reunited with the undisturbed parts of skeletons found in excavation (see further pp. 158–9).

In those areas of churchyard which were always popular for burial—particularly along the south and east sides of the church—graves with be found at their densest, and it can often be seen that within a century, or sometimes less, of these areas being filled to capacity the ground was levelled to erase the evidence of previous grave mounds and a fresh start made. This could happen over and over again, so that as many as ten bodies might theoretically occupy the same plot of ground. As the ground level of the cemetery rose, so the earlier burials became relatively deeper from the surface and were protected from intercutting by later interments. Thus a 'layer cake' of skeletons is formed. This, of course, provides the vertical stratification in the cemetery, and when one grave lies wholly or partly over another the order of burial cannot be in doubt. Close packing in a cemetery inevitably results in graves clipping one another, so that horizontal stratification is thereby provided.

In a large-scale cemetery excavation, where hundreds or even thousands of skeletons are recorded, a long and complex stratigraphical chain may be built up, to which dating techniques can be applied. In such a chain it is common to find that the earliest burials are actually cut by, or underlie, the Saxon or Norman walls of the church and are useful candidates for radio-carbon dating. Next will come graves which can be seen to be contemporary with the earlier phases of the church building. Then, the church might have been expanded, with aisles or other appendages added, sealing burials of the previous phase. The next burial horizon can probably be related at some point to the new building, and so the sequence progresses, until we reach the eighteenth century, when coffin fittings and tombstones become prolific and often provide close dating. In essence, the successful excavation and understanding of a cemetery depends first on the construction of a grave matrix (fig. 65), and secondly on the application of suitable dating techniques and the recognition of datable horizons. Having established the basic chronology of the site, many other aspects can profitably be explored: for example, burial groupings, favoured

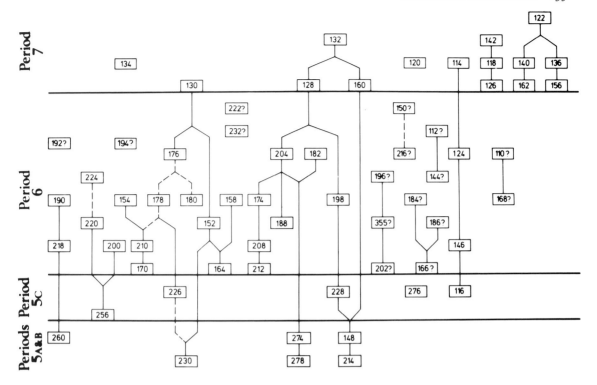

65 Matrix diagram to illustrate burial sequences and phasing in a sample of the graves excavated at Rivenhall. The three horizontal lines divide the series into four main period-groups: Anglo-Saxon (5A and B), Norman (5C), medieval (6) and post-medieval (7). A skeleton number followed by a question-mark indicates uncertainty of period, and broken lines between boxes indicate uncertain stratigraphical relationships. *Drawn by Kirsty Rodwell*

locations, orientations, relationships with boundaries, paths and cemetery structures. The diversity of orientations discernible from the extant post-medieval tombstones (p. 132) represents only the last stratum of topographical influences: many others will only be found through excavation. It was observed at Barton-on-Humber that graves pre-dating the tenth-century church took their alignment from a topographical feature, as yet undiscovered, which differed from the orientation of the church by about eight degrees. Excavation of the cathedral cemetery at Wells revealed graves on two alignments, differing by twelve degrees: burials made after *c.* 1200 followed the alignment of the present cathedral, whereas those of earlier date were in sympathy with the Anglo-Saxon cathedral. Norman graves excavated close to the chancel apse at Rivenhall showed a marked tendency to lie tangentially to the building, contrasting with the more

conventional alignment of graves belonging to the pre-apse and post-apse periods.

The excavation of graves and the examination of their contents will be further discussed in the next chapter, but it should be noted here that small-scale cemetery excavations are fruitless, since they do not yield the chains of stratigraphically related evidence outlined above. A few whole and fragmentary skeletons, and a pile of unstratified bones, all of uncertain date and association, are of no use to anyone.

Although we tend not to think of churchyards as places of activity by the living, they certainly were in medieval times. The churchyard, which was not then so cluttered with stone monuments, was a public meeting area where functions took place, with the consequential loss of personal oddments and the occasional erection of structures for secular functions. In towns markets might spill into churchyards and into the churches themselves, and important street frontages were often developed as ecclesiastical speculations. This is a significant factor to be borne in mind when studying and excavating the environs of urban churches, because their medieval yards often extend beneath adjoining secular buildings in all directions.

Very few detached priests' houses and

chantries survive in English churchyards, yet it is clear from documents that such structures once existed at least in their hundreds. Many disappeared with the Reformation, and although nothing may now be visible above ground, there is every likelihood that excavation would rediscover these and other lost buildings. Furthermore, churchyard excavation will often provide valuable information on the origins of the site and its pre-church use. Evidence for an earlier timber, or even stone-built, church may be recovered, as well as the foundations of miscellaneous ancillary structures such as standing crosses and ground-level bell-cages. Ancillary buildings still survive in some churchyards, such as the priest's house at Muchelney, Somerset, the detached bell tower at Berkeley, Glos., and the timber bell-cage at East Bergholt, Suffolk. A salutary lesson in the discovery of the unexpected was learned at Rivenhall when, although only one twentieth of the medieval churchyard was excavated, some twelve hitherto unknown buildings and structures were discovered, apart from the standing church. The list included: a major Roman villa, a sixth-century post-built hall, a middle Saxon mausoleum/chapel, a late Saxon timber church, traces of a possible priest's house of the eleventh century, three successive medieval priest's houses on another part of the site, a fourteenth-century bell-cage foundation, a medieval latrine hut, a seventeenth-century herring shed, and miscellaneous other features (figs 66a, b). Documentary evidence only attests three structures in the churchyard at Rivenhall, and two of those have not been found: there was a post-medieval sexton's house in an unexcavated corner of the yard, a medieval chantry chapel which remains unlocated, and the herring shed just mentioned (from which a charitable distribution of herrings was made). There is nothing special about Rivenhall churchyard and many other sites might, upon adequate investigation, yield a similar or more complex sequence (Rodwell and Rodwell, forthcoming).

Excavation around the bases of the walls of a church is a delicate matter, for it is here that traces of builders' levels, scaffold pole settings, buried ground surfaces, paths and the like will be found. In most cases there will be numerous graves cut through these layers, particularly against the south and east sides of the church, but nevertheless even small areas of surviving stratification can, under skilful excavation, yield important evidence for the constructional history of the building and its relationship to cemetery phases. These critical archaeological levels, which are no less important than the internal deposits, may only survive for a few few centimetres away from the bases of the walls, but in occasional patches they may extend, even if intermittently, for a metre or more. Should these deposits be completely cut away from the building, either by incompetent excavation or by drainage schemes, the church will have been irreparably severed from its surroundings. Thus whenever a scheme for drainage around an ancient church is proposed it should be preceded by the total, meticulous excavation of a strip at least 2m. and preferably 5m. wide around the walls. Many churches have already had their external achaeological deposits shovelled away during Victorian or modern drainage operations (discussed fully in Rodwell and Rodwell, 1977, section 9), and a number of other important buildings have been the object of inadequate excavations conducted for the purpose of searching for demolished structures. The damage caused to archaeological deposits by a drainage trench dug around the east end of Repton Church has been graphically demonstrated by Prof. Martin Biddle's recent excavation of the site.

We have already noted (pp. 65–6) that some churches have been reduced in the extent of their ground plans, so that the foundations of lost cells now lie beneath the churchyard. Antiquarian excavations of the past, as at the east end of Deerhurst Church or on the north side of Brixworth, were directed solely at the recovery of the plans of missing parts. Modern re-excavation at Deerhurst demonstrated that

66A Rivenhall, development of the churchyard 1:
7th to 9th centuries Chapel (S1) and cemetery established in Roman villa complex (main villa house shown in dotted outline, B2). Probable site of hall (S9) on earthwork platform against north side of villa.
10th century Timber church (B7) built over site of Roman cellar in south wing of villa. Cemetery expands southwards.
11th century New stone church built (B8) and formal boundaries of graveyard established. Traces of possible priest's house (S8).
12th century Apse added to church and new priest's house built adjoining the churchyard (B6).
13th century Priest's house rebuilt (B10) and provided with larger enclosure.
14th century East end of church rebuilt and ground-level bell-cage provided (S4). Priest's house rebuilt again (B9) and latrine hut erected over a ditch (S2)

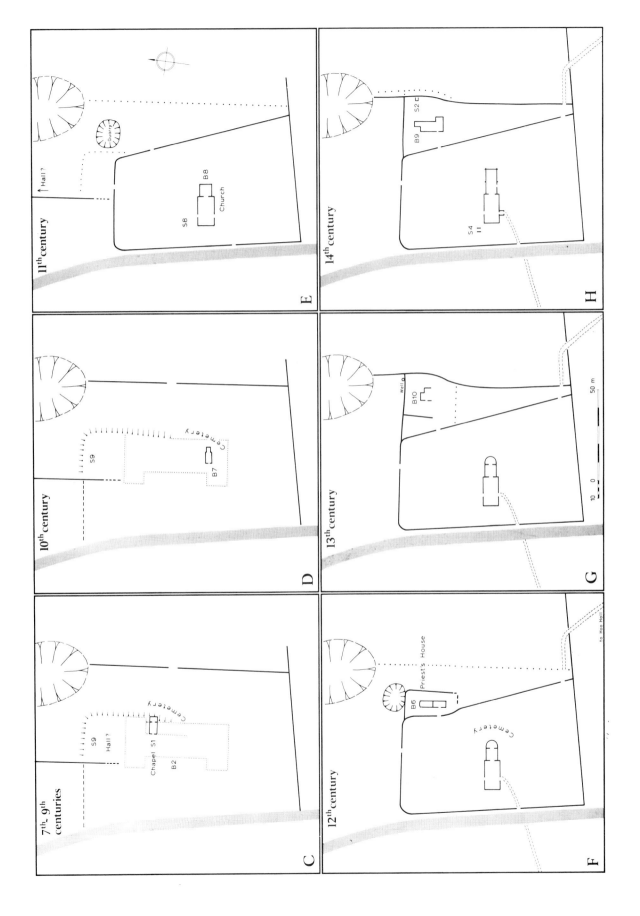

C — 7th, 9th centuries

Hall?
S9
Chapel S1
B2
Cemetery

D — 10th century

S9
Cemetery
B7

E — 11th century

Hall?
Quarry
S8
B8
Church

F — 12th century

Priest's House
B6
Cemetery
to Hoo Hall

G — 13th century

Well
B10
10   0   50 m

H — 14th century

B9
S2
S4
I1

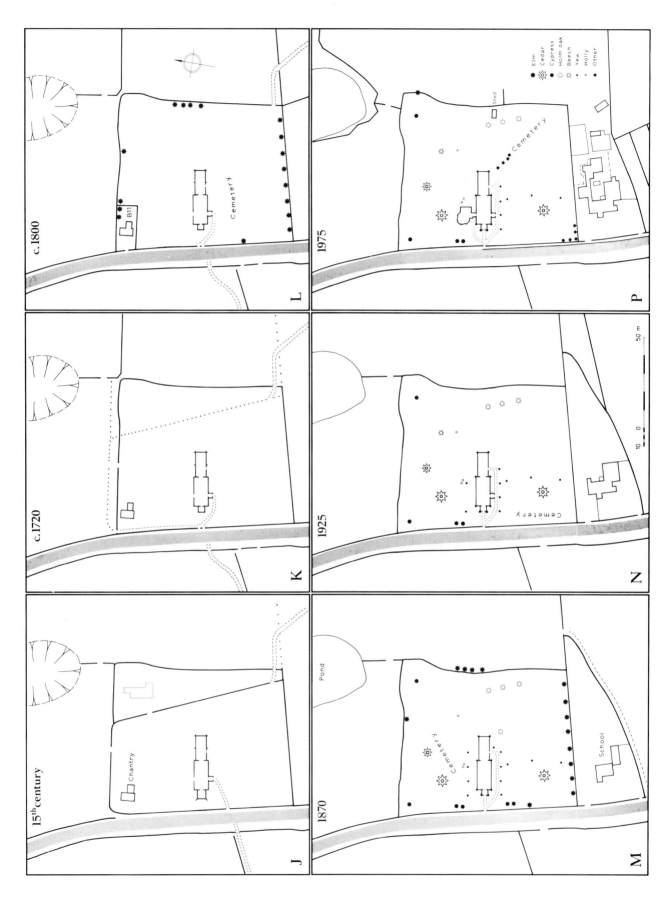

15th century

Chantry

c.1720

c.1800

B11

Cemetery

1870

Pond

Cemetery

School

1925

Cemetery

1975

Shed

Cemetery

Elm
Cedar
Cypress
Holm oak
Beech
Yew
Holly
Other

10   0   50 m

J   K   L

M   N   P

66B Rivenhall, development of the churchyard 2:
15th century Tower added to church, chantry chapel and house probably built in north-west corner of churchyard. Priest's house probably abandonded.
c. 1720 New church tower built and graveyard boundaries redefined. The chantry probably became the Sexton's house.
c. 1800 Sexton's house (B11) and garden defined. Elms planted around churchyard boundaries. Main burial area south of church.
By 1870 Church heavily restored (1838–9) and flanked by rows of yews. Semi-formal planting of other evergreen trees. Main burial area north of church. Church school built.
By 1925 Graveyard depleted of many of its trees. School extended. Main burial area south-west of church.
By 1975 Hall built onto north side of church. School extended again and surrounding boundaries substantially altered. Main burial area south-east of church.

not all traces of the earliest deposits had been destroyed and some crucial evidence remained to be discovered (Rahtz, 1976a). Leaving aside instances where whole cells are known to have been demolished, there seems to be a remarkable number of cases where structural evidence unexpectedly appears outside a church, such as the foundations of previous western towers at Rivenhall and Asheldham or the realigned south wall at Cressing, Essex (Hope, 1974), and there are many examples of scars appearing on external walls in positions suggestive of former porches, vestries, priests' houses, anchorite cells, etc.

Churchyard excavation is never easy and is seldom informative when undertaken on a small scale. Sometimes useful observations can be made when graves or drainage trenches are dug, especially if one is armed with some prior knowledge of the archaeology of the site. It is however important to remember that 'watching brief' observations are dangerously misleading, and often contractors, incumbents and archaeologists peer into a hole and see nothing but so-called 'grave earth' (i.e. undifferentiated dark soil) and some bones. Of all the structures discovered in the churchyard at Rivenhall (p. 136) none, with the exception of the villa, was, or could have been, found by examining graves or contractors' trenches. While casual observation is seldom informative on structural matters, the collection of loose finds from churchyards is extremely valuable. These are rarely spectacular, but they can tell us a good deal about the history of the site: it is not uncommon to examine grave-diggers' spoil heaps and find prehistoric flint tools and flakes, Roman pottery, and post-medieval coffin

fittings. These all contribute to the archaeological understanding of the site, and the locations of the finds must be recorded. The value of this kind of evidence should not be underestimated, and it is the accumulation of material rather than the single find which matters; seldom have I looked over recently backfilled graves, in any ancient churchyard, and not seen archaeological material lying on the surface.

Finally, under excavation, some further mention must be made of boundaries. Their nature, construction and relationship to adjoining features are all significant factors for the elucidation of the age and development of the churchyard as an enclosure. Churchyards have always been well fenced, largely for the practical considerations of excluding cattle and keeping the incumbent's sheep or goats in, and the state of repair of the boundaries is commonly mentioned in archdeacons' visitations (p. 47). In areas where natural stone is abundant, walls were generally built to define the boundaries, but elsewhere banks and ditches were the norm.

Very few churches and churchyards are likely to have been established in terrain which had not already been cleared and settled, with the consequence that roads and some boundaries will nearly always have existed first. Thus it should come as no surprise to discover, upon excavation, that one or more boundaries of a churchyard preceded any Christian activity on the site. At Rivenhall, when the bounds of the yard were formally established in the eleventh century, they followed Roman features on three sides: a road on the west, a bank on the south and the edge of a masonry building on the north (fig. 66). The eastern boundary, a bank and ditch established in the late Saxon period, exhibited some five phases of reconstruction before being abandoned in the fifteenth century in favour of a new boundary further east.

The building of Anglo-Saxon churches alongside Roman roads seems to have been commonplace, although the later encroachment of the churchyard onto the road has often necessitated re-routing, as at Asheldham where one of the ditches flanking the Roman road was found to pass through the churchyard, close to the south side of the building (Drury and Rodwell, 1978).

The excavation of a boundary cannot be satisfactorily undertaken merely by cutting trenches across its line: a substantial length needs to be dissected, say 10m. It will often be found that a bank and ditch have shifted gradually, through recutting, over the course of centuries. The movement is normally outwards from the enclosed area, so that the earliest ditch may lie beneath the present bank or even inside its line. Earthwork boundaries are seldom as simple as they at first appear, and the activities of tree roots, worms, rabbits and moles have usually wrought havoc with the stratigraphy, which is why the excavation of an adequate length of bank and ditch is essential if a reasonably intelligible and comprehensive development sequence is to be obtained. For most churchyards there can be no such thing as a 'typical' section across the boundaries: each side needs to be treated individually, at least in the first instance. In 1980 Prof. Philip Rahtz excavated a section across a remarkably well defined succession of boundaries on the west side of Deerhurst churchyard, which provided stratigraphical links between the yard and the adjacent flood-plain of the river Severn. The other boundaries of that yard are all likely to yield different histories upon investigation.

The opportunity seldom arises to excavate entrances to churchyards, which is unfortunate since these are likely to be informative. It is here that one has the possibility of showing whether the boundary and entrance are contemporary, whether gates or stiles have been provided, whether there is a succession of metalled paths passing through the opening, and so on. The study of entrances, their relationship to the surrounding topography, and the pattern of paths within the churchyard can be very revealing, potentially pointing to lost buildings and other foci.

The origins of churchyards

We have already touched several times on the wider aspects of churchyard archaeology, since we are dealing with different kinds of evidence from those associated with the investigation of the church building itself. There, we were examining evidence in a solid state, but much of the archaeology of the churchyard and its environment is less tangible, with the result that academically based reasoning and inter-pretation become more prominent factors. By their very size, churchyards impose limitations on the amount of excavation which can be tackled, and there are few opportunities for investigation consequent upon restoration and development works. Rivenhall stands almost alone in this respect amongst 'living' churches. However, the stripping of large areas of ancient cemetery at Wharram Percy, Raunds, Clopton, Cambs., and St Helen-on-the-Walls, York, must be mentioned here. While providing large numbers of skeletons for pathological study, York has yielded few details of churchyard bounds and structures. The work at Raunds is not yet complete, but shows promise for boundary studies, while at Wharram Percy a great deal has been learnt about boundaries, entrances and paths. Work continues there too, but when complete it seems likely that Wharram will provide the fullest evidence we have, not only for the history of the boundaries of a rural churchyard, but also for the relationship between the church, the yard, the vicarage and the surrounding settlement. This is one of the bonuses of large-scale excavation on a deserted village site, where everything is available for investigation. Likewise, the excavation of boundaries has been possible on the deserted cathedral cemetery at North Elmham, Norfolk (Wade-Martins, 1980). Here, too, is a graphic demonstration of boundaries determining grave orientation.

In general, however, an understanding of the relationship between a churchyard and the adjacent historic environment must be sought through the techniques of 'landscape archaeology', since excavation is never likely to be practicable on more than a minute number of sites. No general rules can be formulated, but an analysis of the road pattern, land divisions and siting of settlement foci is always a pre-requisite to understanding a rural church in its surroundings. The physical relationships between church, manor, parsonage house and glebe may suggest lines of enquiry. Even without any knowledge of the history of a particular church, it is possible to make an inspired guess at its ancient status in the community by studying topographical relationships. When a church and manor house stand side by side there is little doubt that the former was a proprietary adjunct of the latter. Indeed, it now seems tolerably certain that the great majority of English rural churches came into existence in the later Saxon period as proprietary chapels attached to manors. On the other hand, there is little doubt, from topographical evidence alone, that a large cruciform church standing on an 'island' in the middle of the village was anciently a minster

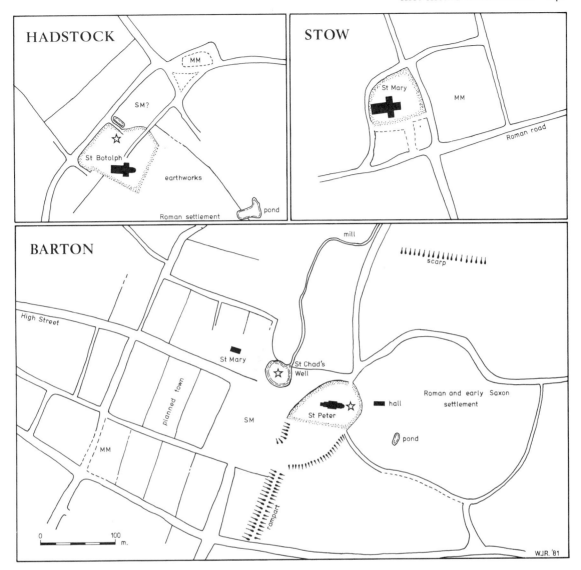

67 Churchyards in settlement history: these three churches were important Anglo-Saxon monasteries or minsters and are shown here in reconstructed landscapes of the mid-eleventh-century. A star (*) indicates a 'holy' well; stippling indicates the bounds of the medieval churchyard. SM—suggested site of Saxon market. MM—site of medieval market or fair.

Hadstock: the church and churchyard are clearly superimposed on an earlier landscape with a distinctive road pattern. The Saxon village seems to have lain to the east of the church, and is now only represented by earthworks; these are contiguous with the Roman settlement.

Stow: the church sits in a planned rectilinear landscape based on a Roman road. Stow had, at various times, been both a minster and a monastery, and presumably the religious precinct occupied the entire western island-block which was later encroached upon.

Barton-on-Humber: the present St Peter's Church may be proprietary in origin, associated with the hall to the east. The alignment and siting, however, suggest that an earlier church, perhaps a monastery, awaits discovery elsewhere in the oval enclosure which includes the present churchyard in its northern half. To the east of the church is an irregular enclosure which contains the Roman and earlier Saxon settlements, but in the late Saxon period the planned town and market were probably laid out on a new site to the west of St Peter's. A market place chapel, originally dedicated to All Saints and later St Mary, was built at the north-west corner to serve those who were not entitled to attend St Peter's Church.

(e.g. Stow, Lincs., or Thame, Oxon., prior to the laying out of the medieval town; fig. 67).

In general, a local lord who desired to found a chapel for the use of his family and retainers would do so on his own land and close to his residence: hence the innumerable church-hall complexes which are so characteristic of eastern England. In these cases the churchyard is likely to be an enclosure created around the church and adopted as a place for burial. If there is evidence for a Roman or early Anglo-Saxon site under or adjacent to the church-hall unit there must be a strong presumption in favour of continuity of occupation from pre-Christian times (Morris and Roxan, 1980). The once-prevalent notion that churches were established on the sites of Roman buildings simply for the supply of materials is no longer tenable: the factors involved are more complex and certainly more positive in terms of settlement development. Unfortunately, in very few instances is the sequence as fully understood as at Rivenhall. Similar sequences can at least be postulated with reasonable confidence on sites such as Roxby, Claxby, Lincs., Kedington, Suffolk, Ruddington, Notts., Rothley, Leics., Lower Halstow, Kent, and West Mersea, Essex.

In deciding exactly where to place a church, proprietary or otherwise, superstition and ancient custom will have played their part, as they have always done in religious matters. Thus, many churches were probably built on the site of pre-Christian religious activity, although archaeological evidence to support such a statement has rarely been obtained (p. 36). There is, however, one class of evidence which is particularly worthy of mention, namely the 'holy wells'.

While natural springs were understandably magnets for human settlement throughout antiquity, they were endowed with religious as well as secular functions in some parts of Britain. Several thousand springs, mainly in western Britain and Ireland, were given an aura of sanctity by dedicating them to saints and, in many cases, by linking them with a church building. Holy wells are therefore a feature of churchyard archaeology, yet they have been largely overlooked by modern scholars (but see Rahtz and Watts, 1979); one of the few excavations on the site of a holy spring was conducted by Sir Cyril Fox on the well-pool adjoining Exeter Cathedral (Fox, 1956); and Prof. Rahtz has investigated the 'Chalice Well'

at Glastonbury (Rahtz, 1964). Much was written in the last century about holy wells, their curative powers and the miracles which are supposed to have been performed in their vicinity (see, for example, Hope, 1893). Quite apart from the folklore, which is a subject of interest to the church archaeologist, there is a serious and practical dimension to the study of holy wells in urgent need of fulfilment. Sometimes the holy well is contained within the churchyard (St Margaret's Well, Binsey, Oxon.), or even inside the church itself (St Ethelbert's Well, Marden, Herefs.); many occur on the boundaries of churchyards (St Mary's Well, Stevington, Beds.) or just beyond (St Catherine's Well, Eskdale, Cumb.); a few are in special enclosures attached to the churchyard (St Faith's Well, Hexton, Herts.); and others are in separate parcels of land a short distance from the church (St Aldhelm's Well, Doulting, Som.). In addition, there are many springs, some with dedications and some with local names, which are not closely associated with churches.

One of the most important holy wells in England is St Andrew's Well, at Wells in Somerset. It is one of a group of five ancient springs which gives the city its name, and excavations in 1978–80 demonstrated the fundamental significance of these natural features to the development of the cathedral complex. First, there was a Roman settlement beside the springs, perhaps a villa, and a Roman-type mausoleum was built a little to the west of what was later to be called the 'holy well'. That mausoleum, which may have been associated with a more extensive cemetery as yet undiscovered, was clearly erected for the burial of an important person, presumably a Christian. In or by the eighth century, the mausoleum had become the eastern focus of a Christian cemetery, and the original occupant was removed from the burial chamber, which then became an ossuary. The bones of about 30 men, women and children were packed into the chamber (fig. 68).

Later, perhaps in the early part of the tenth century, the mausoleum was demolished and a roughly square building erected on its site. This appears to have been a private mortuary chapel into which a series of family burials was inserted, and an altar was erected in the centre of the floor. In the latter part of the tenth century the chapel was encased in the eastern end of a two-celled rectangular building.

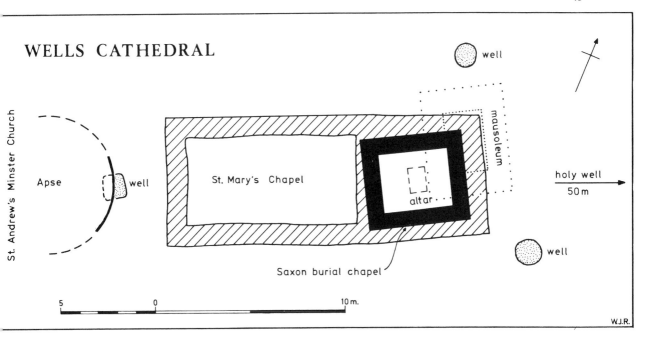

WELLS CATHEDRAL

St. Andrew's Minster Church

Apse

well

St. Mary's Chapel

altar

mausoleum

well

holy well

50 m

well

Saxon burial chapel

5   0   10 m.

W.J.R.

68 Wells: the development of St Mary's Chapel from cemetery structures. The Roman mausoleum is the earliest building on the site; it was followed by a Saxon cemetery and burial chapel, the latter being incorporated in the new St Mary's Chapel in the tenth-century. In addition to the 'holy well' there were three liturgical wells in the cemetery around this complex. *Copyright C.R.A.A.G.S.*

Meanwhile, three new well shafts had been dug around the chapel, presumably to serve liturgical functions. To the west of this complex lay the as yet unexcavated Anglo-Saxon minster church, founded early in the eighth century.

In AD 909 the minster became St Andrew's Cathedral, and the ancient chapel just described is identifiable from later documents and was dedicated to St Mary (Rodwell, 1980c and forthcoming). Throughout these developments the holy well remained the eastern focus of the religious complex, a position which it still occupies today, although the cathedral has been rebuilt and the ancient liturgical axis disrupted. Recent excavations at the church of St Mary de Lode, Gloucester, have hinted at an important sequence, analogous to Wells, where a mausoleum was possibly the first in a succession of religious buildings (Bryant, 1980).

The digging of well-shafts in and around Saxon churches, especially on their east-west axes, was a liturgically-inspired activity about which we know very little, except as a result of recent excavations. At Winchester Old Minster a well-shaft was dug into the centre of the north

porticus and another formed a central feature of the tenth-century eastern apse (Biddle, 1970), while at Barton-on-Humber a group of timber-lined wells and a tank were found in excavation due east of the Anglo-Saxon chancel, where they must have fulfilled a liturgical function, perhaps associated with outdoor baptism. A prolific natural spring, known as St Chad's Well, also rises *c.* 60m. west of the church.

While some monasteries and minsters had to be founded on 'open' ground, there was a marked tendency in the middle Saxon period for Roman walled enclosures to be granted *in toto* to new religious communities, so that a complete but disused fort might constitute the monastic precinct or minster churchyard. Notable examples of this kind of development occur in two areas, the north-west and the south-east. In the former it was the Roman forts on Hadrian's Wall and its hinterland which seem to have been made over to religious use, while in the latter it was the Saxon shore forts of Reculver, Richborough, Burgh Castle, Felixstowe and Bradwell. To what extent there was a resident population at the time of founding these monasteries is unclear, and the same applies, for example, to St Kyneburga's monastery which was built in the yard of the great precinct villa at Castor, Northants.

The establishment of churches in or adjoining enclosed metalled yards is an interesting feature of Roman towns in Britain.

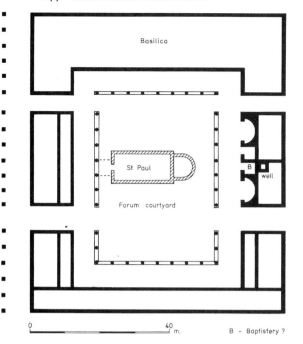

69 Lincoln. Diagrammatic reconstruction of the plan of the Roman forum and church of St Paul-in-the-Bail in the seventh-century. The central siting of the church within the courtyard enabled the Roman well to form an eastern focus, which was liturgically significant. The eastern forum range was probably adapted for religious use, including one of the small chambers adjacent to the well as a baptistery. The plan of the church has close connexions with St. Peter's, Bradwell-on-Sea and, by analogy, was probably entered through a west porch and door. It seems clear that the church was intended to articulate with the columniation of the forum courtyard colonnade; the western range was presumably adapted to serve as an *atrium*, through which the church was approached. *After Gilmour, 1979, and Jones and Gilmour, 1980*

Nor is there any reason to suppose that the siting was accidental. In the Roman period it was usual to set a temple in its own precinct or, in the case of especially important temples, in the forum. When Christianity became the state religion the principal church of a town was not infrequently established in or close to the forum. In Britain we can only see this clearly in the case of the Roman church at Silchester, Hants., where a religious precinct was established on the south side of the forum (Frere, 1975). It can therefore be no coincidence that some very early and important Anglo-Saxon churches were built in the fora of Roman towns, in each case presumably using the forum courtyard as the churchyard. The excavation of the church of St Paul-in-the-Bail, Lincoln (fig. 69), has provided an emphatic

demonstration of this (Colyer and Gilmour, 1978). The churches of St Peter Cornhill, London, St Michael, Verulamium (St Albans) and St Mary Major, Exeter, are exactly analogous. At York the *principia* of the legionary fortress and its courtyard were adopted for the cathedral church. The same probably holds true at Cramond, East Lothian, and Doncaster, Yorks., where the parish churches lie in the respective *principiae* of the forts; in the latter case it is interesting to note that a medieval castle was very aptly built on the site of the *principia*, and that the present parish church was successor to the castle chapel. In these and other related cases, the church appears to have been established first, with the cemetery developing as a secondary feature in the courtyard around. The same is almost certainly true in those urban situations where a post-Roman church emerged from the foundations of a Roman building, as at St Nicholas' and All Saints' churches, Colchester, St Mary's, Silchester, and St Edmund's, Caistor-by-Norwich. At the last mentioned the churchyard would appear originally to have occupied one small *insula* in the south-east corner of the town.

An entirely different situation obtained in the suburbs of Roman towns, where in most instances a pagan Roman cemetery came first. It is not difficult to visualize a christianization of these cemeteries in the later Roman or early Saxon period, leading to the establishment of churches: St Bride's London; St Botolph's, Colchester; St Pancras' and perhaps St Martin's, Canterbury; St Lawrence's and St Cecilia's, Cirencester; St Mary's, Godman-chester, Hunts., and All Saints', Great Chesterford, Essex.

The differences between town and country are significant but as yet ill understood: in particular we do not know to what extent pagan Saxon cemeteries were adopted for Christian burial, and Sancton, Yorks., is one of a relatively small number of examples in this category (Faull, 1976). Others have been recorded in East Anglia, at North Runcton and Hilgay, Norfolk, and Soham, Cambs. But even in these instances it is not certain that the pagan and Christian cemeteries were one: they might have been two adjacent but distinctly separate entities. In urban settings there are many examples of churches and their cemeteries arising on Roman extra-mural burial grounds, while in rural areas there is an observable tendency for several distinct, short-lived cemeteries to be found within a single parish. Thus there may be a truly pagan cemetery of the fifth and sixth centuries, a christianizing one of the seventh to ninth centuries, and finally the church cemetery running through from the tenth century, or earlier. Evidence related to the gradual changeover from pagan rural cemeteries to Christian ones is now coming to light, for example at Winnall, Hants. (Meaney and Hawkes, 1970) and at several Kentish sites.

Although in a class of its own at present, the Northumbrian royal centre at Yeavering has been found to incorporate two cemeteries: the earlier was associated with a north-south oriented building described as a 'temple', and the later with an east-west structure for which the identification of a Christian church has been proposed (Hope-Taylor, 1977). The seventh-century cemetery was enclosed by a wooden fence.

In short, a greater understanding of cemeteries and churchyards, from the late Roman period onwards, is urgently required. Cemeteries were more firmly rooted in the pre-tenth-century landscape than churches and in general terms their archaeology is thus ancestral to that of churches.

9 Bones, Burials and Monuments

There are two extremes of approach to the archaeology of burials. On the one hand, they may be regarded as a nuisance and an interference with the 'real' archaeology of the site, and to be shovelled away as quickly as possible. On the other hand, some excavators lavish enormous effort on the recording of burials, to the detriment of other aspects of the investigation. In both cases these excesses result from a basic misunderstanding of the value of skeletal evidence. It is as well to begin by examining the various methods and forms of burial which are likely to be encountered in church excavations.

Burials inside churches

There can hardly be a parochial church in England which does not have at least a few memorial plaques on its walls or inscribed slabs in its floors; with few exceptions, these betoken burials inside the building, although they provide no guide to the number of interments which has actually taken place. The surviving memorials represent only a tiny fraction, even of the post-Reformation burials, in most churches. Urban churches, some of which are crowded with memorial plaques and slabs, often had scores or even hundreds of burials packed beneath their floors in the last three centuries. Inevitably, this means that ancient floor levels and all that is contained in and under them will have been seriously disturbed. This is an instance where one class of archaeological evidence has been replaced with another.

The practice of burying the dead inside churches increased steadily through the ages, down to the mid-nineteenth century when legislation brought it to an end, owing to public health dangers. Burial in the body of the church was rarely permitted in the Anglo-Saxon period, and thus it is uncommon to find many pre-Conquest graves in the nave; persons of especial reverence or importance could however be interred in subsidiary chapels, or *porticus*, including the chancel. A well-known example is the burial of the early archbishops and kings of Kent in the *porticus* of the church of St Peter and St Paul, Canterbury (Taylor and Taylor, 1965, 134–9). The thorough excavation of several smaller Saxon churches, such as St Pancras', Winchester, and St Peter's, Barton-on-Humber, has demonstrated the sparsity of pre-Conquest burials inside these buildings. Furthermore, in the case of Barton an earlier cemetery on the site was systematically exhumed before the church was built.

The evidence from St Pancras' church provides a picture of intra-mural burial which is probably typical of many churches of its class. There were few, if any, graves dug inside before the later medieval period and those interments that were eventually made occupied the most favoured positions. Thus one grave was in front of the high altar, a string of four ran down the centre of the nave, three lay side by side in the south chapel in front of its altar, and two were set directly under arches of the north aisle arcade (Biddle, 1975a, fig. 16). Church excavations usually demonstrate that areas in front of altars and the central alleys were the first to be colonized by graves. Frequently, there have been several phases of inter-cutting burials at these favoured locations.

Down to the seventeenth century burial inside a church was a privilege enjoyed by the clergy and a few notable lay folk, mainly gentry, but in the eighteenth and nineteenth centuries the desire for indoor burial became an obsession. Merchants, farmers, architects, physicians and a host of others managed to buy their way into the church, a process observed by epitaph writers:

Here lie I by the chancel door,
Here lie I because I'm poor.
The further in, the more you'll pay,
Here lie I, as warm as they. (Kingsbridge, Devon)

Whole families, including babies, were now interred beneath the floors; and those who could afford such luxuries had great underground vaults of brick or stone built to receive their coffins. Vaults vary in size and construction and could be designed to house just one infant or up to twenty coffins. A few noble families caused vaults or crypts of enormous size to be built and fitted with shelving to accommodate tier upon tier of coffins.

The implications of the post-medieval predilection for deep grave digging and vault construction are, first, that many earlier burials have been destroyed or fragmented and, secondly, that sizeable areas of church interiors have been archaeologically sterilized of all but the very latest features. As a rough guide we may say that the larger and more affluent the community served by a church, the greater will be the number of post-medieval vaults. Thus the excavator who is particularly interested in recovering a complete medieval liturgical layout, or succession of layouts, would do well to investigate a church in a rural area where there have been no resident families of substance in the last two or three centuries. Hadstock was a case in point, except that a drastic lowering of the floors in 1884 had removed much of the evidence which would otherwise have survived (p. 107). The scholar who is especially interested in post-medieval burial practice, vault construction, coffin types and furniture, and memorials will find his greatest harvest in the important urban churches. The skeletal material derived from these later burials is highly significant to the palaeopathologist (p. 164).

Indoor burials of the Anglo-Saxon and early medieval periods were as a rule placed in very shallow graves, sometimes in stone, lead or wooden coffins. The lid of a stone coffin was frequently in the form of a sculptured or incised slab which was set flush with the contemporary floor. Some particularly important burials, such as those of bishops in cathedrals, were actually above floor level, being contained in tomb-chests or even in wall-benches (e.g. Bishop Wm. de Marchia at Wells). This meant that decaying corpses were not sealed with a suitable anti-smell layer of earth or clay, so that the alternative of embalming may have been employed fairly regularly, (p. 156).

In the later Middle Ages the fashion for decorated coffin lids set in the floor passed away and burials were often placed slightly deeper in the ground, and not usually embalmed. The increasing popularity of indoor burial after the Reformation must have entailed the constant upheaval of floors in urban parish churches. It is difficult to imagine today the mess which this must have caused: in an important town church there can hardly have been a few weeks pass by without the need to open up some part of the floor. It must have been a dreadful patchwork of materials, always sinking and uneven. The cutting of one grave through another raised no qualms and it is common during excavation to find that half a dozen or more interments have been made on the same spot in those parts of a church which were popular for burial. Disentangling the sequence is seldom easy, and the soil is always brimming with disassociated bones. From time to time one finds an articulated limb or section of backbone which was obviously fairly 'fresh' when dug up inadvertently, and was placed back on top of or beside a newly interred corpse. While the disturbance of corpses in a partially decomposed state might seem repugnant to us, it was clearly a common occurrence, certainly down to the middle of the last century. Shakespeare provides us with an indirect reference to this kind of happening when Hamlet holds up a skull which has just been exhumed by a grave digger and exclaims 'Alas, poor Yorick!—I knew him well' (*Hamlet* Act V, Scene 1). This must be the most often recited Shakespearian line on church archaeology!

By the early nineteenth century few churches can have been without at least a handful of family vaults, while many were nearly filled to capacity beneath the floor. In many instances neither the coffins nor the vaults were sealed in an airtight state permitting the aroma from decomposing bodies to permeate the church. Contemporary records speak of the intolerable stench, particularly in the City of London. It is therefore small wonder that measures were taken not only to stop the practice of intramural burial but also to put sealing layers of clay or rammed chalk over graves before laying new floors. These sealing layers are frequently found below Victorian tiled pavements. Families who could afford it were buried in lead coffins with airtight soldered joints, which made the re-opening of vaults to receive additional interments somewhat less distasteful than it would otherwise have been. Conversely, vaults in churchyards seldom contain burials in lead coffins.

Survival of the evidence

One of the most interesting aspects of burial investigations is the differential survival of evidence, for the skeleton, the body, the funerary wrappings and the coffin. Remarkably little is known about the factors which influence preservation, or the way they interact, resulting in different effects not only within one cemetery but even within a single grave. The survival of bone depends largely on the acidity of the soil: worst of all is acid gravel or brickearth, which dissolves bone at an amazing rate. Within a hundred years of burial, or even less, there may be nothing left of the body except perhaps some tooth-caps, which are more resistant to decay than bone. If the whole skeleton has dissolved the excavator can only attempt to recover a silhouette of the body from which virtually nothing can be learned except perhaps the burial posture and approximate stature. In clean sandy soils brown stains may indicate the positions of the principal bones, but in gravelly brickearth there is commonly no recognizable trace of the body.

At the opposite end of the scale, the preservation of bone in chalky soil may be superb, providing the best possible conditions for detailed osteological study after excavation. The relationship of burials to buildings can also affect bone survival, through the creation of soil micro-climates. Thus a grave situated immediately below a gargoyle may be subjected to a disportionately high impregnation with acid rainwater, whereas a grave cut through a chalk footing, say under a nave arcade, will be surrounded by an alkaline 'cushion'.

When excavating a deeply stratified cemetery it is noticeable how bone preservation also varies with depth: thus skeletons to a depth of, say, one metre may be in a crumbly state, those between one and 1·5m. may be in better condition, and then all below 1·5m. may be excellently preserved. This has little or nothing to do with the antiquity of the grave, and one commonly finds a decayed eighteenth-century skeleton only a few centimetres above an Anglo-Saxon one in good condition. The 'cut-off' point can be very abrupt, and may be associated with a change in the colour of buried bone. At Wells Cathedral the better preserved skeletons from deep-set burials were all stained black; the same was true at Barton-on-Humber. The cut-off line, which is apparently related to the winter water-table in the soil, can be so precise

that it is detectable through differential discolouration within the depth of a single skeleton.

Less clear, however, are the reasons for uneven decay along the length of a skeleton. The skull, the legs, and sometimes the arms and pelvis, may be well preserved, when the vertebrae and rib-cage have decayed to the consistency of a crumbly biscuit. This effect is not the result of differential acidity in the grave fill since it has been noted on skeletons contained within sealed stone coffins, and the decay of the body itself must play a part here. A long experienced grave-digger in a municipal cemetery told me of an interesting experience involving the rapid dissolving of a body. He was reopening a grave to make a second interment some sixty years after the date of the first and expected to alight upon the 'box' in the usual way. He found the coffin handles loose in the soil and when his spade struck timber it was the bottom of the coffin, which was in a sound state of preservation: the corpse and the remainder of the coffin had decayed without visible trace. This has implications for cemetery archaeology.

Given the high mortality rate among babies and young children throughout antiquity, it has lately become of increasing concern to palaeopathologists that the very young seem to be seriously under-represented in many cemetery populations (e.g. Dawes and Magilton, 1980, 27). At the very least there ought to be one child aged less than twelve and one infant for every two adults, yet clearly nothing like this figure obtains in excavated collections of skeletons. One of the largest assemblages from a parochial churchyard is that from St Helen-on-the-Walls, York, where a thorough analysis of the skeletons and disarticulated bones indicated the following maximum numbers of individuals: adults and sub-adults, 724; children 284; babies, 33. Furthermore, it is interesting to note that most of the 21 articulated babies' skeletons were accompanying adults. It is now a demonstrable fact that infants and children (say up to five years of age) are found far less frequently in excavation than they ought to be, especially when buried alone. While many infant graves must have been very shallow and were destroyed by later diggings, the paucity of disarticulated bones asserts that this is only part of the solution to the problem; the remainder have been destroyed by other agencies. Many infants buried in shallow outdoor graves will have been wholly consumed by rats and other burrowing animals. Indeed, when rats penetrated outdoor vaults they could consume adult corpses with alacrity, leaving only a few gnawed bones and coffin fittings for the archaeologist to find.

The second major factor affecting infant burials is dissolution. This has been carefully examined at Barton-on-Humber, with particular reference to sealed post-medieval burials inside the church. Attention was first drawn to the problem by finding grave-like slots which contained nothing except, perhaps, three or four nails. It soon became clear that these slots were infant graves from which the bodies had largely or completely dissolved. There were no silhouettes, only the occasional patch of cream-coloured bone residue or, interestingly, fragment of skull. While no difficulty was experienced in excavating infant graves cut into firm material, there must certainly have been many more contained within the loose, backfillings of post-medieval graves in the central alleys which defied recognition. It is noticeable that infant bones survive best where they are in close contact with an adult skeleton.

A final example may be cited to illustrate the self-destroying powers of an infant corpse under seemingly neutral conditions. A brick vault built to house the coffin of a 10-month-old baby was investigated. It was found to contain a pinewood coffin which was in an excellent state of preservation, apart from the bottom which had rotted badly. Of the infant only a tiny crumb of skull remained.

Under normal conditions of burial in the soil or in vaults bacterial decay brings about the decomposition of all the non-bony material within 10–50 years, but under the special conditions created by embalming and indoor burial skin and hair may survive through a process of dessication. These exceptional conditions were found to obtain in the tomb of Archibishop Godfrey de Ludham at York, which was opened and recorded in 1969 (Ramm, 1971), and in one of the canonical graves opened in the chapter house vestibule at Lincoln in 1955 (Bruce-Mitford, 1976). If suitably alkaline conditions prevail in the soil, gall-stones and bladder-stones may survive, and even fragments of hardened arteries.

More commonly recovered are traces of textiles in graves. These may be from vestments, shrouds or coffin coverings, and

usually survive as a result of contact with metal. Even if the bones have decayed, the micro-chemistry of the soil around metal objects can permit the remarkable survival of textiles, leather and wood. Graves of the pagan Saxon period regularly yield fragments of clothing which owe their preservation to the inclusion of brooches, buckles and weapons with the corpse. The paucity of grave goods in Christian burials greatly reduces the chances of survival of organic materials, except in cases where chalices and patens were placed in priests' graves (fig. 71B). While the cloth itself may not survive in all instances, careful inspection will nearly always reveal the weave-pattern preserved in the products of chemical decay on the surface of the metal. Vestments worn by priests often included gold thread, particularly in the hems, which is recoverable by careful excavation.

Interments in stone or lead coffins permit both the better preservation and easier recognition of organic materials, as evidenced so dramatically in medieval archbishops' tombs at York (Ramm, 1971). A canon's burial in a stone coffin at Wells, included fragments of his leather sanctuary slippers. The post-medieval practice of covering wooden coffins with cloth—often green baize—and applying a variety of fittings over this commonly results in the survival of a 'sandwich' of metal, textile and timber. By contrast with other materials, coffin wood is commonly preserved in damp soil conditions. If the ground is waterlogged, and has always been so since the time of burial, a coffin may survive largely intact, as at Bordesley Abbey (Rahtz and Hirst, 1976, pl. XVII) or York Minster (Phillips, 1976, pl. XII). In conditions where the ground has remained consistently damp over a long period ephemeral traces of timber, or 'coffin stains; are regularly to be found. They are not easily detected in loose, rubbly grave-fills, but in fine soil sand or mortar the outline of the coffin can be perfectly delineated (fig. 70). The lid will not normally be found because it will have collapsed and fragmented under the weight of overlying soil, but the rectilinear outline of the side-boards of the coffin will be seen as a grey stain in the soil, between one and two centimetres in thickness. If metal fittings are present they can be recorded precisely in relation to the stain and, most importantly, details of coffin construction can be worked out.

It has been known, at least since the Roman period, that coffins will last longer in the soil if

70 A (*left*) Grave cut through a rubble foundation with the silhouette of the coffin showing, above the level of the skeleton, as a dark grey line in the pale mortar filling **B** (*right*) Tomb of Bishop Levericus in Wells Cathedral during opening in 1979. The bones are tenth-century, contained in a coffin-like relic box made in 1848, set in a stone cist built in 1914 and covered with a life-sized effigy carved *c.* 1200 *Photos: author. Copyright C.R.A.A.G.S.*

the boards from which they are made are charred in a fire. In other words, the coffin is partially carbonized. While this practice was certainly widespread down to the end of the Saxon period, it seems to have become less common as the Middle Ages progressed. A coffin stain produced by charred timber is much easier to follow in excavation, owing to its black carbonaceous content. This practice should not be confused with that of 'charcoal burial', where the body is covered with a layer of true charcoal. Burials of this kind are not very common and tend to be found in monastic cemeteries of the late Saxon and early medieval periods (e.g. Christchurch, Oxford, St Guthlac's Minster, Hereford, Bath Abbey and St Oswald's Priory, Gloucester).

Our knowledge of early timber coffins and their fittings is extremely limited and will only be enhanced through the meticulous recording of wood stains and metal fittings found in excavation. In the Roman and Saxon periods iron was sometimes used in prodigious quantities in the form of nails, straps, corner plates, handles and so on. Rarely have reconstructions been attempted like those from Winchester (Clarke, 1979) and Kelvedon, Essex. Complex pieces of furniture, apparently including bedsteads, were sometimes placed in graves of the seventh century, such as those at Shudy Camps, Cambs., and Sutton Hoo, Suffolk (Vierck, 1980). also, house-shaped coffins were sometimes constructed, and such

71 Burial rites at Barton-on-Humber
A (*left*) Anglo-Saxon burial in an un-nailed wooden coffin (now decayed), with a pair of large, white flint pebbles used as 'ear-muffs' to keep the skull in place. Note: the 'parallel-sided' effect caused by the body fitting tightly inside the coffin; the distortion of the spine effected during decomposition; and the skull which has become detached from the neck and has rolled over, taking the lower jaw with it.
B (*right*) Medieval burial of a priest, whose hands clasp a chalice and paten of pewter which stand on the stomach. He was wrapped in a shroud, but not contained in a coffin. Note: the spread-out elbows; and the crossed legs, indicative of a military connection. *Photos: author. Crown copyright*

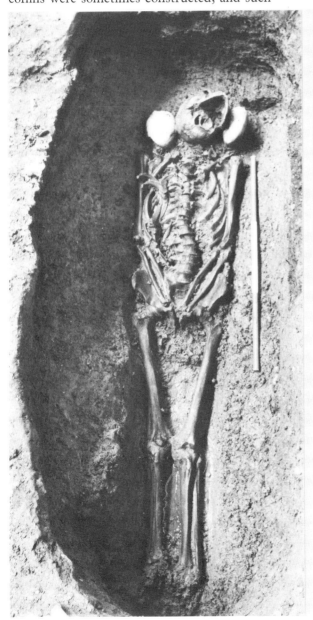

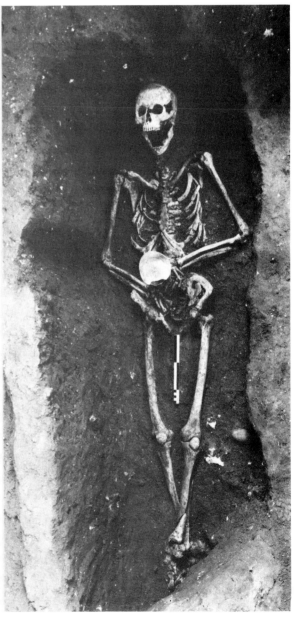

exotic grave furniture in England is known only from the positions of significant iron fittings. More difficult to find and interpret are those coffins which were carefully carpentered, without the use of nails or other ferramenta. They were held together with dovetailed joints and wooden pegs; and such coffins have been found under waterlogged conditions in Roman London. Unfavourable soil conditions or careless excavation can destroy the coffin stain and with it all evidence that the body was ever encoffined. Even more puzzling to the excavator are those graves which yield only a few nails, say no more than half a dozen. A nailed coffin cannot be made with less than a dozen nails; hence it is tempting to regard such graves as uncoffined and the few nails present as strays. But that will not do, since it is clear that some coffins *did* only contain two or three nails. On a fully jointed coffin they were merely used to secure the lid in place and, occasionally, to strengthen a defective joint.

Evidence bearing upon many of the above problems was found at Barton-on-Humber in 1981 with the remarkable discovery of many Saxon timber coffins, some so perfectly preserved that every toolmark and scratch was plainly visible.

Rites of burial

Pagan burial customs are renowned for rites which resulted in the deposition of a variety of grave goods. These customs died slowly, and some of the earliest burials which are probably, or plausibly, Christian could include funeral furnishings: the ship burial at Sutton Hoo, the barrow burial in Taplow old churchyard and the cemetery of five graves at Lower Brook Street, Winchester (Biddle, 1975a) are amongst the more striking examples. The Liudhard medallion of *c*. AD 600 from St Martin's churchyard, Canterbury, is probably a relic from an early Christian grave, and so too the numerous silver coins of the seventh and eight centuries which have turned up in grave digging and, occasionally, in archaeological excavations in south-eastern and southern England (cf. Biddle, 1976). An important recent addition to the corpus of early Christian sepulchral furnishings is the seventh-century hanging bowl from St Paul-in-the-Bail, Lincoln (Gilmour, 1979).

On the whole, grave goods are uncommon in Christian cemeteries, but are certainly not as scarce as is generally supposed: in total, there is a considerable quantity of personal property from English churchyards which may once have been associated with burials. Unexpected lapses into the anachronistic may be stumbled upon: at Barton-on-Humber post-medieval grave goods included dice, various coins, a china dinner plate and a delft-ware sugar bowl!

In a few instances it is possible to determine the kind of wrapping material used (p. 149), although deciding whether that represents clothing, vestments or a simple shroud is another matter. Gold thread suggests vestments, trouser buttons and tie-pins are clear indicators of clothing, and shroud-pins are self-proclaiming. A noticeable tendency in medieval shroud burials is to wrap the corpse tightly, so that the arms and shoulders could not spread out in the natural way; but it is well to be aware that the same effect could derive from a tight-fitting coffin (fig. 71A). A great many medieval churchyard burials, together with some indoor ones, were simply shrouded but uncoffined, a fact frequently demonstrated by the shapes of graves.

Archaeology is demonstrating that there was much more to the art and ritual of grave digging than merely excavating a hole large enough to contain a body. Study of the grave-cut—if it can be detected—will generally make it clear whether there could have been a coffin or not: if the grave is scarcely wider than the body, has an uneven bottom and rounded ends it can safely be assumed that the burial was uncoffined. If, however, the grave is broad, flat-bottomed and square-cut it was probably so shaped to house a coffin. Pieces of stone and tile standing on edge against the sides of the grave are also indicators of the backfilling around a coffin. Some graves, particularly in the Anglo-Saxon period, were provided with side ledges and other features (Hogarth, 1973), while in the medieval period the grave-cut itself could be body-shaped, that is provided with an excavated niche to accommodate the skull.

More common was the body-shaped coffin in stone; externally it might be roughly rectangular, while internally a neatly cut niche was provided for the skull, and the body-space was often tapered. Drainage holes and channels were provided in the floor of the coffin and a carefully shaped recess would be formed in one side to receive a mortuary chalice if the burial was that of a priest. Even a baby could be buried in a stone coffin if the family were willing to entertain the expense.

72 Wells Cathedral: medieval burials in stone-lined cists below the floor of the Lady Chapel-by-the-Cloister. Only a tiny patch of the thirteenth-century glazed-tile floor survived between a group of graves at the top of the picture. Note the massive foundations of the rebuilt chapel (AD 1477) cutting across the earlier cists and foundations on a different alignment. *Photo: author. Copyright C.R.A.A.G.S.*

A solid stone coffin was well beyond the financial means of most families, but some could afford to build a stone-lined cist as a receptacle for a wooden coffin (fig. 72). An even more economical arrangement was simply to apply plaster to the sides of the grave, to give an impression of a stone lining. Many stone coffins were provided with elaborately decorated lids (fig. 77) which were set at floor level inside the church (p. 161); both lid and coffin were often torn up and discarded, or reused for another purpose, within a century of being laid down. Lids were used as floor slabs, door steps, lintels and foundation blocks, while coffins tended to be recycled or used to build buttresses, for which purpose they were often of suitable proportions. The sites of these despoiled tombs are revealed in excavation as large, shallow, flat-bottomed pits; the lower dimensions of the missing coffin can be ascertained from the slight dent which its considerable weight made in the floor of the grave pit.

Lead, as a coffin material, was not frequently employed between the end of the Roman period and the seventeenth century, except for important royal, monastic and episcopal graves: Archbishop de Ludham's tomb at York had a lead lining (AD 1265). An early example (AD 1422) of the use of a sealed lead coffin in a parish church is the so-called 'pickled knight' of Danbury, the discovery of which was reported in the *Gentleman's Magazine* in 1789 (Gomme, 1893, 102).

The use of lead, especially when soldered and airtight, was known to retard the rate of decay of the corpse, giving rise to the recording, from the Anglo-Saxon period onwards, of bodies being discovered in an 'uncorrupt' state, but embalming also played a part in this process (p. 156). The popularity of lead rose sharply in the eighteenth century, with the result that few parish churches are likely to be without some lead coffins, and they are almost invariably associated with vaults of brick or stone. The soldered lead box was nearly always an inner lining to a timber coffin, and could in turn also

73 An example of a rubbing of the punched inscription and incised decoration on a lead coffin recorded by making a careful rubbing, using a wax crayon on detail paper. *Photo: author*

have a timber lining within, creating a 'sandwich' effect. Both the lead and the outer box, usually of elm, could be decorated in an infinite number of ways. The lead might be decorated with a scored pattern, such as an all-over diamond twill, and an inscription punched or engraved into the lid (fig. 73). All this would be hidden by the outer box, covered with cloth or leather, and ornamented with a greater or less number of decorative strips (of pressed tin) plaques, nameplates, arms, corner pieces, etc., all made of iron, tin or brass, according to rank and affluence. Six handles were usually provided on a full-sized coffin.

The archaeology of post-Reformation funeral furniture has hardly been touched and a great deal of recording is necessary before much of the evidence is lost through natural decay and the destruction of vaults which is now commonly taking place. When access to vaults is obtained photographs, measured drawings and careful rubbings of the metal fittings should always be collected as a basic record; if the contents of a vault are to be cleared out, moved or otherwise damaged a much fuller record, including a medical investigation, should be put in hand, and samples of all the coffin fittings must be preserved. The coffin plate, the most individual part of the assemblage, may be very elaborate and beautiful, perhaps with a combination of engraved and respoussé decoration on gilt copper. This may need urgent attention from a conservation laboratory. Plates made from tin are also susceptible to decay under adverse conditions, while those of pressed iron disintegrate most rapidly of all. These last were the cheapest to buy, being mass-produced, with the inscription applied to a blank cartouche in paint or gilding.

The aristocracy of the eighteenth century sometimes caused semi-subterranean mausolea to be built for their family's interment. Some were free-standing buildings in the churchyard (e.g. Hambleden, Bucks.; Britford, Wilts., and Hovingham, Yorks.), while others adjoined the

church, as at Hinton St George, Somerset and Redbourne, Lincs. Here the Dukes of St Albans were buried in elaborate coffins surmounted by their coronets, one of the latest examples of the inclusion of grave goods. Although the vast majority of medieval and later burials did not include funerary accoutrements (p. 149), the clergy were the principal exception. The burials of bishops, priests and abbots are generally recognizable from their contents. A bishop or archbishop was laid out in his full attire, with chalice and paten, crozier and ring. An ordinary priest was provided with the chalice and paten only; and in the post-Reformation era he might have been buried with the opposite orientation to that which was normal: i.e. he had

74 A (*left*) Late Saxon burial at Wells showing the dark staining and exfoliation of the skull, contrasting with the appearance of the rest of the skeleton. This effect is believed to be due to embalming of the face.
B (*below*) The same, showing the top of the skull. There is a clear demarcation between the treated forehead and the untreated scalp, indicating the hair-line. This is also a rare instance where the cause of death is evident in the skeleton; a two-pronged instrument (pitchfork?) pierced the skull. *Photos: author. Copyright C.R.A.A.G.S.*

his head to the east. A simple pectoral cross made of lead was commonly included in the graves of abbots and in some early bishops' graves (fig. 4). Such crosses have been found at St Augustine's Abbey, Canterbury, Bury St Edmunds Abbey and elsewhere. They could be inscribed, providing a precise identification of the corpse, and an interesting one from Canterbury reads, in Latin, 'On 11 March 1063 departed out of this life Wulfmaeg sister of Wulfric the Abbot'. The pectoral cross contained in Bishop Giso's grave (1088) at Wells was inscribed with excerpts from the Latin Mass for the Dead (Rodwell, 1979).

We have briefly touched upon the subject of 'preservation' of the dead, which could be attempted by careful burial or embalming (p. 147). A great deal remains to be learned about the latter, in particular, through archaeological investigation. There seems little doubt that the exfoliated state of certain bones of the Saxon bishops and other early skeletons at Wells results from embalming, particularly of the face (fig. 74). The local surgeon was present at the opening of the tomb containing the 'pickled' body at Danbury in 1779, and he was convinced that embalming had taken place: '. . . the body lying in a liquor or pickle, somewhat resembling mushroom catchup. . . . I tasted, and found it to be aromatic, though not very pungent, partaking of the taste of catchup and of the pickle of Spanish olives . . . feathers, flowers and herbs in abundance were floating, the leaves and stalks of which appeared quite perfect, but totally discoloured' (Gomme, 1893).

The Venerable Bede provides us with many references to the exhumation of well-preserved bodies, where a pre-burial treatment of some kind may have been applied, and at the same time he reminds us that the translation of corporeal remains and the collection of relics were common activities. These have several implications for the archaeological record. The finding of empty graves is not infrequent during excavation (apart from those where dissolution of the bones has taken place p. 148) and in some cases the removal of an important person can be postulated, as at St Paul-in-the-Bail, Lincoln (Gilmour, 1979). The 'cleansing' of the ground—that is the exhumation of previous interments—could take place before building a new church, or making an addition to one. Two examples may be cited from the Saxon period: when Wulfric built his octagon onto the church

of St Peter and St Paul, Canterbury, he is recorded as having 'cleansed' the site, Archaeologically, the evidence should be recoverable, as it was at St Peter's, Barton-on-Humber, where upwards of thirty graves were exhumed before the Anglo-Saxon church was built, but one grave was overlooked and the skeleton was decapitated by a foundation trench.

The reinterment of exhumed skeletons could take place in a crypt, an ossuary (as at Wells, p. 18) or simply in a charnel pit (a hole dug to receive a large quantity of bones). A flourishing trade in bones and other so-called 'relics' existed before the Reformation, and although a great deal of the evidence relating to this activity has perished new discoveries have been made by archaeologists. Most commonly these take the form of relic pits under altars and foundations (p. 122), and just occasionally relics are discovered in places where they were hidden for protection long ago, in walls and tombs. In most cases, we have no clue to the identity of the persons represented by the bones; exceptions do exist, including St Eanswythe whose leaden reliquary was discovered in the fabric of the chancel wall at Folkestone parish church in 1885 (Woodward, 1892). A surprising number of relic chambers still exist in churches, such as the little ground-level cupboard in the east wall, behind the altar, at Martock, Somerset, and doubtless many more have been masked by later alterations but could be revealed through archaeological investigation.

The excavation of graves

The most numerous features encountered during church excavations are graves, and the most prolific finds are bones, both *in situ* and disarticulated (see generally, Brothwell, 1963). The archaeologist has, therefore, to make up his mind, before he begins, how he intends to tackle the problem. And there is a problem, because it is easy to fall into one of the extreme traps mentioned on p. 146. Given the premise that all skeletal material must be recorded and collected, how is this to be done and still achieve the basic aims of the excavation, which will usually be both complex and wide-ranging? First, disarticulated bones, which may comprise 50 per cent of the total, can be collected as 'ordinary' finds, in their stratigraphical context, without detailed recording. The only exceptions, where planning and photography are worthwhile, are bones which seem to have been placed in some significant way in the backfill of a grave, under a foundation or, of course, in a relic pit.

The excavation and recording of whole and fragmentary skeletons poses difficulties which are greatly compounded when individual grave-cuts are not readily distinguishable as work proceeds. This is virtually always the case in long-used outdoor cemeteries: the detection of grave-cuts inside churches can be much easier. It is the outdoor problem which must be tackled in a realistic rather than idealistic manner, and a valuable paper on the subject by Birthe Kjolbye-Biddle (1975) focuses on the cathedral cemetery at Winchester. The various options and the methods adopted are fully discussed, drawing a clear distinction between those graves which were regarded as having a high academic importance and the rest. I have already outlined some of the problems of cemetery excavation in the previous chapter (pp. 134–5), and every excavator has to decide what information he can afford to collect and what he is prepared to sacrifice: to insist that everything will be dug 'properly' is to shirk responsibility (cf. Powlesland, 1980). There is no direct correlation between time taken and the quality of an excavation, and it is worth remembering that the more thoroughly a skeleton is cleaned, either in or out of the ground, the more potential pathological evidence is destroyed in the process. There is no merit in cleaning vast numbers of skeletons, either singly or in multiples, simply to take eye-catching photographs of them, although this regularly happens in cemetery excavations. I have sometimes seen several man-days spent on the excavation and recording of each skeleton, generally an unprofitable exercise. Such a laborious approach is justifiable when the excavation of the cemetery is the only target, and where the preservation of evidence of exceptional medical or other interest is assured. The cemetery at Raunds is perhaps a case in point, but the final results will need to be of unprecedented importance to justify the expenditure of eight man-days on an unaccompanied inhumation (Boddington, 1980).

Once the first glimpse of a skeleton has been seen it should take no more than an hour or two to clean the whole sufficiently well for every bone to be visible for planning, which can be done in an hour or less by an experienced person. For

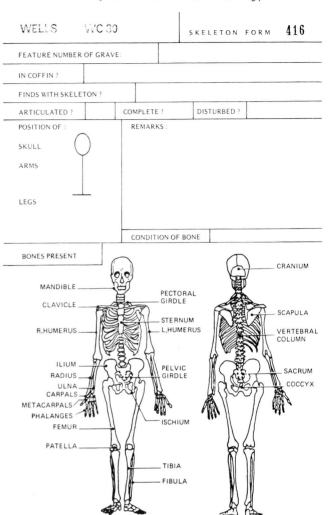

75 Skeleton recording form. Photocopies are made on A4-sized paper and used to record basic details of each skeleton; bones present are marked on the diagrams using a coloured pencil. A form should be completed for every articulated skeleton, however fragmentary, and each receives a serial *skeleton number*, while the grave is given a *feature number*. The skeleton and the grave are separate entities, and should never be conflated into a single *grave number*. Forms are prepared by being stamped with the site name and serial numbers for the skeletons. A self-advancing number-stamp is used to eliminate the problem of duplication or omission of numbers. *After Hirst, 1976*

most skeletons that is a perfectly adequate record of the bones in the ground. If the grave contains objects or coffin stains, or the skeleton exhibits a pathological deformity, or the body is in an unusual posture, more careful cleaning, wet sponging of the bones and photography may be required. The complete process can take up to one man-day. A representative selection of the various grave types and burial postures present on the site should be fully cleaned and photographically recorded.

The skeleton recording form (fig. 75) is a useful means of noting which bones are present and certain other basic details: it is in effect a simple check-list and is completed by the excavator at the time of lifting the skeleton. Using a coloured pencil, he simply shades those bones on the outline drawings which are present in the ground. Marginal notes can also be put on the form, indicating, for example, those bones which disintegrated whilst being lifted. If photographic resources are plentiful, it is possibly worth taking a record shot of each skeleton, or inter-cutting groups, before the bones are lifted; vertical photography is also, under rushed conditions, a substitute for planning skeletons in the field. A good photograph, equipped with locating points, can be used as a basis for planning skeletons after the excavation is completed; the method has its advantages and drawbacks. The greatest saving of time is however to be derived from having a resident palaeopathologist, who knows what is worth devoting effort to and what is not.

Most Christian burials are laid supine, with the head to the west, the legs together and the hands in one of the following positions: beside the pelvis, with the arms straight down; together over the pelvis; together over the abdomen; arms across the chest with each hand by the opposing elbow. Occasionally the hands may be found in an attitude of prayer or irregularly placed. In many cases it is impossible to ascertain the original positioning of the skull: if it faces directly towards the feet, or upwards from the grave, there is no doubt that burial took place with the head resting back in a natural manner. If, however, the skull is turned to one side there is every likelihood that it did so during decomposition. The same is plainly true when the skull has rolled westwards, away from the neck, and now rests on the cranial vault. The lower jaw frequently becomes detached at an early stage of decomposition; likewise, the spine may acquire twists and the legs may become detached from the pelvis and roll outwards, in opposite directions, towards the sides of the grave. Naturally, there is a greater facility for movement if the body is contained within a coffin.

It was an appreciation of the readily detachable nature of the skull that probably led to the making of coffins and graves with niches to contain the head (p. 147). Another method of countering the problem, found in middle and later Saxon cemeteries, in particular, was to place a large stone either side of the skull, inside the coffin, to form a pair of 'ear-muffs' (fig. 71A). Pieces of Roman brick and flat stones could be used as an alternative in uncoffined burials.

At one time it was considered a luxury to have a palaeopathologist (a person who specializes in the study of ancient bones for their medical interest) permanently on hand during the excavation of a cemetery, but it is now appreciated that so much information has been lost that it is a waste of effort to proceed without skilled assistance. Many pathological conditions can be spotted while the skeleton is being uncovered and the recording geared to deal adequately with those. The processes of excavation, washing and packing are so destructive that a skeleton which was of medical interest at the moment of its discovery may be devoid of that interest when it finally reaches the palaeopathologist. The variable state of bone preservation found in most cemeteries naturally leads to the loss of much basic osteological evidence, and many a long-bone which will fall to pieces when lifted from the ground is capable of fairly accurate measurement before it is taken up. The osteometric data need not be lost if a trained person is available to take measurements *in situ*.

Palaeopathology is a developing science: there is much more to the study of ancient cemeteries than merely 'counting heads' (so to speak) and listing ages and sexes. Nor is it just the earliest human remains which are of interest: it is more than doubly valuable to have a long sequence of burials for study, such as that found in the average church excavation which should be continuous from the later Saxon period to the mid-nineteenth century. This is the material from which demographic studies can be made, and the larger the sample the greater is its validity. To date, only a handful of large-scale cemetery excavations have taken place in England where, say, more than a thousand individuals are represented in the material recovered. St Helen-on-the-Walls, York, is the first to be published (Dawes and Magilton, 1980): Winchester and others will follow in due course; and there are about another 20 sites from which skeletal assemblages representing some hundreds of

76 Skull of a late eighteenth-century *post mortem* victim at Barton-on-Humber. A neat saw-cut enabled the vault of the skull to be lifted off for the examination or removal of the brain. Glue was used to re-unite the parts for a 'tidy' burial. *Photo: author. Crown copyright*

individuals have been recovered. The collection of disarticulated bones (p. 148) is important when they form part of a large assemblage of material: they make a considerable difference to the determination of minimum numbers of persons represented; they can sometimes be reunited with the graves from which they were originally derived; and they always add to the general picture of the pathology of the population under study.

At present, we simply do not know what there is to learn from ancient bones, from the point of view of both medical history and archaeology. Rheumatoid arthritis, for example, seems to be a fairly modern disease and its origins may be discovered through archaeology (not to be confused with osteo-arthritis, the commonest of diseases seen in skeletons of all periods). The criteria for assigning ages to skeletons (i.e. age at death) are hotly disputed, since the closing of cranial sutures is not as reliable a guide as was once thought; and claims have been made in recent years for the identification of blood groups in skeletons, but the results obtained, although superficially convincing, appear to be fallacious. New methods of research are certain to be evolved.

Bones recovered from reliquaries may exhibit special features of interest such as the marks of cutting and abrasion, which shed light on medieval liturgical practices concerned with the cult of relics (for an introduction to this complex subject, see Thomas, 1973). Remarkable features have been found in a detailed study of the relics of Anglo-Saxon bishops and others in Wells Cathedral. Two skulls had undergone trepanning operations, one *post mortem*; and another skull had had the *foramen magnum* (hole for the spinal cord) enlarged, apparently to facilitate mounting on a pole for procession or display. Evidence for surgery and anatomical explorations in the early modern period is forthcoming from post-medieval graves, such as one excavated at

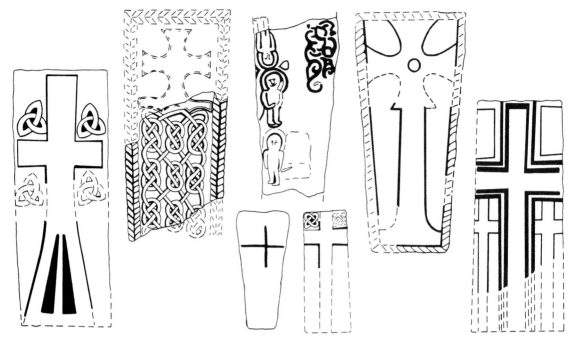

77 Late Saxon gravestones found during excavations by the Lincoln Archaeological Trust on the site of St Mark's Church, Lincoln. The larger slabs were used as horizontal tomb-covers and the small ones as upright grave-markers. *After Colyer, 1976*

Barton-on-Humber in 1980: the cranium had been sawn open to remove the brain, and the entire vertebral column, rib-cage and organs had been removed, leaving the torso as a 'skin bag' with attached arms and legs. In order to make the corpse appear presentable for the funeral, the crown of the skull was glued into position (the joints presumably being masked by the hair), a wooden stake was fitted between the neck and pelvis to replace the vertebral column, the torso was then stuffed, and presumably sewn up (fig. 76).

Monuments and tombstones

In contrast to the modest amount of research which has been undertaken on churchyards in general, and on burials, a great deal of work has been done, relatively speaking, on tombs and monuments of most kinds. They are visually pleasing, easily accessible and have an infinite attraction for the curious. Genealogists have long been interested in collecting data from monuments for the pursuit of family history studies and the recording of inscriptions goes back to Leland's time. For the literary-minded the pursuit of epitaphs has become a popular

study (e.g. Lindley, 1965), for the humorist there is plenty of scope (e.g. Spiegl, 1971), and for the brass-rubber there is a limited stock of precious monuments to be worn away by repeated interference. But the study of a churchyard and its monuments, as a total unit, has received scant attention, and the only work of substance to broach the subject is *English Churchyard Memorials* (Burgess, 1963), also the best introduction to the history of tombstones.

No great volume of memorial sculpture has survived from the early Christian Saxon period, and what has is both fragmentary and mostly displaced from its original locations; but in aggregate, the extant sculpture, memorial and architectural, of the seventh to ninth centuries, particularly from midland and northern England, is an important body of art-historical data (see generally, Baldwin Brown, 1937; Cramp, 1977b; Lang, 1978; Bailey, 1980). Although there is considerable doubt about which pieces are of sepulchral origin, a sculpture such as the 'Hedda stone' in Peterborough Cathedral is most plausibly interpreted as the house-shaped cover or a reliquary. New discoveries of early sculpture, including re-used Roman stones, are occasionally made during church investigations.

Discoveries of new material assignable to the later Saxon and Anglo-Scandinavian periods (ninth to eleventh centuries) are more frequent, with the bulk of the sculpture certainly being of funerary origin. Excavations at St Mark's, Lincoln, at Raunds and elsewhere have brought to light some remarkable headstones and flat tomb covers (fig. 77). Some have been recovered from their original locations, so that it is possible to discover the age, sex and perhaps other details of those who were considered important enough to merit tombstones in an era when permanent markers were not the norm. Grave covers, both plain and decorated, could be placed over an uncoffined body, and conversely stone-lined graves did not always have a marker. In the Saxon cathedral cemetery at Wells heavy stone blocks were found beside two graves, and were probably the bases for small standing crosses. Many burials, from earliest times to the present day, were unmarked other than by the low earth mound over the grave, which normally disappears within about a century. A wooden marker, in the form of an upright board or a cross, has also been used in Christian cemeteries from the Saxon period onwards: the sockets for these are sometimes found in excavation. Despite the general ubiquity of stone memorials in the nineteenth century, wooden 'headboard markers' were used in some parts of England, and a few still survive, although seriously decayed. They are most numerous in Surrey (e.g. at Burstow), a county which lacks good building stone, but they are also to be found in areas of limestone like Somerset. Curiously, the 'headboard' is not placed at the head-end of the grave, but is a longitudinal structure supported on a post at either end; the inscription was usually painted on one or both sides of the board, but virtually all have now been lost through weathering.

Stone monuments of the Dark Age and early medieval periods seldom bear inscriptions, except in parts of western Britain, where some very early inscribed stones have actually survived *in situ*, especially in Cornwall. Pre-Norman stone sculptures, funerary and otherwise, deserve the closest scrutiny and full recording because it is clear, for example, that original paint can survive on Anglo-Saxon tombstones which have been buried for most of their history. Techniques of stone cutting and tooling can also be studied on unweathered sculpture. The traditional art-historical approach to the publication of early sculpture through the means of mediocre photographs needs reconsideration since it is patently

obvious that the finer points of detail are being overlooked. The superb line drawings produced by Victorian antiquaries, in which every nuance of the stone's surface was represented by careful shading, were more informative than a single photograph can ever be. A complex, irregular design can change its form dramatically under different lighting conditions, thus affecting the interpretation. The stone needs, therefore, to be illuminated artificially from many different angles in turn, for drawing and photography.

While this treatment is simple to apply to loose stones whose indoor study can be organized at leisure, it is no less essential for the same recording technique to be extended to sculptured stones in fixed locations, both indoors and outdoors. Slabs of all dates set in church floors are often badly worn and flaked, are impossible to 'rub' properly and are never illuminated adequately by natural light or the available artificial lighting. The installation of movable photo-flood lights seldom fails to reveal unsuspected detail, as well as making photography a worthwhile proposition. Outdoor study of weathered monuments is more difficult, but often more essential because the progress of natural decay cannot be halted. Oblique sunlight may provide perfect illumination for photography, especially of post-medieval gravestones which are clear of obstructions (p. 103), but otherwise artificial lighting for night photography is the only satisfactory means of recording. Owing to the difficulties of arranging outdoor artificial lighting—they appear greater than they really are—few of our most important pre-Norman and Norman sculptures (particularly cross-shafts) have been well recorded, yet they continue to decay before our eyes. Take the Anglo-Saxon circular shaft at Masham, Yorks., for instance; it is steadily being eroded away, but a thorough record of what remains could be made in one evening with a minimum of equipment (fig. 78). If each of the arcaded panels were illuminated in turn, from different angles (left, right and top), a comprehensive set of photographs, about 75 in all, could be assembled and with the aid of these the best possible drawing of the entire decoration assembled.

Mercifully, the majority of medieval tombs and grave covers are inside churches, and those which are not should be moved in when the opportunity arises, after full recording of

78 Masham, Yorks., the Anglo-Saxon cross-shaft
Left Drawing of the shaft in the eighteenth century,
when only three of the 'drums' were visible above the
ground, illustrating the extent to which the level of the
graveyard had risen through many centuries of burial.
After Gough, 1789
Right The shaft as now seen, after being raised and
remounted in the last century. The lowest 'drum' is now
visible and bears a different kind of decoration from the
others. The whole monument is in an advanced state of
deterioration and has never been adequately recorded.
Photo: author

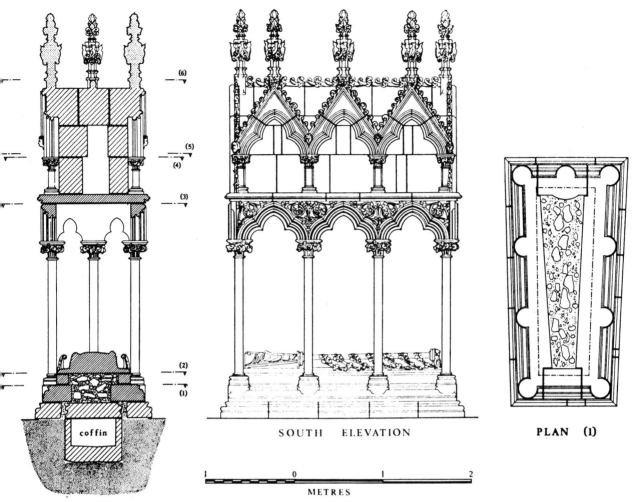

SOUTH   ELEVATION

PLAN   (1)

METRES

79 Examples of some of the measured drawings which were prepared during the restoration of this thirteenth-century tomb at York. Note that plans were made at five separate levels. *After Ramm, 1971*

course. There are three agents of destruction, however, which prevail, singly or in combination, on most medieval monuments: erosion through being walked upon or scuffed by passers-by; exfoliation and disintegration brought about by rising or penetrating dampness; and general wear, tear and mutilation inflicted by visitors, brass rubbers, church cleaners and bored choir boys. All pre-Reformation monuments should be recorded in a comprehensive archaeological manner: brasses, indents, incised slabs, coffin lids, altar tombs, canopied tombs, effigies and inscriptions. It is surprising how many components there can be in an elaborate tomb: some may be re-used or adapted from other

monuments, the whole tomb may have been shifted or rebuilt, and there may be evidence for one or more application of painted decoration. If a tomb is being dismantled for repair and 'restoration', as not a few are every year, the opportunity can be taken to prepare a full set of architectural drawings, and a good example of this kind of recording was carried out on the canopied tomb of Archbishop de Gray (1255) at York, (fig. 79; Ramm, 1971).

All the forms of recording which are used on the architecture of a church—plans, sections, elevations, moulding profiles, photographs and rubbings—may be applied, as appropriate, to monuments. Indeed, some aspects of the recording may have been adequately covered by past enthusiasts of monumental art who prepared illustrations to a quality which cannot realistically be achieved today (e.g. Hodges, 1888 and Chancellor, 1890). Caution is necessary, however, since many aesthetically pleasing drawings are far from technically correct. There is only one class of funerary monument which enjoys the distinction of being well recorded, and that is the incised brass. Through the efforts of the Monumental Brass Society extensive, although not yet fully comprehensive, records have been made county by county of brasses and their indents. This is just as well, since the mania for rubbing, and worse still, for polishing ancient brasses will cause the virtual destruction of some, even before the end of this century.

Post-Reformation wall and free-standing monuments survive in churches in large numbers: many are exquisite, idiosyncratic and highly coloured, being true works of art rather than architecturally derived sculptures. By contrast with most other forms of church recording, photography plays the most important role here, and a set of good photographs (obviously in colour if polychrome is present) will form as comprehensive a record as can realistically be expected. A full drawn record can be produced in the usual way, but this must be regarded as a luxury at a time when too few monuments even enjoy basic photographic coverage. Once again, agents of destruction are ubiquitous and underline the need for recording: concealed iron cramps rust and burst the stone; dampness, dirt and sunlight destroy the paint; and the failure of the gypsum which held small applied parts is causing these to fall to the ground and be smashed beyond recovery. Many a wall plaque is now denuded of its rosettes, swags, cherubs and angels.

Finally, we come to the commonest of memorials—the churchyard tombstone. Very few survive from before the seventeenth century, and the average parish churchyard is only likely to contain one or two ante-dating the early eighteenth century. It was then that the sculptured headstone enjoyed its floruit, at first crude but powerful, becoming more refined and skilful in execution as the century progressed. Then, throughout the nineteenth century the art of monumental masonry steadily declined and was defunct before the First World War. In recent years there has been an upsurge of interest in recording monuments, largely owing to the wholesale destruction of graveyards by parochial church councils and local authorities who are ignorant of the immense body of historical data contained in them; on the general importance and management of churchyards,

see Stapleton and Burman, 1976. There are three broad categories of information recoverable from monuments. First, there are the genealogical, demographic and historical data contained in the inscription; secondly, the art historical and iconographical evidence provided by the design and decoration of the monument as a whole; and thirdly, the 'hidden' archaeological and medical data, which are so often overlooked.

The recording of churchyards began, as an antiquarian pastime, of the Victorian era. Most such records were far from complete, and at the lowest level might simply comprise lists of names and dates. Sometimes interesting inscriptions were copied in full. Very exceptionally a thorough record was compiled, such as that made by the Vicar of Scotton, Lincs., in the middle of the last century: his notebook contains full transcriptions and drawings of tombstones. In the present century the Society of Genealogists has fostered the accurate recording of inscriptions in churchyards, both threatened and un-threatened, and there has been a general realization that irreplaceable evidence is disappearing year by year through the processes of natural decay. York stone, for example, a material much used for monuments in north-east England, is liable to laminate through frost action and to perforate through wind erosion: a complete inscription may fall away from a headstone in a single winter.

The years 1976–7 were notable for the publication of three separate guides to the study of churchyard monuments. The pamphlet issued by the Essex Society for Family History (Rayment, 1977) only caters for the recording of genealogical data contained on tombstones, and does not cover the proper recording of a churchyard or its monuments. The booklet published by the Society of Genealogists (White, 1977) is a good general introduction to churchyard monuments, and discussion of some aspects of their study; it is however defective in matters of basic archaeological importance, such as planning and the full recording of monuments. For those who are interested in pursuing genealogical studies this is required reading, together with the third booklet which is published by the Council for British Archaeology (Jones, 1976; 1979). Here the procedure for making a satisfactory record of a graveyard and its contents is set out, based on sound archaeological principles. A standard

GRAVE MEMORIAL RECORDING FORM

CEMETERY or GRAVEYARD
DEDICATION or DENOMINATION
NAT. GRID REF.
DATE of RECORD
NAME of RECORDER or GROUP
MEMORIAL No. and LETTER
No. of COMPONENTS
ASSOCIATED FORM LETTERS
Memorial type: 1. flat 2. head 3. tomb 4. foot 5. other
MATERIAL and GEOLOGY
STONE MASON or UNDERTAKER
Which faces are inscribed? – compass points
No. of people commemorated
TECHNIQUE of INSCRIPTION
Condition of monument: 1. sound, in situ   2. sound, displaced
3 leaning or falling apart   4. collapsed   5. overgrown
Condition of inscription: 1. mint 2. clear but worn
3. mainly decipherable 4. traces 5. illegible or destroyed

DIMENSIONS   Height
(in mms.)   Width
                    Thickness

PHOTOGRAPH NEGATIVE No.

ORIENTATION   which way
                                               stone faces

PHOTOGRAPH	INSCRIPTION

REMARKS

80 Recording form for graveyard memorials developed by the Council for British Archaeology, available on ready-printed cards of A5-size. The two sides of the form are shown together here. One card is completed for each inscribed tombstone; the system can also be used for indoor memorials. *After Council for British Archaeology*

recording form for monuments, well tried and tested, accompanies the booklet and should be adopted by all graveyard recorders (fig. 80).

The fundamental principle is that the graveyard is a unit, of which an accurate plan is essential (see also p. 131). Within the graveyard are sub-units—the tombs—and each may in turn be composed of several parts: the architectural assemblage, the inscription, art and iconography. Monuments were grouped and oriented meaningfully, even if subconsciously, by their makers giving significance to their inter-relationships. Last, and by no means least, it must be remembered that the corporeal remains of the persons named on a monument lie in the soil beneath it: those

skeletons are therefore named, dated, aged and sexed. They are prime material for future medical and archaeological research, and if monuments are cleared away or permitted to decay without recording their precise original positions the data are all lost. At the time of recording a monument there will probably be not the slightest intention of excavating the remains below it, but in years to come a new parish hall may be built on this spot, the church may be declared redundant or destroyed by some disaster, the churchyard may be sold as a building site for redevelopment. When that happens it is too late to think about recording: a departmental store now stands on the site of St Nicholas' Church, Colchester, where the building contractors used a mechanical excavator 'to pull out the earth, together with foundations, tombs and coffins, just as they came, and made a complete upheaval in which it was almost impossible to recognize what one knew to be there, let alone discover something new' (Hull, 1960).

Under any of the circumstances mentioned above archaeological excavation may take place and if proper recording did not precede destruction, history and medical science will be needlessly deprived of valuable evidence. That has already happened from time to time. At Barton-on-Humber the first spate of churchyard clearance went unrecorded, and the second in 1966 comprised only a list of inscriptions and a sketch plan; the excavation cannot now be meshed with the record. How valuable, for instance, it would have been to have written data on the eighteenth-century *post mortem* (p. 160).

Once a graveyard has been fully recorded, the data are susceptible of numerous forms of analysis, based on family and social groupings, tomb types, orientations, periods of burial in particular areas, and the evolution of iconography and art forms (fig. 81). It is to facilitate these last lines of research that at least one photograph should be taken of every monument prior to 1900. Only for selected stones is it usually feasible to take several photographs, make rubbings and prepare scaled drawings. Wherever they survive, special attention should be paid to tomb railings, especially those before c. 1860, and a good record made. Before the Second World War, England was described as 'a land of railings', but they have since nearly all gone, and those that were spared in the 1940s are now being torn

EARLIEST

DATES SHOWN

ON GRAVESTONES

⊠	ILLEGIBLE
☐	1650 1699
▭	1700 1749
◧	1750 1799
◨	1800 1849
◨	1850 1899
■	1900 ONWARDS

81 Analytical plan of a Welsh Churchyard (Llangar), to show the development of the post-medieval cemetery as evidenced by extant tombstones. The earliest graves are packed closely around the church, particularly on the south side. The alignments of graves near boundaries have been deflected by these. *After Ron Shoesmith, and Jones, 1976*

up or allowed to rot away. Railings are part of the industrial archaeology of churchyards.

It is not an awesome task to record adequately the average churchyard, although comparatively few have so far been completed. There are, unfortunately, some hundreds of churchyards which are claimed to have been recorded, but for which only the genealogical component of the record has been compiled. The would-be recorder should check carefully to ascertain exactly how thorough any previous work has been and, if appropriate, take up the project at the point where the last person abandoned it.

10 Synthesis and Publication: Reconstructing History

Safeguarding the record

The product of any archaeological investigation is the accumulation of information which must be ordered sensibly and interpreted in terms of history. If, at the end of the day, new facts have not been learned about the history of the church, its siting or use, then either the investigation was inconsequential or the interpretation has been at fault. The mindless collection of disparate data is not an end in itself and satisfies nobody, except, possibly, the collector. Furthermore, if the evidence collected is not made permanently available for future reference by researchers it is wholly wasted. Thus the person who surveys a graveyard and keeps the records at home has not only failed to preserve the information in a usable form but has probably done a positive disservice to scholarship by discouraging others from re-recording what he is already believed to have done; likewise, the archaeologist who excavates or records the fabric of a church and does not publish his findings, and the local historian who gathers a wealth of information from written and unwritten sources but never divulges it. Every year, too, thousands of photographs are taken of churches and their fittings, yet not a fraction of one per cent of this effort is preserved in a permanent form.

Obviously, there is no reason why snapshots of weddings and funerals should all become part of the national archive, but there is equally no reason why the invaluable efforts of so many amateur historians and photographers should be utterly wasted. Even worse are those innumerable instances where local enthusiasts set out with the specific intention of recording some discovery, event or evidence which is only available for a brief period. Time and again the people involved use the word 'record', but never stop to think what will have happened to that record a few years or decades hence. In nine cases out of ten it will be lost, destroyed or meaningless within a generation. How much more personal satisfaction there is to be gained through the knowledge that one's efforts, however humble, will be preserved beyond one's own lifetime and will be of value to future generations. When Thomas Phillips climbed the wooden scaffolding at Wells in 1870, struggling with a great brass and mahogany camera, wooden tripod and suitcase of glass slides, to photograph statues which no man had seen at close range for centuries he could have had no idea that his record would play a vital role in a multi-million pound restoration project one hundred years later. By chance, most of his glass plates survived and were looked after, being presented to the cathedral in 1980 by one of Phillips' descendants. By contrast, Messrs. Dawkes and Partridge, also photographers in Wells, recorded the restoration of 1924, but when they died their negatives were dispersed or destroyed and with them an important chapter in the history of Wells Cathedral was lost beyond recall.

Another example, based on the small rural parish of Rivenhall in Essex, is worthy of note, because it is so typical of the way in which local studies can be advanced from scraps of incidental information. When excavations and architectural recording began in 1971 effectively nothing was known of the history of the church fabric, except that it was supposedly 'rebuilt' in 1838–9, and at the same time acquired the finest collection of Norman-French glass in England. Not a single illustration or photograph of the church prior to 1900 was known, nor was the name of the architect responsible for the rebuilding. After two years of investigation it was clear that the site had a long and complex history, and that the Anglo-Saxon church was substantially intact behind a mantle of nineteenth-century stucco (p. 85). How could this be? The historical evidence seemed clear enough: an elaborate brass plaque inside the church recorded the work of 1838–9, announcing that 'Baron Western ... raised this church at his own expense, from a rude and unseemly structure'.

Contemporary newspaper accounts confirmed the 'rebuild'. Archaeology demonstrated how grossly the historical record was distorted: this is a common phenomenon, at all periods.

After a five-year search for material relating to the pre-1838 appearance of Rivenhall church a breakthrough was made. In 1830 the Reverend B. D. Hawkins became Assistant Curate and shortly afterwards began to compile notes on the church and parish. He collected oddmenta of various kinds, including pencil sketches, ink drawings and water colours of buildings and features in the parish, mainly the handiwork of local girls. He also acquired some architects' sketches. His material was assembled into two volumes which he called 'The Annals of Rivenhall': volume one concerned the church and parish, volume two the medieval glass. In 1976 volume one was discovered by chance in a library, uncatalogued and unknown to anybody. The volume contained a superb collection of illustrations of the church in the 1830s, and others post-dating the 'restoration': the medieval and Georgian alterations to the Saxon building were all plainly recorded, together with internal furnishings long since destroyed. Further lines of enquiry yielded other valuable information, including the identity of the architect who designed the mantle of stucco which had deceived modern scholars. He was John Adey Repton, son of the noted landscape architect (fig. 82). One line of enquiry led to another, and soon it was found that Repton had himself been involved in recording archaeological discoveries, not at the church, unfortunately, but elsewhere in the parish: new light was thus shed on other research problems.

A letter with Hawkins' 'Annals' shows how the volume was given to a local antiquary by a descendant and somehow it passed to the library. Its survival and rediscovery were the most fortunate of coincidences, having a fundamental role to play in reconstructing the history of Rivenhall parish and church. But that is only half the story, the rest is in volume two, and that is missing. It was kept by the family and is now lost: it would have told us how Hawkins lighted upon his rich haul of Norman glass, acquired it from the French authorities, shipped it to England and installed it at Rivenhall.

The lesson to be learned from these and countless other examples is clear: the deposition of all records in a place of permanent safety and the publication of a synthesized account of the project, however large or small, are fundamental. First, let us look at the records. Notes, drawings, rubbings, photographs, they are all documents, and their long-term preservation can only be assured if they are stored under archival conditions. Two bodies are equipped to do this: the County Records Office (which normally incorporates all the church records for the area), and the National Monuments Record (NMR) in London. The original records should be deposited with one of these bodies, and a copy with the other; generally it is best to keep the original in the county. The person who made the record can, of course, keep a copy for himself, so that everyone's interests should be satisfied. While many records offices have facilities for micro-filming documents which are loaned to them, they cannot always cope with archaeological and architectural records, but the National Monuments Record can. When originally set up, under the title of National Buildings Record (NBR), this body only collected photographs and architectural drawings, but in recent years the service has expanded to include all kinds of archaeological records, a fact of which some researchers may not be aware. There are three sections in the NMR: Buildings, Archaeology and Air Photography.

It is perhaps worth pointing out that the church archaeologist or recorder can deposit a full copy of his material with the NMR without cost to himself. All records can be microfilmed and returned to the owner at no charge; and the NMR has the finest facilities available for making photographic prints from negatives (a computer scanner gives each part of the negative the correct exposure). When a photographic negative is loaned to the NMR a print is made for the national archive and the negative returned to the owner, who still retains his copyright. As a further incentive for the deposition of photographs in the archive, the NMR may be able to provide the photographer with a

82 Rivenhall, Essex: changes wrought through 'restoration'
A (*upper*) 1835 pencil drawing, showing medieval windows, buttresses and porch set in Saxon walls, and tower of 1717. Note temporary fence to keep sheep off fresh grave mounds in foreground.
B (*lower*) 1841 grey-wash drawing by J. A. Repton who had just completed the 'restoration'. The whole of the early church and the Georgian tower are encapsulated in this. *Photos: John Mead, courtesy of Essex Archaeological Society*

selection of first-rate prints from his own negatives, at no charge. The copyright of all records, photographic or otherwise, remains with the person who made or commissioned them unless he assigns it elsewhere. The National Monuments Record and County Records Offices are always meticulous in their respect for the ownership of copyright.

I would therefore urge all those who have made photographic, architectural or other records of churches, churchyards, monuments and fittings to contact the County Records Office and National Monuments Record (addresses p. 182). Under the terms of the *Parochial Records and Registers Measure 1978* the deposition of most church records in the relevant County Records Office is being arranged, so that it is entirely appropriate for copies of historical and archaeological researches to be deposited in the same place.

Objects or samples derived from excavations and structural investigation are a different matter and should, with very few exceptions, be deposited in an appropriate museum, and never left lying around in the church or the vicarage shed. It would be easy to list some of the losses of important archaeological material from specific churches through carelessness, ignorance and theft: sculpture, glass, medieval tiles, pottery and metal objects, and so on. Once the initial wave of interest generated by a new discovery has passed, the object is vulnerable. Churches are not museums, and, as a general rule, antiquities which are not physically attached to the building should not be kept in them. If it is desired to exhibit a piece of ancient sculpture, for example, it should be properly mounted and fixed, never stood on a window sill or left on the floor up a corner. When depositing objects in a museum a copy of the relevant documentation should always be included with them: archaeological finds must not be divorced from the records relating to their discovery. It should, however, be noted that very few museums are equipped for the proper storage of archival material, just as record offices are not equipped to store objects. A sensible division of the material must be made, with copies as appropriate. The private custody of archaeological material is always to be discouraged.

Analysis and synthesis

While recording or excavation is in progress the archaeologist is thinking constantly about the evidence before him, and its interpretation. On-the-spot preliminary analysis is essential to a proper understanding of any building or site, so that questions can be thrown up and answers sought as work proceeds. Anyone who believes that he can excavate a site or record a building, while leaving interpretation until later, is certain to overlook a great deal of evidence. This is not so serious when studying something which can be re-examined in the future, but if the primary evidence is to be destroyed through demolition, restoration or excavation there is only one opportunity to record it. Equally, no investigation should begin with an anticipated result in mind, or simply with a series of questions to be answered: such approaches inevitably lead to a compression and distortion of the evidence. It is an open and receptive mind which is required, not a pre-conditioned or an empty one.

The process of analysis, initially on site and later at home or in the office with the records, must involve a thorough dissection of the evidence into all its component parts. Ideally, with the investigation of a wall one would consider the relationship of every stone to its neighbours, but in practice it is only feasible to study groups of stones, each making up a 'lift', a patch, an insertion or one man-day's work. No wall is a simple entity, and if its history is to be correctly deciphered, then the minutiae of its construction must first be understood. Similarly, the development of a cemetery is such a complex process that not only must the graves be found, but the subtleties of their inter-relationships must also be worked out. It is not just a matter of stratigraphical sequences, although these are naturally fundamental: relationships can best be expressed graphically by means of a simple matrix diagram (figs 65, 83). Such a diagram should enable the researcher to determine the number of generations of burial in a cemetery and to understand something of its lateral development, even when there are gaps in the securely stratified sequences.

Again, it is worth stressing the fundamental rule that nothing should be assumed when analysing structures (p. 58) and although there is an obvious danger that too many structural phases may be claimed for a building, this is better than too few. It is simple enough to equate and combine pieces of evidence one with another but it is an altogether more difficult

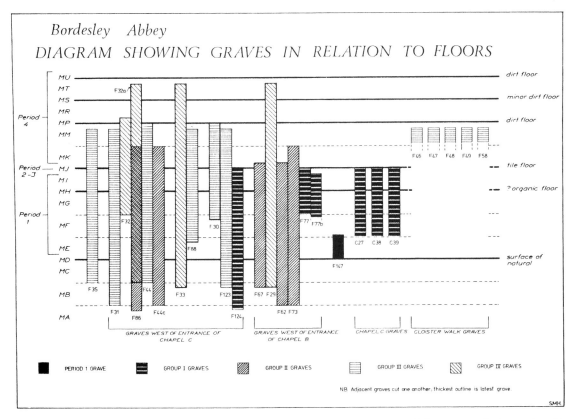

83 Diagram to illustrate the comparative depths of graves in relation to floor levels. It is possible at a glance to determine which graves are sealed by which floors. Note the tendency for the earliest graves to be the shallowest, with progressively deeper burial following in later periods. A depth chart and matrix diagram (fig. 65) are essential for a proper understanding of excavated graves and their relationships, both to one another and to the rest of the site. *After Rahtz and Hirst, 1976*

problem to separate them. In general, there can be no doubt that archaeological and historical interpretations are massively over-simplified, especially by those who favour the 'economy of hypothesis' approach. The true complexities of historical evidence can best be seen and tested through the study of those standing buildings which remain living entities (like most churches) and whose archaeology is visibly being created in our own times.

A wide range of analytical techniques and scientific studies can be applied in church archaeology but they cannot be discussed at length here, and the needs will differ greatly between one project and another. At the simplest level, a survey project on a small church could be undertaken by two or three people with little external assistance. A fairly thorough structural study might be accom-

plished by a team of six, some of whom should possess specialist skills. If an excavation of any importance is to take place, a team of twenty or more will be required, as will access to all the specialist skills shown on the organization diagram (fig. 3). In cases where exceptional conditions result in the preservation of uncommon classes of evidence (e.g. seeds from stomach contents or human parasite eggs in graves) additional specialist assistance will need to be enlisted, as appropriate. In general, the wider the range of expertise which can be brought to bear on the material, the more will be learnt from it.

Perhaps the most difficult question facing the church archaeologist is, where do we stop? This applies both to the collection of evidence and to its analysis. Since churches are such rich stores of historical evidence, and since so much of it is unstudied or under-studied, it is easy to let a minor investigation develop into a major project, which does not always earn the undying gratitude of those who have to endure the disruptions and other consequences! But when a full and thorough investigation is possible, and the co-ordinating archaeologist has the aptitude to pursue numerous diverse lines of

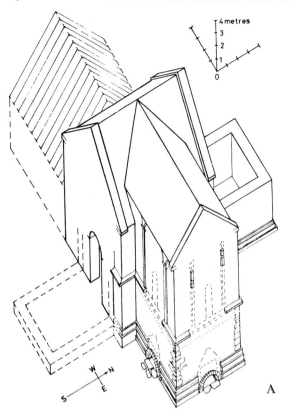

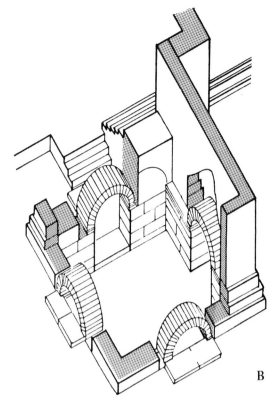

A

B

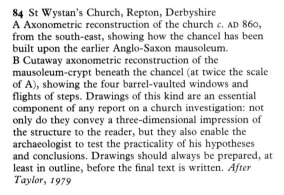

84 St Wystan's Church, Repton, Derbyshire
A Axonometric reconstruction of the church *c.* AD 860, from the south-east, showing how the chancel has been built upon the earlier Anglo-Saxon mausoleum.
B Cutaway axonometric reconstruction of the mausoleum-crypt beneath the chancel (at twice the scale of A), showing the four barrel-vaulted windows and flights of steps. Drawings of this kind are an essential component of any report on a church investigation: not only do they convey a three-dimensional impression of the structure to the reader, but they also enable the archaeologist to test the practicality of his hypotheses and conclusions. Drawings should always be prepared, at least in outline, before the final text is written. *After Taylor, 1979*

enquiry, the results can be extraordinarily rewarding. In so many branches of archaeological study analysis and synthesis of structural remains lead only to the production of a series of 'phase plans', possibly accompanied by hypothetical and very schematic reconstructions, and some general comments on the possible use of various dissociated items found in excavation. A different order of synthesis is possible in church archaeology: reconstruction can be far more detailed and soundly based; nor need it be limited solely to the physical attributes of a

church: liturgical and sociological reconstructions are an integral part of synthesis.

A full appreciation of a church, as a building, can best be achieved by preparing three-dimensional drawings and scale models, so that relationships between evidence recorded in plan and elevation can be seen in context (fig. 84). Liturgy, use and patterns of human movement can be studied to a certain extent through the disposition of furnishings, flooring materials, graves and wear patterns in a church; outside in the churchyard, paths, entrances, buildings, trees, crosses, clusters of graves and grave-free areas all contribute to similar lines of enquiry.

Much progress can often be made towards the reconstruction of a church's internal appearance through the study of decorative materials, of which there are three main categories: flooring, wall covering and windows. In some important medieval churches comprehensive schemes of decoration within one or more cells of the building, such as chapels, were probably implemented, with the result that glazed floor tiles, wall paintings and patterned glass might be conceived as an ensemble. Thus the arms of the family who built a chapel or were the patrons of the living might appear in all three components of the decoration. Window glass, in particular, can sometimes contribute vital links between the upstanding and excavated evidence. Much of the glass which is found during excavation in or around a church is likely to be more or less in the position where it fell when the window was broken. Thus the study of concentrations of excavated glass fragments should not be undertaken in isolation, but should be related to the extant windows and the glazing of the church (fig. 85). Unfortunately, though, it is often found that medieval glass which has long been buried in the ground has decayed disastrously.

Glass studies, even in relation to a simple parish church can be both unexpectedly complicated and rewarding. Once again Rivenhall provides an example of how complex the synthesis can become when all the evidence is taken into account. In terms of location, the glass falls into three groups: first, that which is leaded into windows; secondly, that which was blasted out in 1941 by a parachute mine; and thirdly, fragments recovered during excavation. Upon close examination, it was discovered that all three groups contained inter-related mixtures of material. Thus in group one we have French glass of the twelfth, thirteenth, fifteenth and sixteenth centuries; English glass of the thirteenth, fifteenth, seventeenth and nineteenth centuries; and Flemish roundels of the sixteenth century. Group two comprises English medieval and post-medieval glass and was recovered variously from the excavations, the rectory and a shed in a private garden. Group three, the excavated glass, has a similar composition to group two. Fragments deriving from the same windows or decorative schemes can be matched between all three groups; add to this the fact that in group one some medieval glass is in its original position and some was moved in 1840, when the French and Flemish glass was imported and, finally, everything was re-arranged again in 1948. The study of the Rivenhall glass was almost an archaeological project in its own right, but once the history of the church's glazing had been established, closer dating of certain architectural features and archaeological deposits was achieved than would otherwise have been possible.

When synthesizing the evidence from a church investigation it is advisable to scour the locality for material which has strayed from the

85 Fragments of fourteenth-century painted window glass recovered during the excavation of late medieval floor levels beneath the window from which they must have fallen. This window depicted the Virgin and Child against a latticed background, interspersed with oak leaves. These and other excavated glass fragments provide the sole evidence for the medieval glazing of the north aisle at Barton-on-Humber. *Photo: author. Crown copyright*

churchyard. Start with the vicarage or rectory, where stained glass may be found in its windows, medieval masonry on its garden rockeries, tombstones on the paths, sculptures and small objects on the mantelpieces, larger objects in the shed, garage and attic. Other items of former church fabric or property will almost certainly turn up elsewhere in the locality, and sometimes farther afield. A fine medieval timber screen from St John's, Glastonbury, was recovered in fragments from the demolition of nearby cottages; sections of the great Norman cross-shaft at Castle Hedingham, Essex, continue to be found in unlikely places (one piece served as a ceiling support in the cellar of a public house); Rivenhall's medieval font was discovered in a garden, where it had done duty as a birdbath for a century (fig. 86); and pieces of the galleries

86 A fourteenth-century font rediscovered in a garden where it has served as a bird-bath for over 100 years. *Photo: author*

which were torn out of Beverley Minster in 1824 are to be found in local buildings, while further parts were recently discovered in a house some fifteen miles distant, across the Humber.

Documenting the arrival of extraneous material in a church is as important as tracing dispersed objects. It is not an easy task, especially for pre-Victorian introductions. It is often claimed that furnishings and even major architectural elements, such as roofs and doorways (p. 46), were acquired by parishes at the Dissolution of the monasteries; few examples are authenticated, but careful research might confirm or deny many other claims. It has recently been suggested that the font at St Martin's, Canterbury, might be made from a Norman wellhead formerly at Christ Church Priory (Tatton-Brown, 1980); while the font at Little Baddow, Essex, has for its basin the largest medieval stone mortar (mixing bowl) in England. Churches have been used as repositories of antiquities in the past and have been the recipients of innumerable gifts of secular furnishings, particularly in the seventeenth and eighteenth centuries. Many of these additions have now become part and parcel of the fabric and furnishings of the church, and as such they merit study and record.

The archaeological evidence and all the associated studies which spring from it or contribute to it constitute the first rank of material for the physical study of churches. The second-level material is the drawn and written evidence, both in manuscript and published forms. It is not within the scope of this book to enlarge upon those sources, which has in any case been done amply by other writers (e.g. Pantin, 1958; Molesworth Roberts, 1970; Owen, 1966; 1970; 1975;1976; Butler, 1976). It is of the utmost importance to distinguish between primary records which relate to the contemporary fabric of the church and secondary records, which are generally opinions expressed about the building sometimes after the period to which they refer. It may be helpful to conclude this section with some cautionary comments regarding the use of documentary sources; most publications on the use of documents in church and local history present only the positive side of the subject and do not make it adequately clear that there can be, and often are, yawning gaps between the various types of evidence. Dr John Harvey summarized the situation neatly: 'The evidence drawn from documents and that from the fabric itself must, in any given case, be compatible. Faced with apparent inconsistency between structure and writings, historians commonly emphasize the documentary records and reserve to them alone the description of 'evidence'; while the architect or the field archaeologist may be tempted to fly to the opposite extreme, looking at the physical remains without adequate appraisal of the writings.' He continues, 'As a valid general proposition it must be accepted that structural evidence has primacy over written record; but this applies only when there is a clear clash of epochs. In such cases the discrepancy has to be resolved by rejection of the chronicle as manifestly referring to another (usually earlier) work now lost' (Colchester and Harvey, 1974, 200–1). The same problems had been discussed by Francis Bond, seventy years earlier (Bond, 1898), and the basic principle had been enunciated in the very early days of church

archaeology: 'As to evidence drawn from record only . . . that is of itself insufficient; for although it affords undoubted proof that at the period mentioned a building of some kind then was in existence at that spot, yet it is no proof, nor does it affect to be so, that what remains now is the same' (Simpson, 1828).

Despite these clear warnings, generations of scholars have succumbed to the irresistible urge to equate documented evidence with extant physical remains, and thereby to provide secure 'dates' for buildings when no such deduction is admissible. Anglo-Saxon archaeology has been especially troubled by spurious dating, and St Laurence's Chapel, Bradford-on-Avon, is a classic (Taylor, 1973b, 152). Another, is the very interesting case of the date of building Wells Cathedral, in relation to the rebuilding of Glastonbury Abbey after the fire of 1184. In a famous pair of papers Dr Armitage Robinson and Dr John Bilson argued out the discrepancies between the supposed historical and architectural 'dates' for the commencement of work at Wells (Robinson, 1928; Bilson, 1928). Half a century later the old evidence on both sides was re-assessed, and some new observations added, with encouraging results for the reunion of historical and architectural dating (Colchester and Harvey, 1974).

Scholars who work regularly with ancient records are familiar with those almost routine distortions of the evidence which can cause so much trouble for the unwary: the omission of a church from the Domesday Survey is no evidence against its existence; statements about the 'foundation' of monasteries and churches in the Anglo-Saxon period can seldom be accepted unquestioningly at face value, since 're-foundation' is often meant; the terms 'building' and 'rebuilding', applied to churches of all ages, are often falsely used when 'rebuilding' and 'refurbishing' are respectively meant. In the last century the word 'restoration' was commonly used as a pseudonym for 'virtual rebuilding'. In such cases the writer's intention was to make the work appear more glorious or acceptable than it actually was. Historical deception, conscious or unconscious, is the fact of the matter. Indeed, the body of medieval pseudographia is vast when one considers all the false charters, the spurious genealogies and successions of kings, nobles and bishops, the enchanting but fictitious foundation 'histories' of many early churches and monasteries (Glastonbury Abbey being the *primus inter pares*), and the amazing claims made for the possession and attributes of holy relics.

In many respects more insidious than overtly fraudulent writings are subtly misleading references. In the Middle Ages it was normal to describe a structure as 'new' for 50 or 100 years after its completion, quite properly to distinguish it from an older work which it replaced. The process continues to this day: at Didmarton, Glos., there are two churches in the village, known as the 'old' and the 'new', and the latter appellation has applied since the building was erected in 1872. Wills and other documents providing instructions for something to be done should, *prime facie*, provide dates for building works, yet sometimes we know that the instruction was not carried out, was modified or was long delayed in its execution. Likewise, dates for the completion or dedication of buildings can be grossly misleading: these acts may relate only to unspecified parts. When the 'new' cathedral at Wells was dedicated in 1239 it was certainly not complete, since the twin western towers stood only as stumps.

Discomforting as it may be, we must accept that documented history, however ancient or modern, is merely a collection of recorded statements and opinions, and these may be true, false, unintentionally misleading or downright incomprehensible. Furthermore, the material which survives for study today is but a random selection and minute fraction of the total written record, itself never complete. We would do well never to forget that all materials used for the pursuit of archaeology and history are chance survivals. Human fallibility is a prominent, if not always readily appreciable, element in the archaeological record. A church may owe its irregular plan to nothing more than a miscalculation by the architect; a numeral or a date in a document may be wrongly copied by a scribe; an entry in a parish register may be at variance with the inscription on the corresponding tombstone (quite common); and an antiquarian illustration may suffer from too much 'artist's licence'.

Old maps and illustrations are an invaluable source of information for the church archaeologist, but they must be used with the knowledge that every detail may not be correct: the number of windows in a clerestorey may not appear the same in an engraving as it does in the church; trees and vegetation may be introduced to balance the picture; while subsidiary buildings or other inconvenient obstructions may be omitted from the record. The general reliability of an artist and the degree to which he conventionalizes his depiction may be assessed by studying a selection of his works in relation to known or surviving structures, before making a value judgement on a difficult item. After *c.* 1850 photography became available as a means of record, with the result that Victorian restorations in full spate could be captured on film (fig. 87). The collapse of the central tower at Chichester Cathedral in 1861 was photographically recorded, and so was St Runwald's church which stood in the centre of the High Street at Colchester and was demolished in 1878. Gilbert Scott rebuilt the Chichester tower as a faithful replica, based on the scrutiny of extant photographs and engravings, and on samples of mouldings which he excavated from the debris. The immense body of evidence captured in Georgian and Victorian illustrations has been graphically demonstrated in the history of cathedral restoration (Cobb, 1980).

Publication

Hardly a church in England can be without any published reference: many have been the object of articles in archaeological and historical journals, and have at some time been provided with a guide-book or leaflet. As we have observed (p. 36), published accounts are frequently far from accurate and seldom is the approach comprehensive. Older works often contain, between the lines of antiquarian discourse, miscellaneous observations and facts which are nowhere else recorded and which must be extracted to join the body of collected data. Whenever possible, a new guide-book or other publication should be compiled from a fresh examination of the available evidence, ancient or modern, direct or indirect, and not from a regurgitation of a previous synthetic work, especially if that is not adequately referenced.

There are three levels of report and publication, which may be examined in the order of their academic importance, and that, incidentally, is exactly the reverse order of importance accorded by the general public to such works.

The Archive is the total assemblage of data recovered from any form of investigation and will comprise the material which should be deposited in a suitable place of permanent

87 Bristol Cathedral from the south-east, probably photographed in 1878. This shows G. E. Street's rebuilding of the nave as complete, but the western towers had not yet been raised, nor the central tower restored. Notice also the stock of scaffolding in the masons' yard: planks, square-section putlogs and barrels. Unique and historically important photographs such as this are regularly discovered amongst the stock-in-trade of dealers in prints and books. *Photo: author, from an unattributed original*

custody, as discussed on pp. 167–70. If, for any reason, no publication of the material is envisaged, a note simply to record its existence and whereabouts should be printed in the relevant county archaeological journal. There is no objection to the inclusion of interpretative material, folklore and old manuscripts or published accounts of a church along with the basic data in an archive. Indeed, this is to be encouraged, because the history of antiquarian studies is itself a subject of interest and the raw materials for its pursuit should not be discarded. While we may scorn previous generations' attempts to study the archaeology of a church there is no guarantee that what we dismiss as incorrect or fanciful is necessarily so.

However confident we may be in our own judgements, we can rest assured that future generations will find fault with them. And so the process continues, generating history at every remove.

The Full Report used to be the ultimate goal of every archaeological investigation or other form of academic study, but the costs of publication are now determining otherwise. Never again shall we see superb surveys published like that on Hexham Abbey (Hodges, 1888), or the meticulous work of scholarship on the relics of St Cuthbert (Battiscombe, 1956). It is a matter for concern and regret that the academic world has so readily succumbed to economic pressures and abandoned the century-old *sine qua non* that all excavations, for example, should be adequately, but not necessarily fully, reported in print. It is therefore inevitable that some of the major projects in church archaeology in the 1970s will not receive proper publication even though the reports may have been written (e.g. Rivenhall); while others will only appear in such condensed form that the term 'final report' is inappropriate

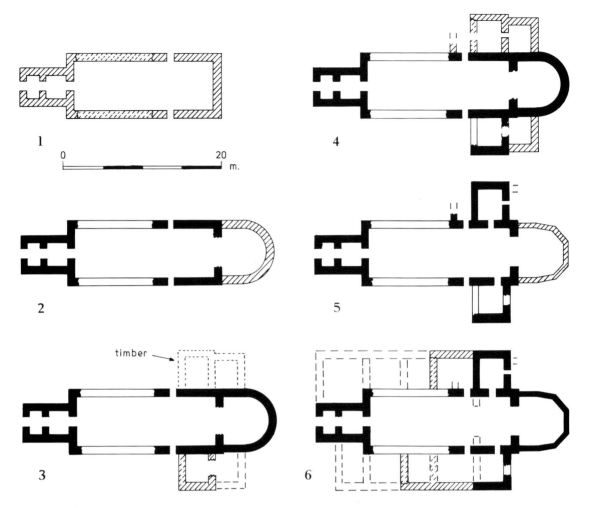

88 St Mary's, Deerhurst, Glos., the development of the Anglo-Saxon church plan, largely revealed through structural archaeology. Investigations so far have been concentrated on the east end of the church, so that the history of the western parts, the tower excepted, awaits elucidation. For the church's development in the vertical dimension, see fig. 89. *After Taylor, 1977a*

(e.g. St Helen-on-the-Walls, York; Magilton, 1980). However, the archive report exists and it is devoutly to be hoped that a future generation will have the inclination and resources to make more readily available the languishing work of the later twentieth-century.

A large part of the publication problem stems from archaeologists' unwillingness to make academic reports attractive and readable to more than the select few. This view is widely held and frequently expressed by the interested and informed public. The problem has gradually worsened over recent decades. Exactly fifty years ago T. C. Lethbridge, in the

preface to his excavation report on three Anglo-Saxon cemeteries, summed up the position with great perspicacity: 'This work is nothing more than a Report on certain excavations, and as such follows the modern fashion of being as colourless as possible. In the last century a similar work would have included musings on the brevity of life, scraps of poetry and various other frills. Now archaeology has become so stern a study that I have not even dared to describe our feelings when a skull at Holywell Row began to walk away with a young rabbit inside it . . .' (Lethbridge, 1931).

A sensible compromise between the long and tedious, and the short and unenlightened, archaeological report should be sought. In a synthetic report it is the selection of relevant data and the skill of synthesis which must tax the writer. The evidence, and the interpretation placed upon it, should be distinguished in the report as far as possible, but in writing the one

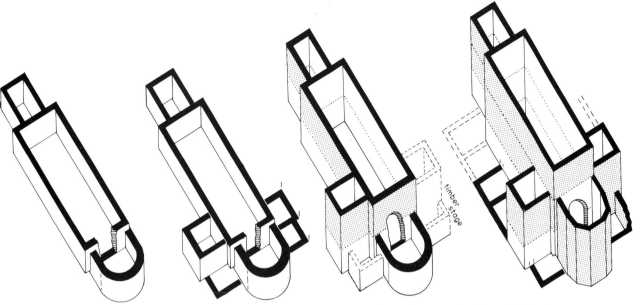

89 The development of the Anglo-Saxon fabric of St Mary's Church, Deerhurst, in the vertical plane; isometric views from the south-east. These show how the church reached its present height in three stages, which are also related to the development of the plan (fig. 88). The analysis of different types of masonry in the walls, particularly 'herringbone' work, was crucial to this study (shown here in stipple on external wall faces). It has also been shown that the eastern *porticus* in phase 3 were apparently of timber in the first instance, later being rebuilt in stone. *After Taylor, 1977a*

we must not lose sight of the other. There is no merit in filling the first part of the report with mortar descriptions, soil colours, grave depths, posthole dimensions and the like if these are not meaningfully related to the synthesis in the second part, and actually contribute something to it. The synthesis or discussion section of an archaeological report is scarcely less important than the preservation of the data: it should never be relegated to an inferior status, or leave the reader in doubt as to the findings and their significance. The discussion is usually the most telling part of a report and from it one may quickly perceive whether the investigator fully understood what he was recording, and whether he is able to interpret his findings in terms of positive information. Good and ample illustrations are a pre-requisite of any archaeological report; the Winchester excavation reports might be followed as a model: *Antiquaries Journal* 44 (1964) to 55 (1975).

The Explanatory Booklet is the presentation most wanted by the interested public. There are two forms of explanatory

publication: the standard guide-book to a building or site, and the account of an investigation or other project which has recently affected the monument. There is no good reason why virtually every ancient church, and some modern ones too, should not be provided with an illustrated guide-book, and useful hints for the would-be compiler of such a work have been published (Dymond, 1977); see also Chapter 5 here.

The second category of explanatory publication is the project-based booklet which seeks to inform the visitor of what is happening, or has happened at the church by way of investigation and discovery. The first essential is for the booklet to be produced promptly and attractively, and to be available while work is actually in progress. Good illustrations, including uncluttered plans and, where possible, reconstructions are at least as important as the text (figs 84, 88–9). If an investigation is undertaken over the course of several seasons a booklet can be produced at the end of the first year and updated annually or bi-annually thereafter. Experience shows that there is a healthy market for project-based booklets and that they continue to sell steadily for years after the investigation has been completed. Most importantly, they are what is wanted and appreciated by the people whose generosity has paid for the project and whose kindness has permitted its undertaking. Some examples related to excavations are: *Under York Minster* (Hope-Taylor, 1971), *The Old*

90 The secular use of a redundant medieval church: an early study in church archaeology by Samuel Prout (undated, but *c.* 1810–20)

Minster: Excavations near Winchester Cathedral (Biddle, 1970b), *4000 Years of Rivenhall* (Rodwell and Rodwell, 1973b), *Under Hadstock Church* (Rodwell, 1974b) and *Wells Cathedral: Excavations and Discoveries* (Rodwell, 1980a); and examples of booklets deriving from structural investigations are: *Deerhurst Studies 1* (Taylor, 1977a) and *Repton Studies 1 and 2* (Taylor, 1977b; 1979).

It is the duty of the archaeologist to make his researches and discoveries available in a readily comprehensible and inexpensive form for the general public, and in so doing he is helping to foster a greater interest in our vast ecclesiastical legacy. That interest in turn generates the desire for more knowledge and facilitates more investigation; it also stimulates an awareness in the minds of those charged with the task of caring for churches, their contents and surroundings, that there is much more to them than meets the eye. There can be little doubt, at least in the minds of those who have been privileged to take part in archaeo-ecclesiastical projects, that churches, cathedrals and monasteries embrace the greatest and most fertile store of untapped archaeological knowledge in England.

Appendix

Institutions and Administration Relevant to Church Archaeology

The following is a select list of the more important institutions and administrative procedures with which the church archaeologist needs to be familiar.

Cathedrals Advisory Commission, formerly **Committee** (CAC)
83 London Wall, London, EC2M 5NA
This body provides expert advice, as and when required, on matters relating to the care and maintenance of cathedrals and their possessions. Architectural historians, art historians and archaeologists serve on the Commission.

Council for British Archaeology (CBA)
112 Kennington Road, London, SE11 6RE
Amongst its many attributes, the CBA has a Churches Committee which provides advice, at national and local levels, on all matters relating to church archaeology. It maintains a network of Diocesan Archaeological Consultants and has published booklets and research reports on church archaeology, including: *How to Record Graveyards* (Jones, 1979), *Historic Churches: A Wasting Asset* (Rodwell and Rodwell, 1977), *The Archaeological Study of Churches* (Addyman and Morris, 1976) and *The Church in British Archaeology* (Morris II, 1981).

Council for the Care of Churches, formerly *Council for Places of Worship* (CCC–CPW)
83 London Wall, London, EC2M 5NA
The CCC is the counterpart of the Cathedrals Advisory Committee for parish churches. It also has the important function of reporting on all Anglican churches for which redundancy is proposed under the provisions of the *Pastoral Measure 1968*. The CCC maintains close liaison with the CBA, with Diocesan Advisory Committees and all other bodies involved in the care and maintenance of parish churches, both living and redundant. It has issued an important series of publications, including *Churches and Archaeology* (Morris II, 1978).

Department of the Environment (DOE)
23 Savile Row, London, W1X 2HE
The Directorate of Ancient Monuments and Historic Buildings (DAMHB) is a division within the DOE which has responsibility for the provision of state funds for rescue archaeology in England,
including work in churches and cathedrals. Within the Directorate is a Churches Section which deals both with archaeology and with the disbursement of Government funds for the repair of historic churches in use. The DOE has also taken into public guardianship various abbeys and churches, which are mainly ruinous but include a few intact buildings.

Diocesan Advisory Committee (DAC)
c/o the local Diocesan Office
There is a DAC for each Diocese and its function is to advise the Chancellor of the Diocese on the granting of Faculties for work in churches. Under the *Faculty Jurisdiction Measure 1938 and 1964* (now under revision) permission has to be sought for all works of repair or alteration in parish churches (cathedrals are excepted); any archaeological investigation which involves tampering with the fabric of the church, or an excavation, requires a Faculty. In many instances an archaeologist serves on the local DAC: he is usually the CBA's Diocesan Archaeological Consultant.

Diocesan Records Office
usually c/o the local County Records Office
This is the place where all church records, registers and related materials, which are not in current use, are stored under archival conditions (see p. 168).

National Monuments Record (NMR)
23 Savile Row, London, W1X 2HE
A section within the RCHM which holds the national archive of architectural and archaeological records. Its photographic collection is of exceptional importance (see p. 168).

Parochial Church Council (PCC)
This is the local management committee for each parish church, usually chaired by the incumbent (vicar or rector). The incumbent, churchwardens and PCC are jointly responsible for the care and maintenance of their church, and have first to give permission for any kind of archaeological investigation, before a Faculty can be applied for.

Redundant Churches Fund (RCF)
St Andrew-by-the-Wardrobe, Queen Victoria Street, London, EC4V 5DE

The Advisory Board for Redundant Churches (ABRC)

Fielden House, Little College Street, London, SWIP 3SH

These two bodies, although separate in reality, are frequently confused. The Advisory Board's function is to consider the possible uses to which a redundant church may be put, in the light of reports and views submitted by various bodies, including the CCC, and to recommend a course of action to the Church Commissioners. It is they who are ultimately responsible for the disposal of property.

The RCF is a guardianship body, funded partly by the Church and partly by the State. Its function is to hold and maintain in sound condition those churches which the Commissioners see fit to vest in it. Both the ABRC and RCF publish *Annual Reports* on their work.

Royal Commission on Historical Monuments (England) (RCHM)

23 Savile Row, London, WIX 2HE

The RCHM has two principal tasks. First, its investigators are working their way slowly across the country, compiling inventories of historic buildings and structures (see list below); and secondly, the RCHM has a duty to record listed buildings and redundant churches which are potentially threatened with destruction or mutilation. Owing to the massive workload this generates for a very small staff, it is seldom possible for the Commission's record to comprise more than a good selection of photographs of those parts of the building which are readily accessible.

The following RCHM county Inventories have been published, wherein all relevant churches are architecturally described. In earlier volumes,

descriptions were often very brief and not accompanied by a detailed plan; furthermore, a cut-off date of 1714 obtained. More recent volumes contain far greater detail (see p. 54).

Hertfordshire (1910)

Buckinghamshire I, South (1912)
                II, North (1913)

Essex I, North-West (1916)
     II, Central & South-West (1921)
     III, North-East (1922)
     IV, South-East (1923)

Huntingdonshire (1926)

London I, Westminster Abbey (1924)
       II, West (1925)
       IV, The City (1929)
       V, East (1930)

Herefordshire I, South-West (1931)
            II, East (1932)
            III, North-West (1934)

Westmorland (1936)

Middlesex (1937)

Oxford, City (1939)

Dorset I, West (1952)
      II, South-East (1970)
      III, Central (1971)
      IV, North (1972)
      V, East (1975)

Cambridge, City (1959)

Cambridgeshire I, West (1968)
            II, North-East (1972)

York II, The Defences (1972)
    III, South-West of the Ouse (1972)

Stamford (1977)

Salisbury I, City, excluding the Cathedral Close (1980)

Bibliography

ADDYMAN, P. V., and MORRIS, R. K., (eds.) 1976. *The Archaeological Study of Churches*. Council for British Archaeology, Res. Rep. 13

ASTON, M. A., and ROWLEY, R. T. 1974. *Landscape Archaeology*

BAILEY, R. N. 1980. *Viking Age Sculpture*

BALDWIN-BROWN, G. 1903. *The Arts in Early England: Life in Anglo-Saxon England in its Relation to the Arts*

BALDWIN-BROWN, G. 1937. *The Arts in Early England, VI: Anglo-Saxon Sculpture*

BARKER, P. A. 1977. *Techniques of Archaeological Excavation*

BATCOCK, N. forthcoming. 'Survey of Ruined and Disused Churches in Norfolk and the Diocese of Norwich'

BATTISCOMBE, C. F., (ed.) 1956. *The Relics of Saint Cuthbert*

BEDE (The Venerable). *Historia Ecclesiastica. A History of the English Church and People.* Translated by L. Sherley-Price (1955; Penguin)

BEDWIN, O. 1975. 'The Excavation of the Church of St Nicholas, Angmering, 1974', *Sussex Archaeol. Coll.* 113, 16–34

BIDDLE, M. 1965. 'Excavations at Winchester, 1964: Third Interim Report', *Antiq. J.* 45, 230–64

BIDDLE, M. 1970a. 'Excavations at Winchester, 1969: Eighth Interim Report', *Antiq. J.* 50, 277–326

BIDDLE, M. 1970b. *The Old Minster: Excavations near Winchester Cathedral, 1961–1969.* Fifth ed. Winchester Excavations Cttee.

BIDDLE, M. 1975a. 'Excavations at Winchester, 1971: Tenth and Final Interim Report: Part II', *Antiq. J.* 55, 295–337

BIDDLE, M. 1975b. 'Little Somborne', *Bull. C.B.A. Churches Cttee.* 2, 17

BIDDLE, M. 1976. 'The Archaeology of the Church: A Widening Horizon', in Addyman and Morris, 1976, 65–71

BILSON, J. 1928. 'Notes on the Earlier Architectural History of Wells Cathedral', *Archaeol. J.*, 85, 23–68

BINNEY, M., and BURMAN, P. 1977a. *Change and Decay: The Future of our Churches*

BINNEY, M., and BURMAN, P. 1977b. *Chapels and Churches: Who Cares* (British Tourist Authority)

BODDINGTON, A. 1980. 'A Christian Anglo-Saxon Graveyard at Raunds, Northamptonshire', in Rahtz, Dickinson and Watts, 1980, 373–8

BOND, F. 1898. 'On the Comparative Value of Documentary and Architectural Evidence . . .', *J. Royal Inst. British Architects*, 26 Nov. 1898, 17–35

BOND, F. 1905. *Gothic Architecture in England*

BOND, F. 1908a. *Screens and Galleries in English Churches*

BOND, F. 1908b. *Fonts and Font Covers*

BOND, F. 1910. *Woodcarving in English Churches: I Stalls and Tabernacle Work; II Bishops' Thrones and Chancel Chairs*

BOND, F. 1913. *An Introduction to English Church Architecture* (2 vols.)

BOND, F. 1914. *Dedications and Patron Saints of English Churches*

BOND, F. 1916. *The Chancel of English Churches*

BRANDON, R., and BRANDON, J. A. 1874. *Analysis of Gothick Architecture* (2nd ed.)

BROOKE, C. N. L., and KEIR, G. 1975. *London 800–1216: The Shaping of a City*

BROTHWELL, D. 1963. *Digging up Bones*

BROWNE, J. 1847. *The History of the Metropolitan Church of St. Peter's, York*

BRUCE-MITFORD, R. L. S. 1976 'The Chapter House Vestibule Graves at Lincoln and the Body of St Hugh of Avalon', in F. G. Emmison and R. Stephens (eds.), *Tribute to an Antiquary*, 127–40

BRYANT, R. M. 1980. 'Excavations at St. Mary de Lode, Gloucester, 1978–79', *Glevensis* 14, 4–12

BURGESS, F. 1963. *English Churchyard Memorials*

BURROWS, J. W. 1953. *The History of Prittlewell Priory* (Sixth ed., Southend Museum Handbook 4)

BUTLER, L. A. S. 1976. 'Documentary Evidence and the Church Fabric', in Addyman and Morris, 1976, 18–21

BUTLER, L. A. S., RAHTZ, P. A., and TAYLOR, H. M. 1975. 'Deerhurst 1971–1974', *Antiq. J.* 55, 346–65

CAMDEN, W. 1586. *Britannia* (1st ed. 1586; 6th ed. 1607). See also R. Gough, 1789

CARR, R. D. 1976. 'A Survey of the Church of St Peter, Ubbeston', *E. Ang. Archaeol.* 3, 155–69

CARTER, J. 1780–94. *Specimens of Ancient Sculpture and Painting.* Issued in parts

CARTER, J. 1798. *History of Gothic and Saxon Architecture in England*

CARVER, M. O. H. 1978. Review of W. and K. Rodwell, *Historic Churches: A Wasting Asset*, in *Bull. C.B.A. Churches Cttee.* 8, 10–12

CASEY, P. J. (ed.) 1979. *The End of Roman Britain.* B.A.R. 71

CAUTLEY, H. M. 1937. *Suffolk Churches and their Treasures* (4th ed. revised, 1978)

CHANCELLOR, F. 1890. *The Ancient Sepulchral Monuments of Essex*

CHRISTIE, H., OLSEN, O., and TAYLOR, H. M. 1979. 'The Wooden Church of St. Andrew at Greensted, Essex', *Antiq. J.* 59, 92–112

CLAPHAM, A. W. 1930. *English Romanesque Architecture before the Conquest*

CLAPHAM, A. W. 1934. *English Romanesque Architecture after the Conquest*

CLARKE, B. F. L. 1969. *Church Builders of the Nineteenth Century* (1st ed. 1938; 2nd ed. 1969)

CLARKE, G. 1979. *The Roman Cemetery at Lankhills* (Winchester Studies 3)

CLIFTON-TAYLOR, A. 1974. *English Parish Churches as Works of Art*

COBB, G. 1980. *English Cathedrals, the Forgotten Centuries*

COLCHESTER, L. S., and HARVEY, J. H. 1974. 'Wells Cathedral', *Archaeol. J.* 131, 200–14

COLES, J. M. 1972. *Field Archaeology in Britain*

COLYER, C. 1976. 'Excavations at St Mark, Lincoln', *Bull. C.B.A. Churches Cttee.* 5, 5–9

COLYER, C., and GILMOUR, B. 1978. 'St Paul-in-the-Bail, Lincoln', *Curr. Archaeol.* 6, 102–5

COOK, G. H. 1954. *The English Medieval Parish Church.* Fourth impression 1970.

COPPACK, G. 1978. 'St Lawrence, Burnham, South Humberside', *Bull. C.B.A. Churches Cttee.* 8, 5–6

CORNISH, V. 1946. *The Churchyard Yew and Immortality*

CRAMP, R. J. 1969. 'Excavations at the Saxon Monastic Sites of Wearmouth and Jarrow, Co. Durham: An Interim Report', *Medieval Archaeol.* 13, 21–66.

CRAMP, R. J. 1970. 'Decorated Window Glass and Millefiori from Monkwearmouth', *Antiq. J.* 50, 327–35

CRAMP, R. J. 1976a. 'St Paul's Church, Jarrow', in Addyman and Morris, 1976, 28–35

CRAMP, R. J. 1976b. 'Monastic Sites', in Wilson, 1976, 201–52

CRAMP, R. J. 1977a. 'The Brixworth Archaeological Research Committee', *J. Brit. Archaeol. Assoc.* 130, 52–4

CRAMP, R. J. 1977b. 'Schools of Mercian Sculpture', in Dornier, 1977, 191–234

CROOME, W. I. (ed.). 1959. *The Conservation of English Wallpaintings* (Council for the Care of Churches)

CUNLIFFE, B. W. 1976. *Excavations at Portchester Castle, II.* Soc. Antiq. Res. Rep. 33

CUNLIFFE, B. W. 1977. *Excavations at Portchester Castle, III.* Soc. Antiq. Res. Rep. 34

CUNLIFFE, B. W. (ed.). 1979. *Excavations in Bath 1950–1975.* (CRAAGS, Bristol)

DAVEY, N. 1964. 'A Pre-Conquest Church and Baptistery at Potterne', *Wilts. Archaeol. Nat. Hist. Mag.* 59, 116–23

DAWES, J. D., and MAGILTON, J. R. 1980. 'The Cemetery of St Helen-on-the-Walls, Aldwark', *The Archaeology of York*, 12/1

DAWSON, D. P. 1977. 'Non-Conformist Chapels in Bristol', *Bull. C.B.A. Churches Cttee*, 6, 4–6

DIRSZTAY, P. 1978. *Church Furnishings* (NADFAS Guide)

DORNIER, A. (ed.) 1977. *Mercian Studies*

DRURY, P. J., and RODWELL, W. J. 1978. 'Investigations at Asheldham, Essex: An Interim Report on the Church and the Historic Landscape', *Antiq. J.* 58, 133–51

DUGDALE, W. 1655/1846. *Monasticon Anglicanum* (1st ed. 1655. Several subsequent editions down to that by J. Caley, H. Ellis and B. Bandinel, 1846)

DYMOND, D. P. 1977. *Writing a Church Guide* (Church Information Office)

ESSEX COUNTY COUNCIL 1976. *Redundant Churches in Essex*

FAULL, M. L. 1976. 'The Location and Relationship of the Sancton Anglo-Saxon Cemeteries', *Antiq. J.* 56, 227–33

FOWLER, P. J. 1981. 'The Royal Commission on Historical Monuments (England)', *Antiquity* 55, 106–14

FOX, C. 1956. 'The Siting of the Monastery of St. Mary and St. Peter in Exeter', in Harden, 1956, 202–17

FRERE, S. S. 1975. 'The Silchester Church: The Excavation by Sir Ian Richmond in 1961', *Archaeologia* 105, 277–302

GILMOUR, B. J. J. 1979. 'The Anglo-Saxon Church at St Paul-in-the-Bail, Lincoln', *Medieval Archaeol.* 23, 214–17

GOMME, G. L. (ed.) 1893. *Topographical History of Durham, Essex and Gloucestershire* (The Gentleman's Magazine Library)

GOUGH, R. (ed.). 1789. W. Camden, *Britannia* (Translated and enlarged edition. 3 vols.)

GRIMES, W. F. 1968. *The Excavation of Roman and Medieval London*

HARDEN, D. B. (ed.). 1956. *Dark-Age Britain*

HARE, M. 1976. 'The Anglo-Saxon Church of St Peter, Tichfield', *Proc. Hants. Field Soc.* 32, 5–48

HARVEY, J. H. 1954. *English Medieval Architects: A Biographical Dictionary down to 1550*

HARVEY, J. H. 1972. *The Medieval Architect*

HARVEY, J. H. 1974. *Cathedrals of England and Wales*

HARVEY, J. H. 1975. *Medieval Craftsmen*

HARVEY, J. H. 1978. *The Perpendicular Style, 1330–1485*

HEIGHWAY, C. M. 1978. 'Excavations at Gloucester, Fourth Interim Report: St. Oswald's Priory,

1975–76', *Antiq. J.* 58, 103–32

HELLIWELL, L. 1958. 'Prittlewell Priory and the Church Site', *J. Brit. Archaeol. Assoc.* (ser. 3) 20–21, 84–94

HEWETT, C. A. 1974a. *Church Carpentry: a study based on Essex examples*

HEWETT, C. A. 1974b. *English Cathedral Carpentry*

HEWETT, C. A. 1978. 'Anglo-Saxon Carpentry', *Anglo-Saxon England VII*, 205–30

HIRST, S. 1976. *Recording on Excavations, 1: The Written Record*

HODGES, C. C. 1888. *The Abbey of St. Andrew, Hexham.*

HOGARTH, A. C. 1973. 'Structural Features in Anglo-Saxon Graves', *Archaeol. J.* 130, 104–29

HOPE, J. H. 1974. 'Drainage Trenches at All Saints' Church, Cressing', *Essex Archaeol. Hist.* 6, 82–9

HOPE, R. C. 1893. *The Legendary Lore of the Holy Wells of England*

HOPE-TAYLOR, B. 1971. *Under York Minster: Archaeological Discoveries, 1966–1971.* The Dean and Chapter of York

HOPE-TAYLOR, B. 1977. *Yeavering: An Anglo-British Centre of Early Northumbria* (HMSO)

HUGGINS, P. J. 1978. 'Excavation of Belgic and Romano-British Farm with Middle Saxon Cemetery and Churches at Nazeingbury, Essex, 1975–6', *Essex Archaeol. Hist.* 10, 29–117

HULL, M. R. 1960. 'The St Nicholas Church Site, Colchester', *Trans. Essex Archaeol. Soc.* (new ser.), 25, 301–28

HUNTER, M. C. W. 1976. 'The Study of Anglo-Saxon Architecture since 1770: An Evaluation', *Proc. Camb. Antiq. Soc.* 66, 129–39

HURST, J. G. 1976. 'Wharram Percy: St. Martin's Church', in Addyman and Morris, 1976, 36–9

JAMES, J. 1979. *The Contractors of Chartres* (Dooralong, N.S.W., Australia)

JESSON, M. (ed.). 1973. *The Archaeology of Churches* (C.B.A.)

JONES, J. 1976 *How to Record Graveyards* (C.B.A. 2nd ed. 1979)

JONES, M. J., and GILMOUR, B. J. J. 1980. 'Lincoln, Principia and Forum: A Preliminary Report', *Britannia* 11, 61–72

KEENE, D. 1977. 'A Note on the proposed Survey of Urban Churches', *Bull. C.B.A. Churches Cttee*, 6, 7–8

KENDRICK, T. 1950. *British Antiquity*

KJØLBYE-BIDDLE, B. 1975. 'A Cathedral Cemetery: Problems in Excavation and Interpretation', *World Archaeol.* 7, 87–110

LANG, J. (ed.). 1978. *Anglo-Saxon and Viking Age Sculpture and its Context.* B.A.R. 49

LEACH, P. J. forthcoming. *Excavations at Taunton* (CRAAGS, Bristol)

LELAND, J. 1710–12. *The Itineraries.* Thos. Hearne, Oxford 1710–12 (New edition by L. T. Smith 1907; reprinted 1964)

LETHBRIDGE, T. C. 1931. *Recent Excavations in Anglo-Saxon Cemeteries in Cambridgeshire and Suffolk.* Cambridge Antiq. Soc.

LINDLEY, K. 1965. *Of Graves and Epitaphs*

LYSONS, S. 1791/1804. *Etchings of Views and Antiquities in the County of Gloucester* (1st ed. 1791; 2nd ed. 1804)

MAGILTON, J. R. 1980. 'The Church of St. Helen-on-the-Walls, Aldwark', *The Archaeology of York*, 10/1

MEANEY, A. L., and HAWKES, S. C. 1970. *Two Anglo-Saxon Cemeteries at Winnall, Winchester, Hampshire* (Society for Medieval Archaeology, Monograph 4)

MOLESWORTH ROBERTS, H. V. 1970. 'Historical Research in Relation to Architecture', *Blackmansbury*, 7, 3–8

MORGAN, D. 1969. *St. Bride's Church, Fleet Street in the City of London* (The St. Bride Restoration Fund)

MORRIS, R. K. (I) 1978. 'The Development of Later Gothic Mouldings in England, c. 1250–1400—Part I', *Archit. Hist.* 21, 18–57

MORRIS, R. K. (I) 1979. 'The Development of Later Gothic Mouldings in England, c. 1250–1400—Part II', *Archit. Hist.* 22, 1–48

MORRIS, R. K. (II) 1977. 'Archaeology', in Binney and Burman, 1977a, 134–40

MORRIS, R. K. (II) 1978. *Churches and Archaeology* (Church Information Office)

MORRIS, R. K. (II) 1979. *Cathedrals and Abbeys of England and Wales*

MORRIS, R. K. (II) 1981. *The Church in British Archaeology* (C.B.A. Res. Rep.)

MORRIS, R. K. (II) and ROXAN, J. 1980. 'Churches on Roman Buildings', in Rodwell, 1980b, 211–42

O'LEARY, T. forthcoming. 'Excavations at the Orange Grove, Bath' (CRAAGS, Bristol)

OLSEN, O. 1976. 'The Legal Situation in Denmark', in Addyman and Morris, 1976, 14–15

OWEN, D. M. 1966. 'How to study your Parish Church from Documents', *Amateur Historian*, 7, No. 1

OWEN, D. M. 1970. *The Records of the Established Church in England* (British Records Assoc.)

OWEN, D. M. 1975. 'Ecclesiastical Jurisdiction in England, 1300–1550: The Records and their Interpretation', *Studies in Church History XI* (Ecclesiastical History Soc.)

OWEN, D. M. 1976. 'Documentary Sources for the Building History of Churches in the Middle Ages', in Addyman and Morris, 1976, 21–5

PALEY, F. A. 1845. *Manual of Gothic Mouldings* (2nd ed. 1847)

PANTIN, W. A. 1958. 'Monuments or Muniments', *Medieval Archaeol.* 2, 158–68

PARKER, J. H. 1836. *Glossary of Gothic Architecture* (3rd ed. 1840; 5th ed. 1850)

PARSONS, D. 1977. 'Brixworth and its Monastery Church', in Dornier, 1977, 173–90

PARSONS, D. 1980. 'A Dated Timber Fragment from Brixworth Church, Northamptonshire', *J. British Archaeol. Assoc.* 133, 30–6

PHILLIPS, A. D. 1975. 'Excavations at York Minster, 1967–73', *The Friends of York Minster, 46th Annual Report*

PHILLIPS, A. D. 1976. 'Excavation Techniques in Church Archaeology', in Addyman and Morris, 1976, 54–9

POWLESLAND, D. 1980. 'The Excavation of Inhumation Burials', in Rahtz, Dickinson and Watts, 1980, 233–8

PRESSEY, W. J. 1940. 'Visitations held in the Archdeaconry of Colchester in 1683', *Trans. Essex Archaeol. Soc.* (ns) 23, 145–64

PUGIN, A. 1823. *Specimens of Gothic Architecture*

RADFORD, C. A. R. 1935. 'Tintagel: the Castle and the Celtic Monastery—Interim Report', *Antiq. J.* 15, 401–19

RADFORD, C. A. R. 1955. *Tintagel Castle* (HMSO)

RADFORD, C. A. R., and SWANTON, M. J. 1975. *Arthurian Sites in the West* (University of Exeter)

RAHTZ, P. A. 1964. 'Excavations at Chalice Well, Glastonbury', *Proc. Som. Archaeol. Nat. Hist. Soc.* 108, 145–63

RAHTZ, P. A. 1976a. *Excavations at St. Mary's Church, Deerhurst, 1971–73.* C.B.A. Res. Rep. 15

RAHTZ, P. A. 1976b. 'The Archaeology of the Churchyard', in Addyman and Morris, 1976, 41–5

RAHTZ, P. A. 1978. 'Grave Orientation', *Archaeol. J.* 135, 1–14

RAHTZ, P. A., DICKINSON, T., and WATTS, L. (eds.). 1980. *Anglo-Saxon Cemeteries, 1979.* B.A.R. 82

RAHTZ, P. A., and HIRST, S. 1976. *Bordesley Abbey, Redditch, Hereford–Worcestershire.* B.A.R. 23

RAHTZ, P. A., and WATTS, L. 1979. 'The End of Roman Temples in the West of Britain', in Casey, 1979, 183–210

RAMM, H. G., *et al.* 1971. 'The Tombs of Archbishops Walter de Gray and Godfrey de Ludham in York Minster, and their Contents', *Archaeologia* 103, 101–47

RAYMENT, J. L. 1977. *Notes on the Recording of Monumental Inscriptions* (Essex Society for Family History)

RCHM 1923. *An Inventory of the Historical Monuments in Essex IV*

RCHM 1926. *An Inventory of the Historical Monuments in Huntingdonshire*

RCHM 1972. *An Inventory of the Historical Monuments in the County of Cambridge II*

RICKMAN, T. 1819. *An Attempt to Discriminate the Styles of Architecture in England from the Conquest to the Reformation* (1st ed. 1817; 2nd ed. 1819; 4th ed. 1835; 5th ed. 1848)

RIGOLD, S. E. 1977. 'Romanesque Bases in and South-East of the Limestone Belt', in M. R.

Apted, R. Gilyard-Beer and A. D. Saunders (eds.), *Ancient Monuments and their Interpretation*, 99–137

ROBERTS, E. 1977. 'Moulding Analysis and Architectural Research: the late Middle Ages', *Archit. Hist.* 20, 5–13

ROBERTS, E. 1979. *A School of Masons in 15th-Century North Hertfordshire.* Herts. Local Studies 2

ROBINSON, J. A. 1928. 'Documentary Evidence relating to the Building of the Cathedral Church of Wells', *Archaeol. J.* 85, 1–22

RODWELL, W. J. 1974a. 'Hadstock Church', *Current Archaeol.* 4, 375–81

RODWELL, W. J. 1974b. *Under Hadstock Church* (Essex Archaeol. Soc.)

RODWELL, W. J. 1976. 'The Archaeological Investigation of Hadstock Church, Essex: An Interim Report', *Antiq J.* 56, 55–71

RODWELL, W. J. 1979. 'Lead Plaques from the Tombs of the Saxon Bishops of Wells', *Antiq. J.* 59, 407–10

RODWELL, W. J. 1980a. *Wells Cathedral: Excavations and Discoveries* (1st ed. 1979; 2nd ed. 1980. Friends of Wells Cathedral)

RODWELL, W. J. (ed.). 1980b. *Temples, Churches and Religion: Recent Research in Roman Britain.* B.A.R. 77

RODWELL, W. J. 1980c. 'Wells: the Cathedral and City', *Curr. Archaeol.* 7, 38–44

RODWELL, W. J. forthcoming. 'The Origins of Wells Cathedral', *Antiquity*

RODWELL, W. J., and MORRIS, R. K. 1976. 'Why Church Surveys?', *Bull. C.B.A. Churches Cttee*, 3, 2–8

RODWELL, W. J., and RODWELL, K. A. 1973a. 'Excavations at Rivenhall Church, Essex: An Interim Report', *Antiq. J.* 73, 219–31

RODWELL, W. J., and RODWELL, K. A. 1973b. *4,000 Years of Rivenhall* (Essex Archaeol. Soc.)

RODWELL, K. A., and RODWELL, W. J. 1976. 'The Investigation of Churches in Use: a Problem in Rescue Archaeology', in Addyman and Morris, 1976, 45–54

RODWELL, W. J., and RODWELL, K. A. 1977. *Historic Churches—A Wasting Asset.* C.B.A. Res. Rep. 19

RODWELL, W. J., and RODWELL, K. A. 1981. 'Barton-on-Humber', *Curr. Archaeol.* 7, 208–15

RODWELL, W. J., and RODWELL, K. A. forthcoming. 'Rivenhall: Investigations on the Roman Villa, Church and Village, 1950–77'

ROUSE, E. C. 1971. *Discovering Wall Paintings* (1st ed. 1968)

SAGE, J., and TAYLOR, R. 1978. 'A Survey of Birmingham Graveyards', *Bull. C.B.A. Churches Cttee*, 9, 2–4

SCHOFIELD, J. 1977. 'Repair not Restoration', in Binney and Burman, 1977a, 153–4

SHARPE, E. 1871. *The Mouldings of the Six Periods*

of British Architecture

SIMPSON, F. 1828. *Ancient Baptismal Fonts*

SPARKS, M. (ed.). 1980. *The Parish of St Peter and St Paul, Canterbury*. The Friends of St Martin's Church

SPIEGL, F. (ed.). 1971. *A Small Book of Grave Humour*

STAPLETON, H., and BURMAN, P. 1976. *The Churchyards Handbook: Advice on their Care and Maintenance* (2nd ed. Church Information Office)

STONES, J. 1980. 'Brixworth Church: Nineteenth- and Earlier Twentieth-Century Excavations', *J. Brit. Archaeol. Assoc.* 133, 37–63

STUKELEY, W. 1725/1776. *Itinerarium Curiosum* (1st ed. 1725; 2nd ed. 1776)

TATTON-BROWN, T. W. T. 1980. 'The Font in St. Martin's Church', in Sparks, 1980, 19–20

TAYLOR, C. C. 1974. *Fieldwork in Medieval Archaeology*

TAYLOR, H. M. 1972a. 'Structural Criticism: a Plea for more Systematic Study of Anglo-Saxon Buildings', *Anglo-Saxon England I*, 259–72

TAYLOR, H. M. 1972b. 'J. T. Irvine's Work at Bradford-on-Avon', *Archaeol. J.* 129, 89–118

TAYLOR, H. M. 1973a. 'The Position of the Altar in Early Anglo-Saxon Churches', *Antiq. J.* 53, 52–8

TAYLOR, H. M. 1973b. 'The Anglo-Saxon Chapel at Bradford-on-Avon', *Archaeol. J.* 130, 141–71

TAYLOR, H. M. 1975. 'Aids to Architectural Measurements', *Bull. C.B.A. Churches Cttee*, 2, 5

TAYLOR, H. M. 1976. 'The Foundations of Architectural History', in Addyman and Morris, 1976, 3–9

TAYLOR, H. M. 1977a. *Deerhurst Studies I: The Anglo-Saxon Fabric, 1971–76* (Privately printed)

TAYLOR, H. M. 1977b. *Repton Studies I: The Anglo-Saxon Crypt, 1974–76* (Privately printed)

TAYLOR, H. M. 1978. *Anglo-Saxon Architecture III*

TAYLOR, H. M. 1979. *Repton Studies 2: The Anglo-Saxon Crypt and Church* (Privately printed)

TAYLOR, H. M., and TAYLOR, J. 1965. *Anglo-Saxon Architecture I and II*

THOMAS, A. C. 1973. *Bede, Archaeology and the Cult of Relics* (The Jarrow Lecture, 1973)

THOMAS, A. C. 1980. 'Churches in Late Roman Britain', in Rodwell, 1980b, 129–64

TUDOR-CRAIG, P. 1977. 'Churches Adapted', in Binney and Burman, 1977a, 177–86

VIERCK, H. 1980. 'The Cremation in the Ship at Sutton Hoo', in Rahtz, Dickinson and Watts, 1980, 343–56

WADE-MARTINS, P. 1980. 'Excavations in North Elmham Park, 1967–72', *East Anglian Archaeol.* 9

WARD, G. 1932. 'The List of Saxon Churches in the Textus Roffensis', *Archaeol. Cantiana* 44, 39–59

WARD, G. 1933. 'The Lists of Saxon Churches in the Domesday Monachorum and White Book of St. Augustine', *Archaeol. Cantiana* 45, 60–89

WHITE, H. L. 1977. *Monuments and their Inscriptions: A Practical Guide*. Society of Genealogists

WILLIAMS, J. H. 1979. *St Peter's Street, Northampton: Excavations 1973–1976*

WILSON, D. M. 1971. 'Medieval Britain in 1970: Pre-Conquest', *Medieval Archaeol.* 15, 124–37

WILSON, D. M. 1973. Review of *Danmarks Kirker, Arhus amt.* in *Medieval Archaeol.* 17, 204–5

WILSON, D. M. (ed.). 1976. *The Archaeology of Anglo-Saxon England*

WOODWARD, M. 1892. *The Past and Present of the Parish Church of Folkestone*

WRIGHT, T. (ed.). 1843. *Letters Relating to the Suppression of the Monasteries*. (Camden Soc. Ser. 26)

Index

Page numbers in italics indicate illustrations.